SCIENTISTS:

The Lives and Works of 150 Scientists

SCIENTISTS:

The Lives and Works of 150 Scientists

Peggy Saari and Stephen Allison, Editors

VOLUME 1

A-F

AN IMPRINT OF GALE

Scientists: The Lives and Works of 150 Scientists

Edited by Peggy Saari and Stephen Allison

Staff

Carol DeKane Nagel, *U·X·L Developmental Editor*
Thomas L. Romig, *U·X·L Publisher*

Shanna P. Heilveil, *Production Assistant*
Evi Seoud, *Assistant Production Manager*
Mary Beth Trimper, *Production Director*

Kimberly Smilay, *Permissions Specialist (Pictures)*

Tracey Rowens, *Cover and Page Designer*
Cynthia Baldwin, *Art Director*

Linda Mahoney, *Typesetter*

Library of Congress Cataloging-in-Publication Data

Scientists : the lives and works of 150 physical and social scientists
/ edited by Peggy Saari and Stephen Allison.

    p.   cm.

    Includes bibliographical references and index.

    Contents: v. 1. A-F – v. 2. G-O – v. 3. P-Z

    ISBN 0-7876-0959-5 (set); 0-7876-0960-9 (v. 1);
0-7876-0961-7 (v. 2); 0-7876-0962-5 (v. 3)

    1. Physical Scientists–Biography. 2. Social scientists–Biography. I.
Saari, Peggy. II. Allison, Stephen, 1969– .

    Q141.S3717 1996
    509'.2'2–dc20

    [B]   96-25579
                                                    CIP

Printed in the United States of America

10 9 8 7 6 5 4

Contents

Albert Einstein

VOLUME 1

VOLUME 2

Scientists by Field of Specialization

Italic type indicates volume numbers.

Ruth Patrick

Botany

Chemistry

Climatology

Computer Science

Medicine

Metallurgy

Meteorology

Microbiology

Microscopy

Molecular Biology

Physiology

Psychiatry

Psychology

Radiology

Rocket Science

Seismology

Sociobiology

Surgery

Virology

Zoology

Reader's Guide

An Wang

Budding scientists and those entering the fascinating world of science for fun or study will find inspiration in these three volumes. *Scientists: The Lives and Works of 150 Scientists* presents detailed biographies of the women and men whose theories, discoveries, and inventions have revolutionized science and society. From Louis Pasteur to Bill Gates and Elijah McCoy to Margaret Mead, *Scientists* explores the pioneers and their innovations that students most want to learn about.

Scientists from around the world and from the Industrial Revolution until the present day are featured, in fields such as astronomy, ecology, oceanography, physics, and more.

In *Scientists* students will find:

- 150 scientist biographies, each focusing on the scientist's early life, formative experiences, and inspirations—details that keep students reading

- "Impact" boxes that draw out important information and sum up why each scientist's work is indeed revolutionary

- 120 biographical boxes that highlight individuals who influenced the work of the featured scientist or who conducted similar research
- Sources for further reading so students know where to delve even deeper
- More than 300 black-and-white portraits and additional photographs that give students a better understanding of the people and inventions discussed

Each *Scientists* volume begins with a listing of scientists by field, ranging from aeronautical engineering to zoology; a timeline of major scientific breakthroughs; and a glossary of scientific terms used in the text. Volumes conclude with a cumulative subject index so students can easily find the people, inventions, and theories discussed throughout *Scientists*.

Acknowledgment

Aaron Saari was an important asset to this project. In addition to conducting research, he wrote the biographical boxes and several main entries.

Suggestions

We welcome any comments on this work and suggestions for individuals to feature in future editions of *Scientists*. Please write: Editors, *Scientists,* U•X•L, Gale Research, 835 Penobscot Bldg., Detroit, Michigan 48226-4094; call toll-free: 800-877-4253; or fax to: 313-961-6348.

Timeline of Scientific Breakthroughs

Donald Johanson and Lucy

1730s **Charles Townshend** introduces innovative farming methods that help spur the Industrial Revolution in England.

1769 **Richard Arkwright** patents the water frame, a spinning machine powered by a water wheel.

1769 **James Watt** patents his design for the steam engine.

1774 **Joseph Priestley** reports the results of his experiments with oxygen, gets credit for discovering the gas.

1789 **William Herschel** completes his revolutionary study of the nature of the universe.

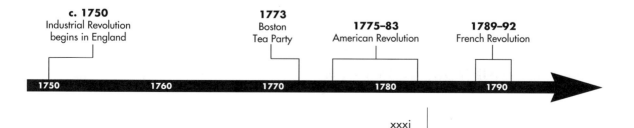

c. 1750
Industrial Revolution
begins in England

1773
Boston
Tea Party

1775–83
American Revolution

1789–92
French Revolution

1750   1760   1770   1780   1790

1789 **Antoine Lavoisier** describes the role of oxygen in animal and plant respiration.

1799 **Carl Friedrich Gauss** discovers the root form of all algebraic equations.

1808 **John Dalton** publishes his view of the atomic theory of matter, marking the beginning of modern chemistry.

1808 **Humphry Davy** invents the carbon arc lamp, initiating the entire science of electric lighting.

1823 **Charles Babbage** begins to build his Difference Engine, predecessor of the modern digital computer.

1831 **Michael Faraday** confirms that electricity and magnetism are a single force.

1847 **James Prescott Joule** publishes his calculation for the mechanical equivalent of heat.

1848 **William Thomson, Lord Kelvin** develops the Kelvin scale of absolute temperature.

1854 **Louis Pasteur** begins his experiments with fermentation that lead to the widespread sterilization of foods.

1856 **Henry Bessemer** patents the converter, a device that will revolutionize the steelmaking industry.

1859 **Charles Darwin** publishes *The Origin of Species by Means of Natural Selection,* "the book that shook the world."

1864–73 **James Clerk Maxwell** devises equations that prove that magnetism and electricity are distinctly related.

1865 **Gregor Mendel** presents his basic laws of heredity.

1867 **Alfred Nobel** patents dynamite.

1869 **Dmitry Mendeleev** formulates the periodic law.

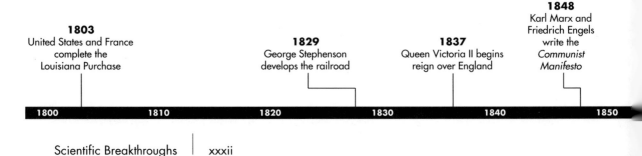

1803
United States and France complete the Louisiana Purchase

1829
George Stephenson develops the railroad

1837
Queen Victoria II begins reign over England

1848
Karl Marx and Friedrich Engels write the *Communist Manifesto*

1800   1810   1820   1830   1840   1850

1871   **Luther Burbank** develops the Burbank potato.

1872   **Elijah McCoy** patents the lubricating cup for steam engines that eventually becomes known as "the real McCoy."

1876   **Alexander Graham Bell** patents the telephone.

1877   **Thomas Alva Edison** invents the phonograph; two years later he demonstrates in public the first incandescent lightbulb.

1884   **Svante Arrhenius** formulates electrolytic dissociation theory, explaining how some substances conduct electricity in solutions.

1887   **Nikola Tesla** perfects the use of alternating-current electricity in his polyphase motor.

1887   **Granville T. Woods** patents the railway telegraph, allowing communication between moving trains.

1892   **Rudolf Diesel** patents an internal-combustion engine superior to the gasoline-powered engines of the day.

1895   **Wilhelm Röntgen** discovers X rays.

1896   **George Washington Carver** joins the Tuskegee Institute, beginning his career in scientific agriculture.

1897   **Guglielmo Marconi** patents the wireless radio.

1898   **Marie Curie** and **Pierre Curie** publish the first in a series of papers on radioactivity.

1899   **Sigmund Freud** lays out the basic principles of psychoanalytic theory in *The Interpretation of Dreams*.

1900   **David Hilbert** sets an agenda of twenty-three problems for mathematicians to solve during the twentieth century.

1900   **Max Planck** formulates the quantum theory, taking the science of physics into the modern age.

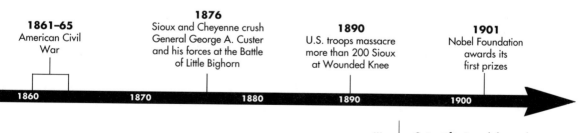

1861–65
American Civil War

1876
Sioux and Cheyenne crush General George A. Custer and his forces at the Battle of Little Bighorn

1890
U.S. troops massacre more than 200 Sioux at Wounded Knee

1901
Nobel Foundation awards its first prizes

1860   1870   1880   1890   1900

1900   **Florence R. Sabin** commences her studies of the human lymphatic system.

1903   **Bertrand Russell** unites logic and mathematics in *The Principals of Mathematics.*

1903   **Wilbur Wright** and **Orville Wright** achieve the first sustained flights in a power-driven aircraft.

c. 1903 **Arthur C. Parker** conducts his first formal archaeological excavation on the Cattaraugus Reservation.

1905   **Albert Einstein** formulates his special theory of relativity, changing forever the way scientists look at the nature of space, time, and matter.

1906   **Lee De Forest** patents the audion tube (triode), crucial to the development of the modern radio.

1910   **Annie Jump Cannon**'s method for classifying stars, known as the Harvard system, is adopted by the astronomical community.

1910   **Ernest Rutherford** determines the structure of the atom.

1912   **Alfred Wegener** proposes the theory of continental drift.

1913   **Niels Bohr** introduces the quantum mechanical model of the atom.

1913   **C. G. Jung** publishes *The Psychology of the Unconscious* and is outcast by the psychoanalytic community.

1919   **Karl von Frisch** discovers that honeybees communicate through ritual dances.

1919   **Karl Menninger** and his father open the Menninger Clinic for psychiatric treatment and research.

1908
Henry Ford introduces
the Model T

1914
World War I
begins

1917
Russian Revolution

1920
19th Amendment
gives American
women the
right to vote

1923
Time magazine
begins publication

| 1910 | 1913 | 1916 | 1919 | 1922 | 1925 |

1920–40 **Edith H. Quimby** conducts studies of the effects of radiation on the body.

1924 **Vladimir Zworykin** patents the kinescope, or the picture tube, which will make television as we know it possible.

1926 **Robert H. Goddard** launches the first liquid-propellant rocket.

1926 **Ivan Pavlov** publishes his masterwork, *Conditioned Reflexes*.

1927 **William Augustus Hinton** develops a test that becomes the standard for diagnosing syphilis.

1928 **Alexander Fleming** discovers penicillin.

1928 **Margaret Mead** publishes *Coming of Age in Samoa*.

1929 **Edwin Hubble** initiates the theory of an expanding universe.

1930s–40s **B. F. Skinner** conducts experiments that convince him that behavior can be controlled through the environment.

c. 1932 **Ruth Patrick** begins studying the presence of diatoms in various marine ecosystems.

1935 **Subrahmanyan Chandrasekhar** rocks the astronomical community with his radical theories on the evolution of white dwarf stars.

1935 **Percy L. Julian** synthesizes physostigmine, a chemical used in the treatment of glaucoma.

1935 **Charles F. Richter** develops the Richter scale to measure earthquake intensity.

1935 **Robert Watson-Watt** develops radar.

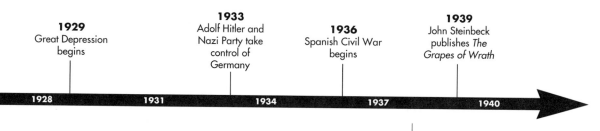

1929
Great Depression begins

1933
Adolf Hitler and Nazi Party take control of Germany

1936
Spanish Civil War begins

1939
John Steinbeck publishes *The Grapes of Wrath*

1928   1931   1934   1937   1940

c. 1935　**Berta Scharrer** and her husband Ernst begin their pioneering work in neuroendocrinology.

1935–38　**Konrad Lorenz** spends his "goose summers" confirming his many hypotheses on animal behavior patterns.

1938　**Lise Meitner,** with Otto Robert Frisch, develops the theory that explains nuclear fission.

c. 1938　**Katharine Burr Blodgett** invents nonreflecting glass.

1939　**Charles Richard Drew** develops a method to process and preserve blood plasma through dehydration.

1939　**Lloyd A. Hall** cofounds the Institute of Food Technologies.

1939　**Ernest Everett Just** publishes his findings on the role protoplasm plays in a cell.

1939　**Linus Pauling** publishes the landmark *Nature of the Chemical Bond and the Structure of Molecules and Crystals.*

1942　**Enrico Fermi** produces the first self-sustaining nuclear chain reaction.

1942　The World Health Organization adopts **Florence Seibert**'s skin test as the standard tool for diagnosing tuberculosis.

1944　**Norman Borlaug** shares agricultural advances with the Mexican government, thus starting the Green Revolution.

1944　**George H. Hitchings** and **Gertrude Belle Elion** begin their twenty-five-year collaboration developing "rational" drugs.

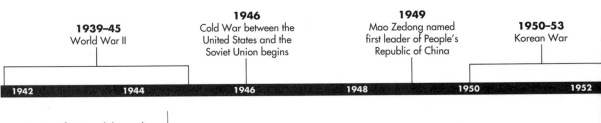

1939–45
World War II

1946
Cold War between the United States and the Soviet Union begins

1949
Mao Zedong named first leader of People's Republic of China

1950–53
Korean War

1942　　1944　　1946　　1948　　1950　　1952

1944 **Barbara McClintock** begins her studies that will lead to her discovery of "jumping genes."

1944 **Vivien Thomas** perfects the surgical technique that will save thousands of "blue babies."

1945 **J. Robert Oppenheimer** sees the culmination of his work as director of the Manhattan Project: two atomic bombs are dropped on Japan to end World War II.

1947 **Carl Ferdinand Cori** and **Gerty T. Cori** share the Nobel Prize for their studies on sugar metabolism, begun in the early 1920s.

1947 **Thor Heyerdahl** crosses the Pacific on the balsa raft *Kon-Tiki.*

1947 **Edwin H. Land** introduces the instant camera.

1947 **William Shockley** and his research team develop the transistor.

1948 **Dorothy Hodgkin** begins using X-ray crystallography to determine the structure of vitamin B_{12}.

1948 **Norbert Wiener** publishes *Cybernetics,* detailing his theories on control and communication in humans and machines.

c. 1948 **Albert Baez,** with Paul Kirkpatrick, builds the first X-ray microscope.

1949 **Maria Goeppert-Mayer** publishes her hypothesis for the structure of atomic nuclei.

1951 **R. Buckminster Fuller** patents the geodesic dome.

1951–52 **Jacques Cousteau,** with the *Calypso,* undertakes his first extensive expedition.

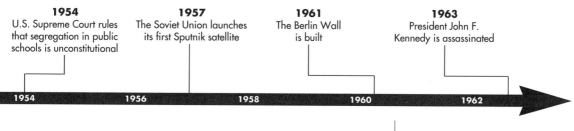

1954
U.S. Supreme Court rules that segregation in public schools is unconstitutional

1957
The Soviet Union launches its first Sputnik satellite

1961
The Berlin Wall is built

1963
President John F. Kennedy is assassinated

1954   1956   1958   1960   1962

1952   Through X-ray diffraction, **Rosalind Franklin** makes a preliminary determination of the structure of DNA.

1952   **Dorothy Horstmann** concludes that the virus that causes polio travels through the bloodstream to reach the nervous system.

1953   **Auguste Piccard** and **Jacques Piccard** set a depth record of almost two miles in their bathyscaphe *Trieste*.

1953   **James D. Watson** and **Francis Crick** unravel the mystery of the structure of DNA.

1954   **Angeles Alvariño** begins groundbreaking studies of marine zooplankton.

1955   **Jonas Salk**'s polio vaccine is pronounced effective, potent, and safe.

1955   **An Wang** patents techniques for developing magnetic core memories in computers.

1956   **Charlotte Friend** isolates the virus responsible for leukemia in mice, thereby pointing the way for future cancer research.

1956   **Chen Ning Yang** and **Tsung-Dao Lee** theorize that the unusual behavior of K-mesons violates the law of conservation of parity.

c. 1956   **Rosalyn Sussman Yalow** codevelops the diagnostic tool radioimmunoassay (RIA).

1957   **Albert Sabin** begins administering his oral polio vaccine to millions of Russian children.

1957   **Chien-Shiung Wu** conducts beta decay experiments that confirm the violation of the conservation of parity.

1958   **James Van Allen** discovers bands of high-level radiation surrounding Earth.

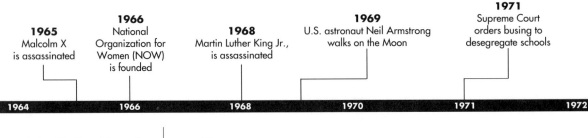

1965 Malcolm X is assassinated

1966 National Organization for Women (NOW) is founded

1968 Martin Luther King Jr., is assassinated

1969 U.S. astronaut Neil Armstrong walks on the Moon

1971 Supreme Court orders busing to desegregate schools

1964   1966   1968   1970   1971   1972

c. 1958   **Meredith Gourdine** develops the formula for electrogasdynamics.

1959   **Luis Alvarez** develops a 72-inch bubble chamber to better study subatomic particles.

1959   **Mary Leakey** finds the 1.75 million-year-old fossilized skull of a hominid that **Louis S. B. Leakey** names "East Africa man."

1959   **Marvin Minsky** cofounds the Artificial Intelligence Project at the Massachusetts Institute of Technology (MIT).

1959   **Robert Noyce** invents the integrated circuit, or microchip, revolutionizing twentieth-century technology.

1960   **George Bass** undertakes the first excavation of an underwater shipwreck site.

1960   **Jane Goodall** establishes a camp in the Gombe Stream Reserve, beginning her long-term studies of chimpanzee behavior.

1960   **Theodore Maiman** constructs the first working laser.

1960s   **Tetsuya Theodore Fujita** develops the F Scale, used to measure the strength of tornadoes.

1962   **Rachel Carson** publishes *Silent Spring,* sparking the beginning of the environmental movement.

1966   **Keiiti Aki** develops the seismic moment, a new method of measuring the magnitude of earthquakes.

1967   **E. Margaret Burbidge** and **Geoffrey Burbidge** publish *Quasi-Stellar Objects,* one of the first surveys of quasars.

1967   **Jocelyn Bell Burnell** discovers pulsars.

1968   **James E. Lovelock** publishes his controversial Gaia theory about Earth's regulation of her ecosystems.

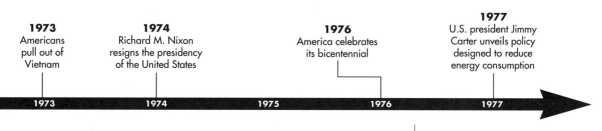

1973
Americans pull out of Vietnam

1974
Richard M. Nixon resigns the presidency of the United States

1976
America celebrates its bicentennial

1977
U.S. president Jimmy Carter unveils policy designed to reduce energy consumption

1973   1974   1975   1976   1977

1968   **Abdus Salam** announces his theory of the electroweak force.

1968   **Edward O. Wilson** confirms his theory of species equilibrium in a study of insect life on six islands off the Florida keys.

1970   **Bruce N. Ames** develops test for measuring the cancer-causing potential of chemicals.

1970   **Sylvia A. Earle** spends two weeks in an underwater chamber to study marine habitats.

1970   **Paul R. Ehrlich** helps found Zero Population Growth, a group that aims to educate people on the environmental dangers caused by overpopulation.

1971   **Fred Begay** begins his research into harnessing the clean, safe power of nuclear fusion.

1971   **Helen Caldicott** first organizes opposition to nuclear weapons, prompting the French government to cease atmospheric testing for a time.

1971   **Geoffrey Hounsfield** tests the first CAT scan machine.

1972   **Stephen Jay Gould** introduces the concept of punctuated equilibrium, contradicting a central tenet of the Darwinian theory of evolution.

1972   **Richard Leakey** unearths a 1.9-million-year-old *Homo habilis* skull, the oldest *H. habilis* specimen discovered so far.

1973   **Shirley Ann Jackson** is the first African American woman to earn a doctorate from MIT.

1974   **Paul Berg** publishes the "Berg letter," warning of the dangers of genetic engineering, a field he pioneered in the late 1960s and 1970s.

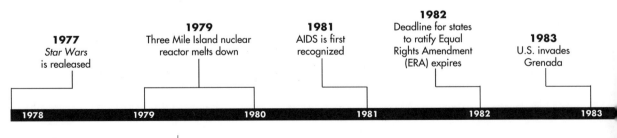

1977
Star Wars
is realeased

1979
Three Mile Island nuclear
reactor melts down

1981
AIDS is first
recognized

1982
Deadline for states
to ratify Equal
Rights Amendment
(ERA) expires

1983
U.S. invades
Grenada

1978   1979   1980   1981   1982   1983

1974 **Donald Johanson** finds Lucy, the oldest fossilized remains of a hominid ever unearthed.

c. 1974 **Stephen Hawking** discovers that black holes emit radiation.

1975 **Sandra Faber,** with Robert Jackson, formulates the first galactic sealing law, used to help calculate distances between galaxies.

1975 **Bill Gates** begins his career as a software designer and entrepreneur when he cofounds Microsoft.

1976 **Maxine Singer** helps formulate guidelines for responsible biochemical genetics research.

c. 1976 **James S. Williamson** supervises the design of the first solar-powered electricity-generating plant in the United States.

1977 **Steven Jobs** and Stephen Wozniak introduce the Apple II computer, touching off the personal computer revolution.

1977 **Louis Keith** and his twin brother found the Center for the Study of Multiple Births.

1978 **Elizabeth H. Blackburn** begins groundbreaking work that leads to the discovery of the enzyme telomerase.

1978 **Patrick Steptoe** produces the first test-tube baby.

1980 **Lynn Conway** publishes *Introduction to VLSI Systems,* which simplifies the way computer chips are produced.

1980 **Levi Watkins Jr.,** performs the first implantation of the automatic heart defibrillator.

1982 **Robert K. Jarvik** implants the Jarvik-7 artificial heart into Barney Clark.

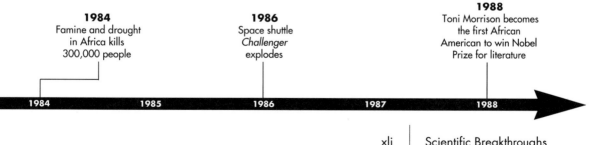

1984
Famine and drought in Africa kills 300,000 people

1986
Space shuttle *Challenger* explodes

1988
Toni Morrison becomes the first African American to win Nobel Prize for literature

1984   1985   1986   1987   1988

1983 **Irene Diggs** publishes *Black Chronology*, focusing on the accomplishments of people of African descent.

1984 **Helene D. Gayle** begins research on the effects of AIDS on children throughout the world.

1984 **Jaron Lanier** founds VPL Research Inc., to provide virtual reality software to the general computer user.

1985 Using technology he calls telepresence, **Robert D. Ballard** discovers the remains of the sunken *Titanic*.

1986 **Sally Fox** opens a mail-order business to sell the naturally colored cotton fibers she developed.

1986 **Margaret Geller** reports finding a "Great Wall" of galaxies, forcing some cosmologists to rethink existing theories of the beginning of the universe.

c. 1986 **Francisco Dallmeier** begins biodiversity research and education programs in several countries.

1987 **Anthony S. Fauci**'s research team discovers how the AIDS virus is transmitted.

1987 **Oliver Wolf Sacks**'s 1973 book *Awakenings,* about his treatment of patients with sleeping sickness, is made into a popular film.

1990 **Walter Gilbert** starts the human genome project to compile a genetic map of the entire human being.

1993 **Mark Plotkin** publishes *Tales of a Shaman's Apprentice,* discussing his excursions into the Amazon rain forest in search of medicinal plants and traditions.

1989
Berlin Wall is destroyed

1990–91
Persian Gulf War

1992
Los Angeles riots

1993
Apartheid is outlawed in South Africa

1989 1990 1991 1992 1993

Words to Know

A

Absolute zero: the theoretical point at which a substance has no heat and motion ceases; equivalent to -276°C or -459.67°F.

Algae: a diverse group of plant or plantlike organisms that grow mainly in water.

Alpha particle: a positively charged nuclear particle that consists of two protons and two electrons; it is ejected at a high speed from disintegrating radioactive materials.

Alternating current: the flow of electrons first in one direction and then in the other at regular intervals.

Amino acids: organic acids that are the chief components of proteins.

Anatomy: the study of the structure and form of biological organisms.

Anthropology: the science that deals with the study of human beings, especially their origin, development, divisions, and customs.

Archaeology: the scientific study of material remains, such as fossils and relics, of past societies.

Artificial intelligence: the branch of science concerned with the development of machines having the ability to perform tasks normally thought to require human intelligence, such as problem solving, discriminating among single objects, and response to spoken commands.

Asteroid: one of thousands of small planets located in a belt between the orbits of Mars and Jupiter.

Astronomy: the study of the physical and chemical properties of objects and matter outside Earth's atmosphere.

Astrophysics: the branch of physics involving the study of the physical and chemical nature of celestial objects and events.

Atomic bomb: a weapon of mass destruction that derives its explosive energy from nuclear fission.

B

Bacteria: a large, diverse group of mostly single-celled organisms that play a key role in the decay of organic matter and the cycling of nutrients.

Bacteriology: the scientific study of bacteria, their characteristics, and their activities as related to medicine, industry, and agriculture.

Bacteriophage: a virus that infects bacteria.

Behaviorism: the school of psychology that holds that human and animal behavior is based not on independent will nor motivation but rather on response to reward and punishment.

Beta decay: process by which a neutron in an atomic nucleus breaks apart into a proton and an electron.

Big bang: in astronomy, the theory that the universe resulted from a cosmic explosion that occurred billions of years ago and then expanded over time.

Biochemistry: the study of chemical compounds and processes occurring in living organisms.

Biodiversity: the number of different species of plants and animals in a specified region.

Biology: the scientific study of living organisms.

Biophysics: the branch of biology in which the methods and principles of physics are applied to the study of living things.

Biotechnology: use of biological organisms, systems, or processes to make or modify products.

Botany: the branch of biology involving the study of plant life.

C

Carcinogen: a cancer-causing agent, such as a chemical or a virus.

Cathode: a negatively charged electrode.

Cathode rays: electrons emitted by a cathode when heated.

Chemistry: the science of the nature, composition, and properties of material substances and their transformations.

Chromosome: threadlike structure in the nucleus of a cell that carries thousands of genes.

Circuit: the complete path of an electric current including the source of electric energy; an assemblage of electronic elements.

Climatology: the scientific study of climates and their phenomena.

Combustion: a rapid chemical process that produces heat and light.

Conductor: a substance able to carry an electrical current.

Conservation biology: the branch of biology that involves conserving rapidly vanishing wild animals, plants, and places.

Conservation laws: laws of physics that state that a particular property, mass, energy, momentum, or electrical charge is not lost during any change.

Cosmic rays: charged particles, mainly the nuclei of hydrogen and other atoms, that bombard Earth's upper atmosphere at velocities close to that of light.

Cosmology: the study of the structure and evolution of the universe.

Cross-fertilization: a method of fertilization in which the gametes (mature male or female cells) are produced by separate individuals or sometimes by individuals of different kinds.

Cryogenics: the branch of physics that involves the production and effects of very low temperatures.

Crystallography: the science that deals with the forms and structures of crystals.

Cytology: the branch of biology concerned with the study of cells.

D

Diffraction: the spreading and bending of light waves as they pass through a hole or slit.

Direct current: a regular flow of electrons, always in the same direction.

DNA (deoxyribonucleic acid): a long molecule composed of two chains of nucleotides (organic chemicals) that contain the genetic information carried from one generation to another.

E

Earthquake: an unpredictable event in which masses of rock shift below Earth's surface, releasing enormous amounts of energy and sending out shockwaves that sometimes cause the ground to shake dramatically.

Ecology: the branch of science dealing with the interrelationship of organisms and their environments.

Ecosystem: community of plants and animals and the physical environment with which they interact.

Electrochemistry: the branch of physical chemistry involving the relation of electricity to chemical changes.

Electrodes: conductors used to establish electrical contact with a nonmetallic part of a circuit.

Electromagnetism: the study of electric and magnetic fields and their interaction with electric charges and currents.

Electron: a negatively charged particle that orbits the nucleus of an atom.

Entomology: the branch of zoology dealing with the study of insects.

Environmentalism: the movement to preserve and improve the natural environment, and particularly to control pollution.

Enzyme: any of numerous complex proteins that are produced by living cells and spark specific biochemical reactions.

Epidemiology: the study of the causes, distribution, and control of disease in populations.

Ethnobotany: the plant lore of a race of people.

Ethnology: science that deals with the division of human beings into races and their origin, distribution, relations, and characteristics.

Ethology: the scientific and objective study of the behavior of animals in the wild rather than in captivity.

Evolution: in the struggle for survival, the process by which successive generations of a species pass on to their offspring the characteristics that enable the species to survive.

Extinction: the total disappearance of a species or the disappearance of a species from a given area.

F

Fossils: the remains, traces, or impressions of living organisms that inhabited Earth more than ten thousand years ago.

G

Gamma rays: short electromagnetic wavelengths that come from the nuclei of atoms during radioactive decay.

Gene: in classical genetics, a unit of hereditary information that is carried on chromosomes and determines observable characteristics; in molecular genetics, a special sequence of DNA or RNA located on the chromosome.

Genetic code: the means by which genetic information is translated into the chromosomes that make up living organisms.

Genetics: the study of inheritance in living organisms.

Genome: genetic material of a human being; the complete genetic structure of a species.

Geochemistry: the study of the chemistry of Earth (and other planets).

Geology: the study of the origin, history, and structure of Earth.

Geophysics: the physics of Earth, including studies of the atmosphere, earthquakes, volcanism, and oceans.

Global warming: the rise in Earth's temperature that is attributed to the buildup of carbon dioxide and other pollutants in the atmosphere.

Greenhouse effect: warming of Earth's atmosphere due to the absorption of heat by molecules of water vapor, carbon dioxide, methane, ozone, nitrous oxide, and chlorofluorocarbons.

H

Herpetology: the branch of zoology that deals with reptiles and amphibians.

Hominids: humanlike creatures.

Hormones: chemical messengers produced in living organisms that play significant roles in the body, such as affecting growth, metabolism, and digestion.

Horticulture: the science of growing fruits, vegetables, and ornamental plants.

Hybridization: cross-pollination of plants of different varieties to produce seed.

I

Immunology: the branch of medicine concerned with the body's ability to protect itself from disease.

Imprinting: the rapid learning process that takes place early in the life of a social animal and establishes a behavioral pattern, such as a recognition of and attraction to its own kind or a substitute.

In vitro fertilization: fertilization of eggs outside of the body.

Infrared radiation: electromagnetic rays released by hot objects; also known as a heat radiation.

Infertility: the inability to produce offspring for any reason.

Invertebrates: animals lacking a spinal column.

Ion: an atom or groups of atoms that carries an electrical charge-either positive or negative-as a result of losing or gaining one or more electrons.

Isotopes: atoms of a chemical element that contain the same number of protons but a different number of neutrons.

L

Laser: acronym for light amplification by stimulated emission of radiation; a device that produces intense light with a precisely defined wavelength.

Light-year: in astronomy, the distance light travels in one year, about six trillion miles.

Limnology: the branch of biology concerning freshwater plants.

Logic: the science of the formal principles of reasoning.

M

Magnetic field: the space around an electric current or a magnet in which a magnetic force can be observed.

Maser: acronym for microwave amplification of stimulated emission of radiation; a device that produces radiation in short wavelengths.

Metabolism: the process by which living cells break down organic compounds to produce energy.

Metallurgy: the science and technology of metals.

Meteorology: the science that deals with the atmosphere and its phenomena and with weather and weather forecasting.

Microbiology: branch of biology dealing with microscopic forms of life.

Microwaves: electromagnetic radiation waves between one millimeter and one centimeter in length.

Molecular biology: the study of the structure and function of molecules that make up living organisms.

Molecule: the smallest particle of a substance that retains all the properties of the substance and is composed of one or more atoms.

Mutation: any permanent change in hereditary material, involving either a physical change in chromosome relations or a biochemical change in genes.

N

Natural selection: the natural process by which groups best adjusted to their environment survive and reproduce, thereby passing on to their offspring genetic qualities best suited to that environment.

Nervous system: the bodily system that in vertebrates is made up of the brain and spinal cord, nerves, ganglia, and other organs and that receives and interprets stimuli and transmits impulses to targeted organs.

Neurology: the scientific study of the nervous system, especially its structure, functions, and abnormalities.

Neurosecretion: the process of producing a secretion by nerve cells.

Neurosis: any emotional or mental disorder that affects only part of the personality, such as anxiety or mild depression, as a result of stress.

Neutron: an uncharged particle found in atomic nuclei.

Neutron star: a hypothetical dense celestial object that consists primarily of closely packed neutrons that results from the collapse of a much larger celestial body.

Nova: a star that suddenly increases in light output and then fades away to its former obscure state within a few months or years.

Nuclear fallout: the drifting of radioactive particles into the atmosphere as the result of nuclear explosions.

Nuclear fission: the process in which an atomic nucleus is split, resulting in the release of large amounts of energy.

O

Oceanography: the science that deals with the study of oceans and seas.

Optics: the study of light and vision.

Organic: of, relating to, or arising in a bodily organ

Ozone layer: the atmospheric layer of approximately twenty to thirty miles above Earth's surface that protects the lower atmosphere from harmful solar radiation.

P

Paleoanthropology: the branch of anthropology dealing with the study of mammal fossils.

Paleontology: the study of the life of past geological periods as known from fossil remains.

Particle physics: the branch of physics concerned with the study of the constitution, properties, and interactions of elementary particles.

Particles: the smallest building blocks of energy and matter.

Pathology: the study of the essential nature of diseases, especially the structural and functional changes produced by them.

Periodic table: a table of the elements in order of atomic number, arranged in rows and columns to show periodic similarities and trends in physical and chemical properties.

Pharmacology: the science dealing with the properties, reactions, and therapeutic values of drugs.

Physics: the science that explores the physical properties and composition of objects and the forces that affect them.

Physiology: the branch of biology that deals with the functions and actions of life or of living matter, such as organs, tissues, and cells.

Plankton: floating animal and plant life.

Plasma physics: the branch of physics involving the study of electrically charged, extremely hot gases.

Primate: any order of mammals composed of humans, apes, or monkeys.

Protein: large molecules found in all living organisms that are essential to the structure and functioning of all living cells.

Proton: a positively charged particle found in atomic nuclei.

Psychiatry: the branch of medicine that deals with mental, emotional, and behavioral disorders.

Psychoanalysis: the method of analyzing psychic phenomenon and treating emotional disorders that involves treatment sessions during which the patient is encouraged to talk freely about personal experiences, especially about early childhood and dreams.

Psychology: the study of human and animal behavior.

Psychotic: a person with severe emotional or mental disorders that cause a loss of contact with reality.

Q

Quantum: any of the very small increments or parcels into which many forms of energy are subdivided.

Quasar: celestial object more distant than stars that emits excessive amounts of radiation.

R

Radar: acronym for radio detection and ranging; the process of using radio waves to detect objects.

Radiation: energy emitted in the form of waves or particles.

Radio waves: electromagnetic radiation.

Radioactive fallout: the radioactive particles resulting from a nuclear explosion.

Radioactivity: the property possessed by some elements (as uranium) or isotopes (as carbon 14) of spontaneously emitting energetic particles (as electrons or alpha particles) by disintegration of their atomic nuclei.

Radiology: the branch of medicine that uses X rays and radium (an intensely radioactive metallic element) to diagnose and treat disease.

Redshift: the increase in the wavelength of all light received from a celestial object (or wave source), usually because the object is moving away from the observer.

RNA (ribonucleic acid): any of various nucleic acids that are associated with the control of cellular chemical activities.

S

Scientific method: collecting evidence meticulously and theorizing from it.

Seismograph: a device that records vibrations of the ground and within Earth.

Seismology: the study and measurement of earthquakes.

Semiconductor: substances whose ability to carry electrical current is lower than that of a conductor (like metal) and higher than that of insulators (like rubber).

Shortwave: a radio wave having a wavelength between ten and one hundred meters.

Sociobiology: the systematic study of the biological basis for all social behavior.

Solid state: using semiconductor devices rather than electron tubes.

Spectrum: the range of colors produced by individual elements within a light source.

Steady-state theory: a theory that proposes that the universe has neither a beginning nor an end.

Stellar spectra: the distinctive mix of radiation emitted by every star.

Stellar spectroscopy: the process that breaks a star's light into component colors so that the various elements of the star can be observed.

Sterilization: boiling or heating of instruments and food to prevent proliferation of microorganisms.

Supernova: a catastrophic explosion in which a large portion of a star's mass is blown out into space, or the star is entirely destroyed.

T

Theorem: in mathematics, a formula, proposition, or statement.

Thermodynamics: the branch of physics that deals with the mechanical action or relations of heat.

Trace element: a chemical element present in minute quantities.

Transistor: a solid-state electronic device that is used to control the flow of electricity in electronic equipment and consists of a small block of semiconductor with at least three electrodes.

V

Vaccine: a preparation administered to increase immunity to polio.

Vacuum tube: an electric tube from which all matter has been removed.

Variable stars: stars whose light output varies because of internal fluctuations or because they are eclipsed by another star.

Variation: in genetics, differences in traits of a particular species.

Vertebrate: an animal that has a spinal column.

Virology: the study of viruses.

Virtual reality: an artificial computer-created environment that seeks to mimic reality.

Virus: a microscopic agent of infection.

W

Wavelength: the distance between one peak of a wave of light, heat, or energy and the next corresponding peak.

X

X ray: a form of electromagnetic radiation with an extremely short wavelength that is produced by bombarding a metallic target with electrons in a vacuum.

Z

Zoology: the branch of biology concerned with the study of animal life.

Zooplankton: small drifting animal life in the ocean.

SCIENTISTS:

The Lives and
Works of
150 Scientists

Keiiti Aki

Born March 3, 1930
Yokohama, Japan

Japanese-born American seismologist Keiiti Aki has made several innovative contributions to the science of seismology. Perhaps his most important achievement was the 1966 discovery of a new method of measuring the magnitude of an earthquake. Called the seismic moment, it was a refinement of the less precise Richter scale invented by **Charles F. Richter** (see entry). Aki's discoveries have helped scientists to better anticipate earthquakes and to control casualties from seismic events. He has also pursued research in the propagation of seismic waves, discovery of geothermal energy sources, and analysis of the earth's crustal structure.

Keiiti Aki discovered the seismic moment, a new way of measuring the magnitude of an earthquake.

Embarks on impressive career

Aki was born in Yokohama, Japan, on March 3, 1930, the son of Koichi and Humiko Kojima Aki. He was educated at the University of Tokyo, where he earned a bachelor's degree in 1952 and a doctorate in geophysics in 1958. In 1956 he married Haruko Uyeda, the sister of geophysicist and tectonics expert Seiya Uyeda. They would later have two sons.

After receiving his doctorate, Aki came to the United States as a Fulbright resident fellow in geophysics at the California Institute of Technology (Cal Tech) in Pasadena. He remained for two years, then returned to Japan, where he joined the Earthquake Research Institute at the University of Tokyo. He was first a research fellow in seismology from 1960 to 1962, and then an associate professor from 1963 to 1965. He returned briefly to Cal Tech for the academic year 1962–63 as a visiting associate professor of geophysics, and came to the United States permanently in 1966, when he joined the geophysics faculty at the Massachusetts Institute of Technology (MIT). After becoming a U.S. citizen in 1976, Aki remained at MIT for seven years.

Adds to earthquake knowledge

At Cal Tech and MIT Aki gained prominence as one of the world's foremost seismologists, a scientist who studies and measures earthquakes. An earthquake is an unpredictable event in which masses of rock shift below the earth's surface, releasing enormous amounts of energy and sending out shock waves that sometimes cause the ground to shake dramatically. Not all earthquakes cause calamity, but they are known to be one of the earth's most destructive forces. Entire structures, including buildings and dams, have been known to collapse in an earthquake.

Earthquakes occur along fault lines, which are boundaries of different layers, or plates, of rock masses on the crust of and within the earth. The movement of one immense plate can shift great masses of weight and pressure onto other weak layers. When this pressure gives way, an earthquake can take

place. An earthquake's power can be measured in two ways: by intensity and by magnitude. The intensity of a quake is usually described through people's perceptions and the severity of building destruction.

Around 1930 the United States adopted and revised an early European method of judging earthquake intensity called the Mercalli scale. The Modified Mercalli scale has twelve

A section of the Golden Gate Highway after a powerful earthquake rocked the San Francisco area in 1994.

Keiiti Aki

Waverly Person, American Geophysicist

In January 1994 a major earthquake rocked the Los Angeles, California, area, killing sixty-one people and leaving more than three thousand homeless. One of the first experts called upon for information and advice was Waverly Person (1927–), director of the National Earthquake Information Center (NEIC) at the U.S. Geological Survey, headquartered in Golden, Colorado. A veteran seismologist and geophysicist, Person has worked in the field of earthquake studies for more than thirty years. He is also the first African American to hold such a prominent position in the U.S. Department of the Interior.

As chief of the NEIC, Person is responsible for locating earthquakes and computing their magnitude. Satellites and a host of sophisticated measuring devices record the quakes—as many as fifty a day worldwide. Person and his staff are charged with interpreting the information and disseminating it quickly and effectively to emergency crews, government officials, and the news media throughout the world.

different ratings, ranging from Level I, which is described as "barely felt except by a very few," to, for example, Level X, when many structures completely collapse. The magnitude is measured by using a seismograph, a device that records vibrations within the earth and of the ground. Today seismologists use the Richter scale to express earthquake magnitude. It was named after its inventor, Charles F. Richter, who was a professor of seismology at the California Institute of Technology, where Aki taught during the 1960s.

Makes major contributions to seismology

Aki's most important contribution to the science of seismology was his introduction, in 1966, of a new method of measuring the magnitude of an earthquake. Called the seismic moment, it is calculated using three types of information: geodetic (mathematical calculations), geologic, and seismic. Aki's innovation is a refinement over the less precise Richter scale.

Aki considers his most original innovation, however, to be the concept of coda waves. These waves are named after the musical term *coda,* which is the section of a composition that brings a musical piece to a close. An earthquake generates several kinds of waves that radiate outward from the epicenter (the part of the earth's surface directly above the focus, or origin, of an earthquake) in all directions. When the waves have receded, the earth near the epicenter continues to vibrate, and the remaining vibrations (the "tail" of the waves, or very ends) are called coda waves. Analysis of the waves reveals information about the source of the earthquake and the geology of the places where the recording instruments are located.

Develops seismic tomography

In the 1970s Aki developed an idea that is now called seismic tomography. Tomography is a method of producing a three-dimensional image of the internal structure of an object. Seismic tomography is similar to medical tomography in that it provides a means for scientists to create three-dimensional models of the interior of the earth, much as physicians can do with the human body. More recently, Aki formulated models to explain the "harmonic tremor" that accompanies volcanic eruptions. He also developed a technique called the Aki-Larner method, which calculates seismic motion in places in the earth's crust with irregular or unstable layers. In addition, Aki has applied fractal geometry (the study of curves or shapes that repeat themselves) to investigations of fault systems.

Receives awards and honors

Aki has served as an adviser to many scientific organizations, including the Los Alamos National Laboratory, the Nuclear Regulatory Commission, and the U.S. Geological Survey. He has also acted as an advisor to the United Nations. In 1984 he became the W. M. Keck Foundation Professor of Geological Sciences at the University of Southern California at Los Angeles.

Aki's book *Quantitative Seismology* became a standard textbook for advanced seismology students. He has edited numerous other books, as well, with subject matter ranging from the process of mountain development to the seismology of volcanoes. He is a member of the National Academy of Sciences, the American Geophysical Union, and other scientific organizations, and is an honorary member of a number of international societies, such as the Royal Astronomical Society and the Seismological Society of Japan. In 1987 he received a medal from the Seismological Society of America, and six years later he was honored by the University of Southern California for the creativity of his research. Aki became director of the Southern California Earthquake Center in 1991.

Further Reading

Aki, Keiiti, and W. D. Stuart, eds., *Intermediate-Term Earthquake Prediction,* Birkhäuser, 1988.

Yong-Gang Li, John E. Vidale, Keiiti Aki, and others, "Fine Structure of the Landers Fault Zone," *Science,* July 15, 1994.

Yong-Gang Li, Peter Leary, Keiiti Aki, and Peter Malin, "Seismic Trapped Modes in the Oroville and San Andreas Fault Zones," *Science,* August 17, 1990.

Luis Alvarez

Born June 13, 1911
San Francisco, California
Died September 1, 1988
Berkeley, California

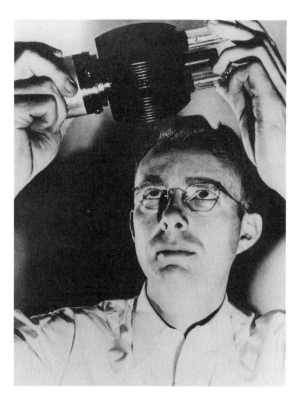

L uis Alvarez made several contributions to World War II military technology. Among them were a narrow-beam radar system that assists in landing airplanes in foggy weather and a radar target detection device for aerial bombing. Alvarez was one of the scientists who participated in the top-secret Manhattan Project, which produced the atom bombs that the United States dropped on Japan in 1945 at the end of World War II. He is also remembered for his controversial theory about the disappearance of dinosaurs. Alvarez's development of giant bubble chambers used to detect a variety of subatomic particles earned him the 1968 Nobel Prize for physics.

Luis Alvarez earned the title "prize-wild idea man" because of his involvement in a wide variety of research activities.

Shows early scientific aptitude

Luis Walter Alvarez was born in San Francisco, California, on June 13, 1911, to Dr. Walter Clement Alvarez, a medical researcher at the University of California at San Francisco, and Harriet Skidmore Smythe Alvarez. While living in San Francisco he attended grammar school and Polytechnic High School, where he avidly studied science. When his father accepted a position at the prestigious Mayo Clinic, the family moved to Rochester, Minnesota. Noticing his son's growing interest in physics (the science of matter and energy), Dr. Alvarez hired a machinist at the Mayo Clinic to tutor him privately on weekends. Alvarez enrolled at the University of Chicago in 1928 with plans to major in chemistry. During his junior year he changed his major to physics and received his bachelor of science degree in 1932. He stayed at Chicago for work on master's and doctoral degrees with Nobel laureate Arthur Compton.

Discovers east-west effect

For his doctoral dissertation Alvarez studied the diffraction of light (the spreading or bending of light waves as they pass through a hole or slit), a topic considered relatively trivial. His other graduate work, however, proved to be more useful. In one series of experiments, for example, he and a few colleagues discovered the "east-west effect" of cosmic rays (particles from outer space). They were able to explain that the number of cosmic rays reaching Earth's atmosphere differed depending on the direction from which they came. The east-west effect furnished evidence that cosmic rays consist of positively charged particles.

A few days after passing his oral examinations for his Ph.D., Alvarez married Geraldine Smithwick, a senior at the University of Chicago, with whom he later had two children, Walter and Jean. Less than a month after their wedding the Alvarezes moved to Berkeley, California, where Alvarez became a research scientist with Nobel Prize-winning physicist Ernest Orlando Lawrence. Thus began an association with the University of California that would continue for forty-two years.

Pursues wide range of interests

Alvarez soon earned the title "prize-wild idea man" from his colleagues because of his involvement in a wide variety of research activities. Within his first year at Berkeley, for instance, he discovered K-electron capture, the process in which atomic nuclei undergo decay by absorbing one of the electrons in their first orbital (part of the nuclear shell). Alvarez and a student, Jake Wiens, also developed a mercury vapor lamp consisting of the artificial isotope mercury-198. (Isotopes are atoms of the same element with differing numbers of neutrons in their nuclei.) The wavelength of the light emitted by the lamp was adopted as an official standard of length by the U.S. Bureau of Standards. In his research with Nobel Prize-winning physicist Felix Bloch, Alvarez developed a method for producing a beam of slow-moving neutrons, which was used to determine the magnetic moment of neutrons. (The magnetic moment is the strength of the turning force exerted by a magnetic field.) And shortly after the outbreak of World War II in Europe, Alvarez discovered tritium, a radioactive isotope of hydrogen.

IMPACT

Although physicist Luis Alvarez won the Nobel Prize for his work in developing the giant bubble chambers used to detect subatomic particles, he and his son Walter will probably be best remembered for sparking controversy in 1980 by suggesting that the extinction of dinosaurs was the result of an asteroid collision with Earth sixty-five million years ago. Since Alvarez's death additional evidence has been obtained to provide strong support for this theory, which is now referred to as the Cretaceous catastrophe.

Invents radar systems

World War II interrupted Alvarez's work at Berkeley. In 1940 he began research for the military at the Massachusetts Institute of Technology (MIT) radiation laboratory on radar (radio detecting and ranging) systems. Over the next three years he was involved in the development of three new types of radar systems. The first made use of a narrow radar beam that assists a ground-based controller in directing the "blind" landing of an airplane. The second system, code-named "Eagle," was a method for locating and bombing targets on the ground that could not be seen by a pilot. Alvarez's third invention became known as the microwave early-warning system, a mechanism for collecting images of aircraft movement in overcast skies.

Helps build first nuclear weapons

In 1943 Alvarez left MIT to join the Manhattan Project research team working in Los Alamos, New Mexico. His primary accomplishment with the team was the development of the detonating device used on the first plutonium bomb. Alvarez was aboard a B-29 bomber with a team that observed the first test of an atomic device at Alamogordo, south of Los Alamos. Three weeks later he flew in a B-29 that followed the bomber *Enola Gay* as it dropped the first atomic bomb on Hiroshima, Japan.

Like most scientists associated with the Manhattan Project, Alvarez was stunned and horrified by the destructive power of the weapon he had helped to create. Nonetheless, he never expressed any doubts or hesitation about the decision to use the bombs, since they brought a swift end to the war. Alvarez became one of a small number of scientists who felt strongly that the United States should continue its nuclear weapons development after World War II was over.

Builds particle accelerator

In the mid-1940s Alvarez returned to Berkeley, where he had been promoted to full professor. Determining that the future of nuclear physics lay in high energy research, he focused his attention on powerful particle accelerators (devices that accelerate electrons and protons to high velocity). His first project was to design and construct a linear accelerator for use with protons. Although his machine was similar to the electron accelerators that had been available for many years, the proton machine encountered a number of new problems. By 1947, however, Alvarez had solved those problems, and his forty-foot-long proton accelerator began operation.

Over the next decade the science of particle physics (the study of atomic components) developed rapidly at Berkeley. An important factor in that progress was the construction of the 184-inch synchrocyclotron at the university's radiation laboratory. The synchrocyclotron was a modified circular particle

accelerator capable of achieving much greater velocities than any other type of accelerator. The science of particle physics involves two fundamental problems: the creation of particles to be studied in an accelerator, and the detection and identification of those particles. As the result of a chance meeting with physicist Donald Glaser in 1953, Alvarez's interests shifted to particle detection.

Glaser had recently invented the bubble chamber, a device that detects the path of subatomic particles as they pass through a container of super-heated fluid. As the particles move through the liquid, they form ions—atoms that have gained or lost one or more electrons—that act as nuclei on which the super-heated material can begin to boil. A track of tiny bubbles then forms, showing the path taken by the parti-

Luis Alvarez in his Berkeley laboratory in 1946 with a Geiger counter, used to measure radioactivity.

Robert T. Bakker, American Paleontologist

Dinosaurs were not killed off by a sudden global climate change or by a monumental meteor strike, according to paleontologist Robert T. Bakker. He believes they underwent a series of extinctions—eight to twelve of them over a 185-million-year period—triggered by the formation of land bridges that exposed dinosaur species to other animals that may have been enemies, competed for food, or carried deadly diseases. During the 1980s, as he excavated in south-central Wyoming, Bakker found fossils indicating that 130 million years ago, between the Jurassic and Cretaceous periods, many of the large dinosaurs were dying out while small animals—turtles, crocodiles, lizards, salamanders, mammals, and a gull-sized pterodactyl—were thriving. He knew the dramatic shift was not caused by a meteor strike or a global climate change: both events would cause falling temperatures, dark skies, and similar changes more dangerous to small animals than to large ones. Bakker published his findings in 1990, but his theory has not yet gained widespread acceptance.

cles. In talking with Glaser, Alvarez realized that the bubble chamber could be refined and improved to track the dozens of new particles then being produced in the giant synchrocyclotron at Berkeley. Among these particles were some with very short lifetimes, known as resonance states.

Wins Nobel for bubble chamber

Improving Glaser's original bubble chamber involved a number of changes. First, Alvarez decided to use liquid hydrogen for the super-heated fluid, since it would be a more sensitive material than the diethyl ether employed by Glaser. In addition, he realized that sophisticated equipment would be needed to respond to and record the resonance states that often lasted no more than one-billionth of a second. The equipment he developed included relay systems that transmitted messages at high speeds and computer programs that could discard insignificant events and save significant events for analysis. Alvarez aimed at constructing larger and larger bubble chambers to record a greater number of events. Over a period of about five years, his chambers grew from a simple one-inch glass tube to his most ambitious instrument, a seventy-two-inch chamber that was first put into use in 1959. With these devices Alvarez eventually discovered dozens of new elementary particles, including the unusual resonance states.

The significance of Alvarez's work with bubble chambers was recognized in 1968, when he was awarded the Nobel Prize for physics. Accompanying him to the Nobel ceremonies was his second wife, Janet Landis, whom he had married in 1958. (They later had two children, Donald and Helen.) Apparently as a result of being separated during the war, Alvarez and his first wife had divorced.

Starts geological debate

Advancing years failed to reduce Alvarez's curiosity about a wide range of topics. In 1965 he was in charge of a joint Egyptian-American expedition whose goal was to search for hidden chambers in the pyramid of King Kefren at Giza, Egypt. The team aimed high energy muons (subatomic particles produced by cosmic rays) at the pyramid to look for regions of low density, which would indicate the presence of possible chambers. However, none were found.

Alvarez shared his last major scientific achievement with his son Walter, who was then a professor of geology at Berkeley. In 1980 the Alvarezes accidentally discovered a band of sedimentary rock in Italy. (Sedimentary rock is formed by sand, stones, and other matter carried and deposited by water, wind, or ice.) The rock contained an unusually high level of the rare metal iridium. Dating techniques set the age of the layer at about sixty-five million years. The Alvarezes hypothesized that the iridium came from an asteroid that struck Earth, thereby sending huge volumes of smoke and dust (including the iridium) into the atmosphere. The dusty cloud covered the planet for an extended period of time, blocked out sunlight, and caused the widespread death of plant life on Earth's surface. This loss of plant life, they speculated, may have brought about the extinction of plant-eating dinosaurs. While the theory has been accepted by many scientists—and has been confirmed to some extent by additional findings—it is still the subject of considerable debate.

Alvarez pursued scientific interests in other areas. He even assisted the Warren Commission in the investigation of the 1963 assassination of President John F. Kennedy. Among Alvarez's twenty-two patented inventions were a system for color television and an electronic indoor golf-training device developed for President Dwight D. Eisenhower. Luis Alvarez died of cancer in Berkeley on September 1, 1988.

Further Reading

Alvarez, Luis, *Alvarez: Adventures of a Physicist* (autobiography), Basic Books, 1987.

Current Biography, H. W. Wilson, 1947, pp. 9–10; 1988, p. 88.

Wasson, Tyler, ed., *Nobel Prize Winners,* H. W. Wilson, 1987, pp. 12–14.

Weber, Robert L., *Pioneers of Science: Nobel Prize Winners in Physics,* American Institute of Physics, 1980, pp. 212–14.

Angeles Alvariño

Born October 3, 1916
El Ferrol, Spain

Angeles Alvariño greatly contributed to the understanding of the ecology and geographic distribution of marine zooplankton and other marine organisms. During the course of her forty-year career as a research biologist, Alvariño discovered twenty-two new ocean species.

Aspires to become a doctor

Angeles Alvariño was born on October 3, 1916, in El Ferrol, Spain, to Antonio Alvariño Grimaldos, a physician, and Maria del Carmen González Diaz-Saavedra de Alvariño. An intelligent and curious child, Alvariño often explored her father's library, especially enjoying books on natural history. She wanted to become a physician like her father, but he discouraged such a choice. He did not want her to experience, as he had, the distress involved in treating patients whose suffering could not be alleviated.

Spanish-born American marine biologist Angeles Alvariño has discovered twenty-two new ocean species.

As an undergraduate at the University of Santiago de Compostela, Spain, Alvariño studied a wide range of courses in physical and natural sciences, social science, and the humanities. After passing final examinations and completing two dissertations for baccalaureate degrees in both science and humanities, she graduated with highest honors in 1933. Though Alvariño still longed to study medicine, her father continued to oppose her decision. Therefore, in 1934, she entered the University of Madrid (now known as the University Complutense) to study natural sciences. Her studies were interrupted, however, when the university was closed from 1936 to 1939 as a result of the Spanish Civil War.

Studies natural sciences

In 1940 Alvariño married Sir Eugenio Leira Manso, Captain of the Spanish Royal Navy and Knight of the Royal and Military Order of Saint Hermenegild. Continuing her studies at the University of Madrid, Alvariño earned a master's degree in natural sciences in 1941. For the next seven years she taught biology, zoology, botany, and geology in various colleges in El Ferrol.

In 1948 Alvariño left teaching to become a research biologist with the Spanish Department of Sea Fisheries in Madrid. Although the Spanish Institute of Oceanography, which was also located in Madrid, officially banned women, Alvariño conducted research and studied oceanography there. The quality of her work persuaded officials at the institute to admit her as a student researcher in 1950. The following year she received a doctoral certificate in experimental psychology, chemistry, and plant ecology from the University of Madrid.

Investigates zooplankton

After successfully competing in an examination for a position as a marine biologist-oceanographer, Alvariño joined the Spanish Institute of Oceanography in 1953. A year later she received a British Council Fellowship that enabled her to conduct research on zooplankton (small drifting animal life in the ocean) at the Marine Biological Laboratory in Plymouth, England. While working at the Plymouth lab she met Frederick Stratten Russell, an expert on hydromedusae (pronounced HI-dro-mih-DYOO-see; jellyfish), who directed her attention to chaetognaths (KEET-og-naths; arrow-worms), jellyfish, and siphonophores (sie-FAHN-uh-fores; small, free-swimming water organisms). For the study of these animals, which had received little attention, Alvariño designed and made plankton nets that she provided to Spanish fishing vessels and research ships so they could collect zooplankton samples.

Conducts groundbreaking research

In 1956 Alvariño was awarded a Fulbright Fellowship for research at the Woods Hole Oceanographic Institute on Cape Cod in Massachusetts. The president of the first U.S. Oceanographic Congress, Mary Sears, was impressed with Alvariño's work and recommended her to Dr. Roger Revelle at the Scripps Institute of Oceanography at La Jolla, California. Revelle appointed Alvariño to the position of biologist at the institute. During her years of research at Scripps, Alvariño produced a significant body of work focusing on chaetognaths, siphonophores, and hydromedusae. In 1967 she earned a doctor of sciences degree with highest honors from the University of Madrid.

Continues marine work

To further expand her research opportunities, in 1970 Alvariño became a fisheries biologist with the Southwest Fisheries Science Center in La Jolla, California, a division of the newly formed National Marine Fisheries Service. Continuing her study of predatory chaetognaths, siphonophores, and hydromedusae, she concentrated on their relationship to larval fish survival. Although Alvariño officially retired in 1987, she has continued her work, adding to the body of knowledge about zooplankton.

In 1993 Alvariño was awarded the Great Silver Medal of Galicia by King Carlos I and Queen Sophia of Spain. She participated in numerous expeditions aboard the research vessels of various countries, becoming the first woman to serve as a scientist on a British research vessel. Alvariño and her husband live in La Jolla; their daughter and only child, Angeles Leira-Alvariño, is an architect and city planner.

Further Reading

Adiyodi, K. G., and R. G. Adiyodi, eds., *Reproductive Biology of Invertebrates,* Volumes 1–2, Wiley & Sons, 1983; Volumes 4–5, Oxford & IBH Publishing, 1990–1992.

Bruce N. Ames

Born December 16, 1928
New York, New York

Bruce N. Ames, a biochemist and molecular biologist, is known for the Ames test, an indicator of the cancer-causing potential of chemicals. He has been at the center of numerous controversies involving the scientific and environmental policies relevant to cancer prevention. In the 1970s Ames was a staunch advocate of strict government control of synthetic (man-made) chemicals. By the 1980s, however, the discovery that many natural substances also caused gene mutation, and possibly cancer, led him to reverse his original position.

Bruce N. Ames is best known for developing the Ames test, which helps in the detection of cancer-causing chemicals.

Receives early science education

Bruce Nathan Ames was born on December 16, 1928, in New York City, the son of Dr. Maurice U. Ames, a high school teacher and administrator, and Dorothy Andres Ames. After graduating from the Bronx High School of Science in 1946, he went on to Cornell University in Ithaca, New York, where he received a B.A. degree in biochemistry in 1950. Three years

The scientific community was just beginning to make advancements in the study of cancer when Bruce Ames developed his test. The Ames test showed that over 80 percent of organic chemicals known to cause cancer in humans were mutagens, meaning they caused increased cell mutation. This result supported the theory that somatic cell mutation causes cancer. It also helped to validate the use of the Ames test for identifying mutagens when considering synthetic chemicals for industrial and commercial use. In addition to these practical results, the research of Ames and a colleague, H. J. Whitfield, led to important advances in understanding how mutation takes place.

later he earned a Ph.D. in the same field from the California Institute of Technology in Pasadena. From 1953 to 1967 Ames worked at the National Institutes of Health, primarily in the National Institute of Arthritis and Metabolic Diseases. In 1968 he moved to the Department of Biochemistry and Molecular Biology at the University of California at Berkeley as a full professor, later becoming the department chair. He was also named director of the university's National Institute of Environmental Health Science in 1979. Back in 1960 he married Dr. Giovanna Ferro-Luzzi, a biochemist who is also on the faculty at Berkeley. They have two children, Sofia and Matteo.

Develops Ames test

In the 1960s and early 1970s Ames devoted his energies to the development of the Ames test, a measure of the degree to which synthetic chemicals cause gene mutation, or a change in deoxyribonucleic acid (DNA), the molecule that carries genetic information. He began by deliberately mutating a *Salmonella* bacterium. The mutated bacterium could not produce an amino acid called histidine that normal bacteria manufacture in order to survive. Next Ames added just enough histidine to his altered *Salmonella* sample to allow the bacteria to live; at the same time he introduced one of several synthetic chemicals he was testing. If the added chemical caused genetic mutation, the abnormal gene of the *Salmonella* bacteria would undergo a fundamental change and again be able to produce histidine. Any mutation-causing test chemical was marked as a suspected carcinogen (cancer-causing agent), since cancer is associated with somatic cell mutation. (A somatic cell is a type of body cell that composes tissues, organs, and other parts, with the exception of egg and sperm cells.)

Makes other contributions

Beyond his work in genetic toxicology (the study of genetic poisons), Ames made important discoveries in molecular biology, including groundbreaking studies on the regulation of the histidine operon (the gene that controls histidine) and the role of transfer ribonucleic acid (RNA) in that regulation. In the 1980s Ames set up a database of animal cancer test results with colleague Lois Swirsky Gold. The database includes information on whether a chemical has tested positive as a carcinogen and, if it has, gives the degree of its virulence. From these data Ames developed a method for measuring the potential cancer-causing danger of a chemical. Called the daily Human Exposure dose/Rodent Potency dose (HERP), it compares the daily dose of a chemical known to cause cancer in test animals with the estimated daily dose of the chemical to which humans are normally exposed. The result is a percentage that suggests the degree of carcinogenicity (cancer-causing power) of a chemical for humans.

Reverses position on government regulations

During the 1970s Ames actively supported government policies to regulate the environmental use of synthetic chemicals. He believed that even small amounts of mutagenic chemicals might cause cancer. For instance, the Ames test showed that *tris* phosphate, a chemical used as a flame retardant on children's pajamas, was a mutagen. Ames was instrumental in persuading the U.S. government to ban the chemical. Similarly, when he found that some hair dyes contained mutagens, his advocacy led to governmental regulations that forced cosmetics companies to eliminate cancer-causing chemicals from their products.

In the early 1980s, however, Ames reversed his position, arguing that the government should not control the use of synthetic substances. He cited scientific studies showing that humans absorb only small doses of cancer-causing chemicals from manufactured products. Ames made this about-face partly as a result of learning that even chemicals found in nature can cause cancer. Concluding that more scientific evidence was needed, he called for increased research instead of government regulations that might hurt American economic competitiveness.

Argues against animal testing

Ames and Gold have also taken a stand against the use of bioassays (animal tests) in determining whether chemicals might cause cancer in humans. In a typical bioassay, rats are given a daily "maximum tolerated dosage" (MTD) of a particular chemical for a period of time (such as a year). The MTD is as much as the animal can be given without immediately becoming ill or dying. At the end of the time period, the number of animals that have developed cancers is tabulated as an indicator of the cancer-causing potential of the chemical being tested. Ames suggested that it is often the large dosage itself, rather than the nature of the particular chemical, that induces cancers in rats. He argued that the tests are not really valid for predicting human cancers because humans are not normally exposed to such large doses. His critics note, however, that he has not offered any substitute for animal testing.

Causes controversy

No one has successfully proven that low dosages of synthetic chemicals do not cause cancer. Ames and his critics agree that—since cancer is not yet fully understood—there is no perfect test for predicting the potential of many substances causing cancer in humans. Ames himself has described his public policy activism as a mere hobby, pointing to his most recent scientific work, which includes studies in the biochemistry of aging.

Receives recognition

Elected to the National Academy of Sciences in 1972, Ames has received several awards, including the Eli Lilly Award of the American Chemical Society in 1964, the Mott

Prize of the General Motors Cancer Research Foundation in 1983, and the Gold Medal of the American Institute of Chemists in 1991. He is the author or coauthor of more than 250 scientific articles.

Further Reading

Ames, Bruce N., and Lois Swirsky Gold, "Too Many Rodent Carcinogens: Mitogenesis Increases Mutagenesis," *Science,* August 31, 1990, pp. 970–71.

Bloyd-Pleshkin, Sharon, Richard Wiles, and Bruce N. Ames, "Pesticides: Pro and Con," *Vegetarian Times,* November 1995.

Edelson, Edward, "The Man Who Upset the Apple Cart," *Popular Science,* February 1990, pp. 64–68.

Marx, Jean, "Animal Carcinogen Testing Challenged," *Science,* November 9, 1990, pp. 743–45.

Moseley, Bill, "Interview: Bruce Ames," *Omni,* February 1991, pp. 75–106.

Spenser, Leslie, "Ban All Plants—They Pollute," *Forbes,* October 25, 1993.

Weinstein, I. Bernard, "Mitogenesis Is Only One Factor in Carcinogenesis," *Science,* January 25, 1991, pp. 387–88.

Richard Arkwright

Born December 23, 1732
Preston, Lancashire, England
Died August 3, 1792
Cromford, Derbyshire, England

By trade a barber and wig maker who had little formal education, Richard Arkwright developed machines and organized factories for the automatic spinning of cotton yarn.

As the textile industry began to expand in England in the eighteenth century, Richard Arkwright recognized the need for machines that would accelerate the spinning of cotton into yarn. Cotton manufacture had been introduced into England in the seventeenth century, yet a hundred years later yarn spinners were still using distaffs (a staff that holds the unspun cotton) and spinning wheels that dated back to the Middle Ages. This equipment could spin only one strand of yarn at a time. Fifty thousand spinners worked in Lancashire in Arkwright's time and still could not keep up with the demand for yarn from weavers.

Other inventors had tried with limited success to develop faster ways to spin yarn. In 1738 Lewis Paul and John Wyatt developed a machine that used rollers to spin cotton. Unfortunately, the design was flawed. Twenty-six years later James Hargreaves invented the spinning jenny, a hand-operated machine that could spin eight strands of yarn at a time. However, the yarn produced by this machine could be used only for the woof (or lateral threads) in cotton cloth. The warp (or longitudinal threads) were made from linen, a stronger material. Hargreaves's efforts were finally doomed because the spinning jenny provoked riots among textile workers who feared that the machines would put them out of work.

Becomes barber and wig maker

Arkwright was born on December 23, 1732, the youngest of thirteen children in a poor family in Preston, Lancashire, in northwestern England. As a child he received little if any schooling. Despite his lack of formal education, however, he gained a reputation for having a quick mind, a powerful curiosity, and great skill in improving upon the ideas of others. When Arkwright was still a teenager he was apprenticed to a barber and learned to make wigs out of human hair. In 1750 he moved to Bolton and joined the established wig-making company of Edward Pallit.

While working for Pallit, Arkwright developed a method for dyeing hair that was superior to any available at that time. He later sold his secret to other wig makers, earning enough money to start his own shop. Barbering and wig making did not provide Arkwright with a sufficient income, so for a time he owned a public house (or restaurant and tavern). In the mid-1750s he married Patience Holt, who died shortly after giving birth to a son. Arkwright later remarried twice.

Invents water frame

Sometime after his second marriage Arkwright began to experiment with mechanical objects as a hobby. In 1766, probably in the course of his own mechanical experiments, he became acquainted with John Kay, a mechanic and clock maker. The two men began working together to build a spinning machine, and Arkwright spent virtually every spare minute of his time on the project. Finally they were able to demonstrate the device in the home of a local schoolmaster in Preston. Known as the "water frame" because it was powered by a water wheel, the spinning machine consisted of two pairs of rollers that pulled cotton fibers taut and twisted them into a strong, fine thread. The diameter of the thread could be controlled by varying the tension and speed of the rollers.

Builds factories

In 1768 Arkwright moved to Nottingham, a center of the hosiery industry, where John Smalley, a liquor merchant and painter, and David Thornley joined him as partners. The next year Arkwright took out a patent on the water frame, claiming to be its inventor. He enlisted two stocking manufacturers, Samuel Need and Jedediah Strut, as financial backers. Together they built a small mill but did not have immediate success.

For the first few years of the mill's operation, the Arkwright family lived in poverty. Nevertheless, Arkwright was determined to expand the business. In 1771 he and his backers decided to build a mill at Cromford in Derbyshire, England. Although Cromford was somewhat isolated, the Derwent River provided water power for the machinery, and the families of local miners offered a potential labor force. The Cromford mill began operation in 1772.

Increases efficiency

In an effort to raise the output of the mill, Arkwright searched for more efficient ways to process raw cotton. In 1775 he patented a machine that would card (or comb and straighten) cotton by passing it over a roller covered with metal teeth. As the cotton was fed into the machine, the roller combed it into parallel fibers that were then formed into rovings (or bundles) and fed into the water frame to be spun into yarn.

Richard Arkwright's improved water frame, circa 1775.

As business gradually increased, Arkwright used his profits to build new factories. His prosperity aroused the anxiety of laborers at Birkacre, who in 1779 destroyed one of the mills. That factory was not rebuilt, but others were added to the Arkwright industries. By the following year he had established mills in Scotland and was selling water frames and carding machines to other business people throughout Britain. Arkwright earned high royalties for the use of the machines under a licensing arrangement.

Uses steam engines

Always intent on finding better ways to spin cotton yarn, Arkwright considered using steam engines to power the spinning frames. In 1786, after nine years of experimentation, he

Henry Ford, American Inventor

Henry Ford (1863–1947), the inventor of the Model T automobile, perfected the mass-production concepts Richard Arkwright had introduced more than a century earlier. Before Ford implemented assembly-line techniques, it took twelve and a half hours to build a single car. After the inventor's innovations were in place, the time required to build each Model T was reduced to a little more than an hour and a half. Thus, between 1908 and 1926 the cost of an automobile was lowered from $950 to an affordable $290.

Ford's new production method called for a worker to stand at one place while the automobile was moved along the "assembly line" on a conveyer belt. The parts the worker needed were brought to the work station on another conveyor. Bodies were built on one line, the chassis and drive train on another, and the two sections were bolted together at final assembly. Ford's mass-production techniques ultimately revolutionized modern industry.

installed steam engines in two of his factories. Next he arranged for all the operations in the manufacture of cotton yarn to be housed together in one building. Typically, his workers spent thirteen hours a day—six days a week—in the factory and earned ten to twelve shillings each week.

Prospers in spite of problems

As cotton manufacturing expanded during the 1780s, other business people using Arkwright's equipment tried to avoid paying him royalties. Some simply refused to pay, while others took out patents for machines similar to those he had patented. Arkwright sued several manufacturers over the use of his milling equipment, and he even appealed to the British Parliament for defense of his patents.

Although Arkwright eventually lost his carding machine patent and the patent on his water frame expired, he continued to prosper. He sold his machines, which he continued to improve, and joined in partnerships that gave him controlling interests in several companies. His shrewd business judgment and ability to organize factories and workers resulted in great success. In 1786 Arkwright was knighted by King George III. That year he began building his family a mansion named Castle, which was not completed until 1793, a year after his death.

Further Reading

Cardwell, Donald, *The Norton History of Technology,* Norton, 1995.

Fitton, R. S., *The Arkwrights: Spinners of Fortune,* Manchester University Press, 1989.

Lipson, E., *The History of the Woolen and Worsted Industries,* Frank Cass & Co., 1965.

Svante Arrhenius

Born February 19, 1859
Vik, Kalmar, Sweden
Died October 2, 1927
Stockholm, Sweden

Swedish physicist and chemist Svante Arrhenius was one of the founders of physical chemistry and a pioneer in the study of the greenhouse effect.

Svante August Arrhenius was instrumental in establishing the connection between physics (the study of matter and energy) and chemistry and is now regarded as one of the founders of the science called physical chemistry. In 1903 he was awarded the Nobel Prize in chemistry for his research on electrolytic dissociation, a theory that had won the lowest possible passing grade for his Ph.D. two decades earlier. During his later years Arrhenius became interested in the origin of life on Earth, arguing that life had arrived on the planet by means of spores blown through space from other inhabited worlds. He was also one of the first scientists to study the greenhouse effect.

Shows early aptitude

Arrhenius was born on February 19, 1859, in Vik (also known as Wik or Wijk), in the district of Kalmar, Sweden. His mother was the former Carolina Thunberg, and his father was

Svante Gustaf Arrhenius, a land surveyor and overseer at the castle of Vik on Lake Målar, near Uppsala. Showing evidence of intellectual brilliance at an early age, Arrhenius taught himself to read by the time he was three. He learned to do arithmetic by watching his father keep books for the Vik estate. When Arrhenius was eight he entered school in the fifth-grade class at the Cathedral School in Uppsala. After graduating in 1876, he enrolled at the University of Uppsala.

Arrhenius concentrated on mathematics, chemistry, and physics at the university, passing the candidate's examination for a bachelor's degree in 1878. He then began a graduate program in physics at Uppsala but left after three years of study. He was said to be dissatisfied with his physics adviser and was not impressed with the only adviser available in chemistry. In 1881 he transferred to the Physical Institute of the Swedish Academy of Sciences in Stockholm, where he studied electrical theory under Erik Edlund. After three years of research Arrhenius returned to Uppsala to present his doctoral dissertation and earn his degree.

Tries to solve electrical mystery

For the topic of his dissertation Arrhenius chose the electrical conductivity of solutions, a problem of considerable interest at the time. Scientists had known for a century that some substances would conduct electricity when dissolved in water. (They were nonconductors in their dry state.) These compounds were called electrolytes. Substances that would not conduct electricity when dissolved were called nonelectrolytes. In the early 1800s **Humphry Davy** (see entry) had shown that chemical compounds could be broken down into their elements through electrolysis. This process involved dissolving a substance and then passing an electric current through the solution. **Michael Faraday** (see entry) had used the term *ion* to refer hypothetically to particles of electricity, just as particles of matter are called atoms. But no one had explained what an ion was or why some solutions would conduct an electric current and others would not.

Arrhenius decided the key to this mystery lay in the nature of the dissolved substance itself. He performed hundreds of experiments measuring the conductivity of various compounds in solution. Studying how the properties of the solutions varied with the amount of compound dissolved, he also measured the boiling points and freezing points of the solutions. Arrhenius knew water would freeze at lower temperatures when a nonelectrolyte, such as sugar, was dissolved in it. If the quantity of sugar in a solution were doubled, the freezing point would be lowered twice as much—the more particles in a solution, the lower the freezing point. But for an electrolyte such as sodium chloride (salt), the freezing point was twice as low as it should be. Arrhenius concluded that each molecule of sodium chloride produced two particles. For larger, more complex compounds, such as barium chloride and sodium sulfate, each molecule lowered the freezing point of the solution three times as much, meaning that three particles had been created.

Proposes revolutionary theory

To explain this behavior Arrhenius devised a simple but revolutionary answer: he proposed that when a molecule of an electrolyte dissolves in a solution, it separates into charged particles called ions; the electrical charges carried by the ions enable the solution to conduct electricity. Salt, for example, separates into two ions—a positively charged sodium ion and a negatively charged chlorine ion. Arrhenius proposed that during electrolysis ions migrate through the solution, the negative ones being attracted to the positive electrode and the positive being attracted to the negative electrode. When an ion reaches an electrode, its charge is then neutralized to produce uncharged atoms of the element.

Idea rejected

In 1884 Arrhenius submitted his thesis. The doctoral committee that heard his presentation in Uppsala was totally unimpressed by his ideas. Among the objections raised was the

question of how electrically charged particles could exist in water. In the end, the
committee granted Arrhenius his Ph.D., but
with a score so low that he did not qualify
for a university teaching position. Convinced
that he was correct, Arrhenius had his thesis
printed and sent it to a number of Europe's
top physical chemists, including Friedrich
Wilhelm Ostwald, who was part of a group
of researchers working on problems that
overlapped chemistry and physics. (They
developed a new discipline that would ultimately be known as physical chemistry.)
From this group Arrhenius received a much
more encouraging response than he had been
given by his doctoral committee. In fact,
Ostwald met with Arrhenius in Uppsala in
August 1884 and offered him a job at the
Polytechnikum in Riga. Although he was
flattered by the offer, Arrhenius eventually
declined. His father was gravely ill (he died
in 1885), and the University of Uppsala
decided at the last moment to offer him a
lectureship in physical chemistry.

Awarded Nobel Prize

Arrhenius remained at Uppsala only briefly, however, as
he was offered a travel grant from the Swedish Academy of
Sciences in 1886. The grant allowed him to spend the next
two years visiting major scientific laboratories in Europe and
working with Ostwald and other prominent scientists. In 1891
he accepted a teaching job at the Technical University in
Stockholm, where he was promoted to professor of physics
four years later. In 1903, during his tenure at the Technical
University, Arrhenius was awarded the Nobel Prize in chemistry for his work on the dissociation of electrolytes—the
same theory his professors had scorned less than twenty years
earlier.

Bert Bolin, Swedish Meteorologist

World-renowned meteorologist Bert Bolin (1925–) was among the first scientists to call international attention to the existence of acid rain and has continued to warn people about the dangers of global air pollution. In 1979 Bolin was selected to be a member of a U.S. National Academy of Sciences committee charged with assessing what impact carbon dioxide introduced into the atmosphere by humans has on the climate. The committee's final report confirmed the possibility of a future climate change brought about by humans. In 1982 Bolin proposed an additional assessment that included chemical and biological factors and how the climate change would impact the environment. The 550-page report, *The Greenhouse Effect, Climate Change, and Ecosystems,* ultimately led to the planning of the United Nations Conference on the Environment and Development, popularly known as the Second Earth Summit, held in Rio de Janeiro, Brazil, in June 1992.

Arrhenius remained at the Technical University until 1905, when he became director of the physical chemistry division of the Nobel Institute of the Swedish Academy of Sciences in Stockholm. He continued his association with the Nobel Institute until his death in Stockholm on October 2, 1927.

Makes other unique contributions

Although he will always be remembered best for his work on dissociation, Arrhenius was a man of diverse interests. While researching solutions he became intrigued by the influence of temperature on the speed of chemical reactions. In 1889 he found that reactions would take place much faster when heat was applied. Arrhenius suggested that molecules had to be "activated," or energized, in order to engage in a reaction. The speed of the reaction would depend on the number of activated molecules present and would therefore be related to the "energy of reactivation" (the quantity of energy that must be added to molecules to trigger the reaction). Arrhenius developed an equation for this relationship that explains chemical reaction rates. This concept has become essential to the modern theory of catalysts (accelerators of chemical reactions).

During the first decade of the twentieth century Arrhenius became interested in the application of physical and chemical laws to biological phenomena. In 1908 he published a book titled *Worlds in the Making,* in which he theorized about the transmission of life forms from planet to planet in the universe by means of spores (single-cell reproductive bodies produced by plants). Arrhenius's name has also surfaced in recent years because of the work he did in the late 1890s on the greenhouse effect. He theorized that carbon dioxide in the atmosphere has the ability to trap heat radiated from Earth's surface, causing a warming of the atmosphere. He also suggested that changes over time in the concentration of carbon dioxide in the atmosphere would have profound effects on Earth's climate and might explain major climatic variations over millions of years. In its broadest outlines, the Arrhenius theory sounds similar to current speculations about climate changes resulting from global warming.

Honored for achievements

Among the honors accorded Arrhenius in addition to the Nobel Prize were the Davy Medal of the Royal Society in 1902, the first Willard Gibbs Medal of the Chicago section of the American Chemical Society in 1911, and the Faraday Medal of the British Chemical Society in 1914.

Further Reading

Dictionary of Scientific Biography, Volume 1, Scribner, 1975, pp. 296–302.

Fleck, George, "Svante Arrhenius," in *Nobel Laureates in Chemistry: 1901–1992,* edited by Laylin K. James, American Chemical Society and the Chemical Heritage Foundation, 1993, pp. 15–22.

Oesper, Ralph, "Svante Arrhenius," in *Great Chemists,* edited by Eduard Farber, Interscience, 1961, pp. 1095–1109.

Wasson, Tyler, ed., *Nobel Prize Winners,* H. W. Wilson, 1987, pp. 34–35.

Charles Babbage

Born in 1792
Totnes, Devonshire, England
Died October 18, 1871
London, England

A brilliant student of mathematics, Charles Babbage spent most of his professional life attempting to create machines for calculating mathematical and astronomical tables. His plans for such calculators, which he called the "Difference Engine" and the "Analytical Engine," were never fully realized but are nonetheless regarded as important groundwork for the later development of computers.

"I am thinking that all these tables might be calculated by machinery."

Overcomes illness

Charles Babbage was born at Totnes in Devonshire, a county in southwest England, in 1792. He was one of two surviving children of Benjamin Babbage and Betty Plumleigh Teape Babbage, both of whom came from prosperous families. Although Babbage suffered frail health from infancy, he discovered early in life that he could endure illness more easily by focusing his mind on an activity. At the age of eleven he was sent to study with a clergyman in the nearby town of

Although Charles Babbage's efforts to build a calculating machine were ultimately unsuccessful, he is still considered a pioneer in computer science. And he made significant contributions to other fields in British science and industry as well. Babbage constructed a table of logarithms of greater accuracy than any then in use, and he developed a new branch of the mathematics of analysis. At one time he even became interested in efficient postal delivery, proposing a standard charge for delivering a letter, regardless of its destination. He also suggested that the English postal service deliver packages as well as letters—an idea that prefigured the establishment of parcel post service. His far-reaching effects on the transportation industry include improving rail travel by conducting detailed studies of how to increase the stability and comfort of railcars. And he delved into the field of medicine, inventing the ophthalmoscope, an instrument used for viewing the interior of the eye.

Alphington, where his parents hoped the clearer air would improve his strength. Their instructions were that he relax and that his studies not be made too taxing. Babbage therefore had considerable free time, which he used to devise experiments and question old ideas. During his later school years Babbage was fond of organizing nonsensical clubs, such as the Ghost Club and the Extractor's Club. He had many friends, whom he often entertained at parties of two or three hundred people.

Pursues interest in mathematics

When he was nineteen Babbage entered Trinity College at Cambridge University; he later graduated from another Cambridge college, Peterhouse. In 1811 he had purchased a book on calculus by the French mathematician Sylvestre Lacroix. After reading the book Babbage decided that English mathematics, which was dominated by the notation system and the ideas of English physicist and mathematician Isaac Newton, was lagging behind the progress being made in the field in France. To encourage mathematics education in England, Babbage and two friends, John Herschel and George Peacock, decided to translate Lacroix's work into English.

Babbage was also interested in logarithms. (A logarithm is an exponent to which a number is raised to produce another number.) As he was concentrating on logarithm tables one evening, a friend asked him what he was thinking about. "I am thinking that all these tables might be calculated by machinery," he replied. It would be ten years before he would begin to build such a machine.

Works on calculating machine

At the time he graduated from college, Babbage envisioned machines that could carry out the mathematics involved in astronomical calculations. He became convinced such a machine was necessary when he discovered inaccuracies in the astronomical tables used in England at the time. If only the necessary calculations could be done by a machine and the results printed out automatically, Babbage reasoned, the tables would be more accurate and science could advance more rapidly.

By 1820 Babbage had made progress in developing a machine that would calculate more exact values for such mathematical functions as tables of logarithms and sines and cosines (used in measuring the area of a triangle). Drawing hundreds of plans and hiring mechanics to help him, he began to build a model of a machine he called the Difference Engine. After the Royal Society, a scientific organization, approved his work in 1823, the British government decided to provide him with financial support.

Progress delayed by tragedy

Although Babbage had hired the best mechanics and engineers to help with the construction of his calculating device, after five years of work the machine was still not finished. One problem was that instrument making was not yet refined enough to craft the hundreds of precisely calibrated rods and gear wheels required to carry out exact calculations. Another difficulty was that Babbage, like many brilliant thinkers, was unable to concentrate his efforts on one activity. He was constantly altering the plans for the machine and making improvements while the mechanics were trying to work.

In 1826 Babbage joined the Royal Society. Then followed the lowest point in his life. During the course of a single year—1827—he lost his wife, Georgiana, whom he had married in 1814, as well as two of their children and his father. These deaths, along with the failure to complete his machine, led Babbage to a near-nervous breakdown. He decided to take an extended trip to Europe, where he studied advanced production facilities and met with many of the learned minds of the day. He returned with ideas for improving British industry, which he published in an influential book, *On the Economy of Manufactures and Machinery.*

Plans more complex machine

When Babbage was ready to resume work on his calculating machine he found that his chief mechanic had quit, taking with him many of the plans and the special tools designed for the project. The mechanic claimed he was owed £7,000, a charge Babbage and the government did not dispute. The loss of tools and plans did not matter by this time, however, because Babbage had decided he wanted to make a calculating machine with much greater capability. Called the Analytical Engine, the new machine would be able to begin a problem and then examine several different alternatives to a solution. In addition it would perform one mathematical operation after another according to instructions punched onto cards as tiny holes, thus allowing fine steel wires to operate the appropriate switches.

Although many of Babbage's ideas would later be used in modern computing, in his day few people understood what a calculating machine would do—and even fewer could see why such a machine was needed. One person who did understand was Lady Ada Lovelace (see box), the daughter of English poet George Gordon, Lord Byron. She encouraged Babbage, planned problems for the machine, and reviewed the inventor's calculations. Lady Lovelace is now known as the world's first computer programmer.

Dream unfulfilled

Babbage did not live to see the production of a machine capable of rapid and accurate constructions of vital mathematical and astronomical tables. He had angered the Royal Society by insisting that the mathematical notations of German

philosopher and mathematician Gottfried Leibniz were easier to work with than those devised by Newton. At one point Babbage had even suggested the Royal Society itself was an obstacle to increased knowledge and should be abandoned. Having alienated many members of the scientific community, he received virtually no encouragement from philosophers and scientists when he proposed building the Analytical Engine.

Ada Lovelace, English Mathematician

Augusta Ada King, Countess of Lovelace (1815–1852), was a mathematician who recognized the importance of Charles Babbage's work. They began a lifelong friendship in 1833 after Lovelace attended a series of Babbage's lectures on the Difference Engine and asked to meet him. In 1843 she published her translation of a French study of Babbage's analytical engine, *The Sketch of the Analytical Engine,* and included her notes and comments as well.

Lovelace encouraged Babbage's scholarly pursuits, and even suggested improvements for the design of the analytical engine. Elaborating on his plans, she developed her own method for automatically repeating steps to produce complex calculations. Unfortunately, Babbage and Lovelace ran into financial problems that led to some desperate schemes. For instance, to raise money they built machines capable of playing chess and tic-tac-toe. Their most unusual venture was an attempt to create an infallible system for betting on horse races— an experiment that failed and left both of them heavily in debt.

Although Babbage continued to work on his ideas until at least the mid-1850s, neither the Difference Engine nor the Analytical Engine was ever finished in England. However, an engineer in Sweden named Georg Scheutz read a magazine article that described the Difference Engine. Working from the article, Scheutz made a perfectly workable machine, although it was not quite capable of the mathematical precision Babbage envisioned. Only after Babbage's death did mathematicians begin to appreciate fully the advanced thinking represented by the Babbage "computers."

Leaves important legacy

Even in his old age Babbage remained curious and interested in human progress. At the time of his death on October 18, 1871, from a lingering illness, he had written more than eighty books and articles. He had published his log tables and followed them with a book of mathematical problems and solutions. He also left a lasting mark on British manufacturing and marketing and stirred British science with a book titled *Reflections on the Decline of Science in England and on Some of Its Causes.* In his last years he wrote an autobiography titled *Passages from the Life of a Philosopher.*

Further Reading

Campbell, Kelley Martin, ed., *The Works of Charles Babbage,* New York University Press, 1988.

Moseley, Maboth, *Irascible Genius: The Life of Charles Babbage,* Henry Regnery, 1964.

Thomas, Shirley, *Computers: Their History, Present Applications, and Future,* Holt, Rinehart & Winston, 1965.

Albert Baez

Born November 15, 1912
Puebla, Mexico

Mexican-born American physicist Albert Baez built the first X-ray microscope.

Albert Baez's pioneering work with X rays not only laid the foundation for the newly developing science of X-ray imaging optics, it would have important applications for many years to come. Baez, the creator of the first X-ray microscope, would go on to become an outstanding and highly effective promoter of science education worldwide.

Builds first X-ray microscope

Albert Vinicio Baez was born in Puebla, Mexico, on November 15, 1912, the son of Alberto Baez, a Methodist minister, and Thalia Baez. He grew up in Brooklyn, New York, where his mother was a social worker for the Young Women's Christian Association (YWCA). Baez earned a bachelor's degree in mathematics and physics from Drew University in Madison, New Jersey, in 1933. Two years later he received a master's degree in mathematics from Syracuse University in Syracuse, New York. He then taught physics and mathematics at colleges in New Jersey and New York. In 1936 Baez married Joan C. Bridge; they had three daughters: Pauline, Joan (who would become the well-known folksinger), and Mimi. The scientist became a naturalized U.S. citizen in 1938.

Baez joined the faculty of Stanford University in Stanford, California, during World War II. After the war he stayed at Stanford, teaching and conducting graduate research under Paul Kirkpatrick. Baez later recalled earning thirty-five cents an hour for searching through the physics machine shop debris for materials with which to build laboratory equipment. With some of that equipment Kirkpatrick and Baez built the first X-ray microscope, which used mirrors to produce the first focused X rays. The team coined the term "X-ray optics" for Baez's dissertation, for which he received a Ph.D. in 1950.

Modifies X-ray microscope

Baez was professor of physics at the University of Redlands in Redlands, California, from 1950 to 1956, but he took a one-year leave in 1951 to teach physics at the University of Baghdad in Iraq. At Redlands, Baez attempted to make an X-ray hologram (a three-dimensional image produced by a split beam of radiation) using an X-ray source with a very small focal spot. However, he found that X rays (any of the electromagnetic radiations having an extremely short wavelength) could not be focused finely enough to create a hologram. In 1960 he began developing a single Fresnel zone plate (a flat device for focusing radiation using concentric circular elements) that could focus X rays, while he did a stint at the Smithsonian Astrophysical Observatory in Cambridge, Massachusetts. He also modified the X-ray microscope principle by using nested arrays of curved mirrors, a concept that was later incorporated in the plans for an X-ray telescope intended for use in space in the 1990s.

Promotes science education

After the launch of the Soviet satellite *Sputnik* in 1957 focused attention in the United States on the teaching of sci-

Although Albert Baez earned recognition in the imaging optics field for creating the X-ray microscope, his greatest accomplishment might possibly be his advancement of the teaching of science in schools worldwide. After the Soviets launched the satellite *Sputnik* in 1957, many Americans began to place more value on the education of their children. Baez left his position as professor of physics at the University of Redlands and began devoting himself to the science education of schoolchildren. After advising on numerous science educational films for Britannica, he headed the Division of Science Teaching of UNESCO, where he oversaw the development of science and math curricula for developing nations and promoted innovative methods for teaching science.

ence, Baez increasingly devoted himself to science education. From 1958 to 1960 he was the studio physicist for the first films produced by the newly formed Physical Science Study Committee, aimed at improving the teaching of high school physics. This led to an invitation from the United Nations Educational, Scientific, and Cultural Organization (UNESCO) to be the first director of the Division of Science Teaching in Paris. From 1961 to 1967 Baez oversaw programs that helped developing nations design science and math curricula adapted to their cultures and individual conditions and also promoted innovative methods for teaching science. From 1967 to 1974 Baez produced nearly one hundred educational physics films for the Encyclopedia Britannica Educational Corporation.

Receives awards and honors

During his career Baez was also associated as a teacher or researcher with Harvey Mudd College, England's Open University, the University of Maryland, Harvard University, the University of California's Lawrence Hall of Science, the Algerian Institute of Electricity and Electronics, and the National Polytechnic Institute of Mexico. At Harvard, Baez was a member of the summer school faculty and honorary research associate from 1967 to 1971. Both Drew and Open Universities awarded him honorary doctoral degrees. He also chaired and acted as consultant to a number of bodies concerned with science education. Toward the end of the 1970s, after he had already retired, Baez was drawn into the environmental movement after becoming chairman of the Commission on Education of the International Union for Conservation of Nature and Natural Resources.

In 1986 Baez became president of Vivamos Mejor/USA, an organization that sponsors improvements in health, housing, and nutrition as well as environmentally beneficial technologies in Latin America. (*Vivamos Mejor* means "Let Us Live Better.") He went on to lecture throughout the world on topics such as holography (the art or process of making or using a hologram), the physics of music, and science education. In 1991 Baez and Kirkpatrick were awarded the Dennis Gabor Award of the International Society for Optical Engineering in recognition of their pioneering contributions to the development of X-ray imaging microscopes and telescopes.

Further Reading

Baez, Albert, *Innovation in Science Education—World-Wide,* UNESCO, 1976.

Baez, Albert, and Joan Baez, Sr., *A Year in Baghdad,* John Daniel, 1988.

Baez, Albert, John Smyth, and Gary Knamiller, eds., *The Environment and Science and Technology,* Pergamon, 1987.

Robert D. Ballard

Born June 30, 1942
Wichita, Kansas

"I am an explorer who's a geologist. I'm an explorer who loves the ocean. And I'm an explorer who loves technology.... I love the pursuit of anything, and the pursuit of truth is very noble."

Around 1 A.M. on September 1, 1985, Robert D. Ballard was summoned to the command center aboard the U.S. Navy research ship *Knorr* by fellow scientists who had come across something they wanted him to see. Staring at one of the many video screens displaying pictures of the ocean below, Ballard saw what he and his colleagues had hoped to find: the remains of the *Titanic*. The ill-fated steamship struck an iceberg and sank in the North Atlantic on April 15, 1912, carrying more than fifteen hundred people to their deaths. Coming after years of research in robotics—the technology involved in designing, constructing, and operating robots—the discovery was the culmination of Ballard's near-obsession with the most famous shipwreck in history.

Becomes deep-sea researcher

Born on June 30, 1942, in Kansas but raised in California, Ballard is the son of Harriet Nell May and Chester Patrick

Ballard, an aerospace engineer. Ballard's passion for the sea began when he was a teenager in San Diego, where he spent many hours swimming, scuba diving, and surfing along the beach near his home. In 1965 he earned a B.S. degree in both chemistry and geology at the University of California at Santa Barbara. After briefly pursuing graduate study in Hawaii and California, in the late 1960s Ballard joined the U.S. Navy and headed east. He served in the Office of Naval Research as liaison officer with the Woods Hole Oceanographic Institute, a nonprofit marine research facility headquartered on Cape Cod in Massachusetts. After his naval assignment ended in 1969, he remained at Woods Hole for more than a decade, conducting research in marine geology.

Designs underwater vessel

During the early 1980s Ballard switched from exploration to engineering. By this time he had made important discoveries in deep-sea exploration and had earned a Ph.D. from the University of Rhode Island. He was now committed to the idea that unmanned exploration of the ocean would be less expensive and more productive than manned missions. He decided to expand on the rather primitive technology of the equipment he had designed for earlier research trips. Ballard envisioned a deep-sea submersible vessel loaded with technologically advanced robotic gear, which would eliminate the need for human passengers. He referred to his invention as "telepresence, of being able to project your spirit to the bottom, your eyes, your mind, and being able to leave your body behind."

With funds primarily from the U.S. Navy and the National Science Foundation, Ballard formed the Deep Submergence Laboratory at Woods Hole in 1981. Within a few years he had designed the *Argo-Jason* system, which contains three video cameras that are so sensitive they can film in almost total darkness. Images transmitted from the *Argo* are immediately visible on video screens on a main ship, which scientists monitor around the clock. The *Argo* has an assistant, *Jason,* a smaller, self-propelled robot "eye" with mechanical arms that can be sent out from the *Argo* whenever it detects an item of special interest.

IMPACT

The technology of "telepresence" —video images produced by remote-control cameras—that enabled Robert D. Ballard to explore the sunken *Titanic* also helped him observe two other important shipwrecks. In 1989 he discovered the *Bismarck,* a sunken World War II German battleship, and in 1993 he discovered the *Lusitania,* an ocean liner sunk by a German U-boat (submarine) in World War I. Ballard emphasizes that the use of telepresence is not limited only to deep-sea exploration; he predicts that machines will one day "climb the mountains, or ride the rocket at blast-off."

Searches for the Titanic

Although Ballard was convinced his system would revolutionize underwater exploration, some of his colleagues at Woods Hole were not ready to give up on manned missions. In order to prove his critics wrong, he decided to test the *Argo* and *Jason* in a dramatic fashion: he announced he would explore the *Titanic,* the supposedly "indestructible" ocean liner that sank on her maiden voyage after hitting an iceberg. Ballard organized Operation *Titanic* in the summer of 1985 with a group of French scientists. The U.S. Navy furnished the research ship *Knorr* as well as detailed maps of the sea floor where the *Titanic* was believed to have come to rest.

Ballard brought along the *Argo* and the *Angus,* a ship he had used in his first experiments. He searched for the submerged vessel from on board the *Knorr.* On September 1, 1985, the cameras of the *Argo* captured the image of one of the distinctive boilers on the *Titanic.* Ballard instantly recognized it from his extensive research on the ship. After celebrating their good fortune, the crew aboard the *Knorr* paused for a moment of silence in memory of those who had perished aboard the luxury liner.

Opens new era

Over the next eight days cameras on the *Angus* and the *Argo* took more than twenty thousand still and videotape pictures of the wreckage. Revealed in vivid color were poignant images of hundreds of different artifacts, including bottles of wine, china plates, and a silver serving tray. The Operation *Titanic* team received a hero's welcome upon their return to Woods Hole on September 9. In a speech to the crowd assembled to greet them, Ballard took a firm stand against any attempts to salvage the ship, saying that it should remain as an

international maritime memorial. He later reflected on the expedition: "To me, the finding of the *Titanic* has two meanings. It is epilogue—an ending to the unfinished maiden voyage. But it is also prologue—the beginning of a new era in exploration. The *Titanic* is the first pyramid to be found in the deep sea. There are thousands of others, waiting to tell their tales."

Robert D. Ballard in 1986, holding a model of the Titanic, *indicating where the iceberg gashed the hull of the ocean liner.*

Makes other contributions

In addition to his exploration of the *Titanic,* Ballard has made several underwater discoveries that rank among the most significant of the century. In the 1970s he supplied geological evidence that helped prove the then-revolutionary theory of plate tectonics, which maintained that segments of the earth's outer crust are in constant motion. Next, during exploration off the coast of Ecuador, he discovered hydrothermal vents—sites on the ocean floor where mineral-rich hot water is discharged —which he called "black smokers." His stunning photographs of these geyser-like phenomena revealed large colonies of never-before-seen underwater creatures. Ballard's findings amazed marine biologists who did not think anything could live in those sunless depths and thus sparked new debates about the origin of life.

Ballard is unusually adept at communicating scientific knowledge to a lay audience—a colleague describes him as a "Carl Sagan with gills." (Carl Sagan is a popular American astronomer and writer best known for his book and television program *Cosmos*.) Ballard has presented lectures, appeared on television, and written books and magazine articles about his discoveries. He also established the Jason Foundation for Education and the Jason Project, a program designed to foster interest in science among students by enabling them to work side-by-side with scientists using underwater exploration equipment at research sites around the world.

Further Reading

American History Illustrated, April 1986, pp. 33–37.

Archbold, Rick, *Deep Sea Explorer: The Story of Robert Ballard, Discoverer of the "Titanic,"* Scholastic, 1994.

Ballard, Robert D., *Discovery of the Titanic: Exploring the Greatest of All Lost Ships,* Warner Books, 1989.

Ballard, Robert D., and Malcolm McConnell, *Explorations: My Quest for Adventure and Discovery Under the Sea,* Hyperion, 1995.

National Geographic, April 1994, pp. 68–85.

George Bass

Born December 9, 1932
Columbia, South Carolina

George Bass has been investigating ancient shipwrecks since the 1960s. An archaeologist first and a diver second, he has no interest in gold or treasure for their monetary value. Instead, he and his coworkers are interested in history. By slowly and carefully uncovering the remains of centuries-old ships and their cargoes, they seek clues about how people lived and worked in the past.

Trains as archaeologist

George Bass was born on December 9, 1932, in Columbia, South Carolina. When he was eight his family moved to Annapolis, Maryland, where his father, Robert, taught at the U.S. Naval Academy. His mother, Virginia Wauchope Bass, worked as a writer and editor. When Bass began college at Johns Hopkins University in Baltimore, he majored in English. During a trip to Spain and Italy in his second year, however, he saw ancient Greek and Roman ruins and decided to change his major to archaeology. Bass graduated from Johns Hopkins

The father of underwater archaeology, George Bass has shed light on sea-faring life through the ages.

53

University in 1955, then spent two years at the American School of Classical Studies in Athens, Greece. In 1959, after serving two years with the U.S. Army in Korea, he started graduate school at the University of Pennsylvania.

Organizes underwater expedition

During his first semester as a graduate student Bass learned about a journalist and diver named Peter Throckmorton, who believed that ancient shipwrecks could be a valuable source of information about the past. Throckmorton had written to the Council of Underwater Archaeology in San Francisco, urging that a scientific expedition be sent to investigate a wreck off Cape Gelidonya on the southwest coast of Turkey. Throckmorton had dived at the site, and the objects he recovered revealed enough evidence to date the ship to the late Bronze Age, sometime between 1600 and 1100 B.C. That would make it the oldest shipwreck ever discovered.

Throckmorton's letter was passed on to Bass's academic adviser, who offered Bass the chance to lead the expedition. Bass eagerly accepted and immediately met with Throckmorton to make preparations for the venture. Although archaeologists had worked underwater before, no one had ever excavated an underwater site. Bass and Throckmorton, however, wanted to use the same slow, careful techniques that had been perfected on land. Before flying to Turkey with Throckmorton, Bass returned to South Carolina to marry Ann Singleterry, a music student he had met in German class; she would later join him on the expedition.

Excavates Bronze Age ship

In early June 1960 the team sailed to Gelidonya and set up camp under the harsh sun along a narrow, rocky beach. Bass made his first dive into deep water, almost 100 feet, to the site of the wreck. There was little to see: centuries of sea growth and a mineral crust called concretion covered everything. Bass and his team developed procedures for excavating items from the wreckage. Smaller objects would be uncovered underwater and carried to the surface. Loose sand would be waved away with a diver's hand, but larger amounts of sand would need to be shifted with an air lift, basically a large underwater vacuum cleaner suspended from the boat above. And large chunks of concretion would be raised with lifting balloons, then wrestled to the beach to be carefully fitted back together.

Identifies tinker's ship

As the chunks of the wreckage were slowly chipped apart, each object inside was drawn or photographed as it appeared. The objects were left sitting on the beach in the same positions they had been in inside the ship. By the end of the summer, the excavation of the Bronze Age ship was complete. Next came the hours of library research needed to figure out exactly what had been found. Returning to Philadelphia, Bass began the research that would, in the end, give him a picture of the ancient vessel and its mission.

IMPACT

A major goal of the Institute of Nautical Archaeology (INA) is "to excavate one merchant ship from every century of antiquity," its founder, George Bass, told an interviewer. Then Bass would like to move on to warships and other vessels. Such a series of excavations would amount to a history of seafaring, shipbuilding technology, and technology in general. This information would shed light on how seafaring cultures traded goods—along with ideas and ways of life—through the ages.

Bass and his team found copper ingots (molds for casting metals), four-handled lumps of raw copper, and piles of broken bronze tools, along with other instruments for shaping and sharpening newly made bronze tools. All this evidence led Bass to conclude that the ship had belonged to an ancient tinker or metalsmith, a traveling craftsman who made bronze tools and weapons. He believes that the Gelidonya ship was not Greek at all, but of Canaanite or Phoenician origin.

Founds institute

Over the next decade Bass organized and carried out several more underwater excavations, while simultaneously pursuing a teaching career. He and his wife also had two sons who would later participate in excavations. Throckmorton eventually left the group to continue exploring wrecks on his

own, but others stayed on, forming a core of experienced divers who trained new students. By the mid-1960s Bass was the leader of a large and sophisticated operation. However, the stress of running the business by himself in his spare time led him to abandon underwater archaeology in 1970.

Soon Bass realized he had made a mistake. In 1973, with support from donors, including the National Geographic Society, he founded the Institute of Nautical Archaeology (INA) at Texas A&M University, where it remains today. By the 1980s the INA had located about eighty ancient shipwrecks near the Turkish coast. Findings ranged from ancient Roman and Greek ships to vessels from the Middle Ages and later, all of which are housed at the Museum of Underwater Archaeology in Bodrum.

Uncovers another ancient ship

In 1984 the INA made a major discovery. Off a small point of land called Uluburun on the southern coast of Turkey, they found a Bronze Age ship even older and better preserved than the one found at Cape Gelidonya. It also held a much richer cargo. Thousands of tools, pots, pieces of jewelry, and other items were brought up, including the oldest book ever found. Excavating the Uluburun wreck took ten years; many more years of library work are necessary before the importance of the wreck can be fully understood.

Bass has won many awards for his work, including the National Geographic Society's 1988 Centennial Award. Although he continues to spend time at excavation sites, he currently focuses most of his energy on teaching and research.

Further Reading

Bass, George, *Archaeology Beneath the Sea*, Walker, 1975.

Bass, George, "Oldest Known Shipwreck Reveals Splendors of the Bronze Age," *National Geographic*, December 1987, pp. 693–732.

Bass, George, "Ship of the Bronze Age," *Omni*, December 1987, pp. 71–108.

Facing page:
George Bass (left) and two members of his team survey the wreck, discovered in 1970, of an eighteenth-century Dutch merchant ship that sunk on its maiden voyage near Hastings, Sussex, England.

Fred Begay

Born c. July 2, 1932
Towaoc, Colorado

"A scientist looks at the world like a child always wondering what it is made out of. What are the pieces of the pieces of the pieces?"

Native American nuclear physicist and educator Fred Begay has conducted extensive research on the Sun and atomic energy and on the physics of plasma, a type of gas used in nuclear power plants. A staff member of the laser fusion division of the Los Alamos National Laboratory in New Mexico since 1971, Begay has applied lasers to nuclear fusion technology in an effort to make nuclear power safer. As a teacher and lecturer on science education, Begay has advised the Navajo Nation in science and technology matters and has encouraged numerous young Native American students to pursue careers in science and mathematics.

Early nomadic life

Begay was born in 1932 on the Ute Mountain Indian Reservation in Towaoc, Colorado. His mother was Navajo and Ute and his stepfather was Navajo and Piute. Both his parents practiced Navajo medicine and provided traditional health care to Navajo communities in the northern regions of the Navajo Reservation. Since his parents were nomadic, some of Begay's earliest memories are of hunting barefoot and sleeping in the open with his four brothers and sisters.

When Begay was about ten years old, his parents sent him to the U.S. Vocational Indian School, a government-run boarding school, in Ignacio, Colorado, where he was given the last name of "Young" and the estimated birth date of July 2, for record-keeping purposes. He was taught farming and to speak English, but after ten years he graduated with only an elementary ability to read or write the language.

Continues his education

In 1951 Begay joined the U.S. Army Air Corps and served as a non-commissioned officer in an air-rescue squadron in Korea. The following year he married Helen Etcitty from Lukachukai, Arizona; they would have seven children (two boys and five girls). In 1955, at age twenty-three, Begay enrolled in the University of New Mexico at Albuquerque and studied intensively to improve his ability to read and write English. Working part time, Begay graduated with a bachelor's degree in physics and mathematics in 1961. Two years later he received a master's degree in physics. When he earned a doctorate in physics in 1971, he became the first Navajo to earn that degree.

Applies lasers to nuclear fusion technology

Begay worked as a research physicist at the Air Force Weapons Laboratory at Kirtland Air Force Base in New Mexico from 1963 to 1965, and later for the National Aeronautics and Space Administration (NASA), conducting satellite experiments and designing atomic particle detector systems for research on the Sun. Begay was invited in 1971 to join the physics staff at Los Alamos National Laboratories.

For more than twenty-five years Begay has devoted his efforts at Los Alamos to understanding plasma physics. In his

Fred Begay has devoted his research efforts to harnessing the power of nuclear fusion, considered a cleaner, safer power source than standard fission reactors. Away from the lab, he is active in the Navajo community. He has been a science and technology adviser to the Navajo government, and he has made a great effort to encourage Native American students to stay in school.

research he seeks to harness the power of nuclear fusion, or the production of energy by combining atoms of lower weights with larger atoms. Nuclear fusion is considered a cleaner, safer power source than the output of standard fission reactors, which produce energy by splitting atoms into smaller parts. To control the energy produced in a fusion reactor, Begay has investigated the use of a laser, a device that produces a narrow beam of light made up of one wavelength of color that can be directed over small and large distances. His other research interests include general relativity, mathematical physics, and quantum theory—the study of the various energy levels contained in atoms.

In addition to his work at Los Alamos, Begay taught at Stanford in 1975 and spent a sabbatical at the University of Maryland during the academic year 1987–88. He has published numerous articles on experimental and theoretical physics topics.

Away from the lab Begay devotes much of his time to maintaining Navajo/Ute language, traditions, and culture and to encouraging minority students to complete their education. He has advised the Navajo government on science and technology matters. For two years, beginning in 1974, he was chairperson of the Navajo Nation's Environmental Protection Commission, and since 1974 he has served as president of the Navajo Science and Engineering Research Council. Beginning in 1991 he has served as a principal investigator with the National Science Foundation-funded minority undergraduate science and mathematics project at Arizona State University, which provides an opportunity for students to conduct basic and applied research at the university and at government and industrial research laboratories.

For his efforts in science education and human resource development, Begay was awarded the American Indian Science and Engineering Society's Ely Parker Award in 1992 and the National Science Foundation's Lifetime Achievement Award in 1994. Begay's life as a physicist and educator was the subject of two films, *Nation Within a Nation* (1972) and *In Our Native Land* (1972), and a *Nova* program titled "The Long Walk of Fred Young" (1978).

Further Reading

"The Long Walk of Fred Young," *Nova* (television program; produced by BBC-TV in 1978), Journal Graphics, 1979.

National Geographic, Volume 172, Number 5, 1987, p. 602.

Native American Biographies, Globe Fearon, 1994.

Science, Addison-Wesley, 1989.

Alexander Graham Bell

Born in 1847
Edinburgh, Scotland

Died in 1922
Cape Breton Island, Nova Scotia,
Canada

Alexander Graham Bell revolutionized communications with the invention of the telephone.

Alexander Graham Bell is remembered today as the inventor of the telephone, but he was also an outstanding teacher of the deaf, a prolific inventor of other devices, and a leading figure in the scientific community. He invented the graphophone, the first sound recorder, as well as the photophone, which transmitted speech by light rays. Among his other innovations were the audiometer, a device for the deaf; the induction balance, used to locate metallic objects in the human body; and disc and cylindrical wax recorders for phonographs. The prestigious journal *Science,* which became the official publication of the American Association for the Advancement of Science, was founded primarily through his efforts. Bell was also involved in establishing the National Geographic Society.

Trains teachers of the deaf

Bell was born in Edinburgh, Scotland, to a family of speech educators. His father, Alexander Melville Bell, had invented visible speech, a code of symbols for all spoken sounds that was used in teaching deaf people to speak. Young Bell began studying at Edinburgh University in 1864 and assisted his father at University College, London, from 1868 to 1870. During these years he became deeply interested in the study of sound and the mechanics of speech, inspired in part by the acoustic experiments of German physicist Hermann von Helmholtz, which gave him the idea of telegraphing speech.

After Bell's two brothers died of tuberculosis, his father took the family to the healthier climate of Canada in 1870. The following year Bell journeyed to Boston, Massachusetts, to join the staff of the Boston School for the Deaf. In 1872 he opened his own school in Boston for training teachers of the deaf; by 1873 he had become a professor of vocal physiology at Boston University and was also tutoring private pupils.

Experiments with harmonic telegraph

Bell's interest in speech and communication led him to research the transmission of sound over wires. In particular, he experimented with the development of the harmonic telegraph, a device that could send multiple messages simultaneously over a single wire. Bell also worked on the transmission of the human voice, experimenting with vibrating membranes and an actual human ear. He was backed financially in his investigations by Gardiner Hubbard and Thomas Sanders, fathers of two of his deaf pupils.

Early in 1874 Bell met Thomas A. Watson, a young machinist at a Boston electrical shop. Watson became Bell's indispensable assistant, bringing to his experiments the crucial ingredient that had been lacking: technical expertise in electrical engineering. Together the two men spent endless hours experimenting.

Although Bell formed the basic concept of the telephone on his own in 1874—using a varying but unbroken electrical current to transmit the sound vibrations of human speech— Hubbard insisted that the inventor focus his efforts on the harmonic telegraph instead. Bell followed Hubbard's advice. When he patented one of his telegraph designs in February

After Alexander Graham Bell invented the telephone in 1876, use of the new device spread rapidly. Over the next century technological improvements were made to Bell's basic design, thereby enabling people to communicate by telephone throughout the world. Among the advances were switchboard systems, coin-operated models, a handheld transmitter-receiver, long distance service, transcontinental cable lines, submarine cables, and international direct dialing. Beginning in 1962 orbiting communications satellites were used to relay and amplify telephone transmissions; fiber-optic transmitting systems were introduced in the 1980s; and mobile telephones using cellular radio technology came into use in 1982. Experiments with the video telephone—transmitting images along with voice—began in 1927 and continue today.

1875, however, he found that American inventor Elisha Gray (see box) had patented a multiple telegraph two days earlier. Greatly discouraged, Bell traveled to Washington, D.C., to consult with Joseph Henry, a prominent inventor and the first secretary of the Smithsonian Institution. Henry urged Bell to resume his work on a device for transmitting speech, assuring him it had the potential of becoming a great invention.

Accidentally invents telephone

Back in Boston, Bell and Watson continued to experiment with the harmonic telegraph but still kept the telephone in mind. Then, on June 2, 1875, the critical breakthrough on the telephone accidentally came about while they were working on the telegraph. When a stuck reed on Watson's transmitter changed an intermittent current into a continuous current, Bell, who had extraordinarily sharp hearing, picked up the sound on his receiver in another room. This event confirmed what Bell had previously suspected: only continuous, varying electrical current can transmit and reconvert continuously varying sound waves. (By contrast, the electric telegraph operates with pulses of current.)

Bell immediately sketched a design for an electric telephone, and Watson built it. The partners experimented all summer but failed to actually transmit voice sounds. Although Bell began to write the patent specifications for the telephone in the fall of 1875, he delayed application. Hubbard finally filed for the patent on February 14, 1876, just hours before Gray, their greatest competitor, appeared at the same patent office to file an intent to patent his own telephone design. Bell's patent was granted on March 7, 1876.

Three days later, as Bell tested a new transmitter, Watson, who was in an adjoining room with a receiver, clearly heard Bell's summons: "Mr. Watson, come here, I want you!" It was the first message transmitted by telephone. The new invention was exhibited at the Philadelphia Centennial Exposition the following June. The scientific judges were impressed, and the emperor of Brazil, Dom Pedro, was astonished: "My God—it talks!" he reportedly exclaimed.

In an undated photo Alexander Graham Bell places the first call on the New York-Chicago telephone line.

Founds Bell Telephone Company

Watson and Bell spent the rest of the year perfecting their new device and arranging public demonstrations to promote the commercial potential of the telephone. Together with financial backers Hubbard and Sanders they formed the Bell

Elisha Gray, American inventor

Elisha Gray (1835–1901) was Alexander Graham Bell's great rival. Gray patented an improved telegraph relay, a telegraph switch, an "annunciator" for hotels and large business offices, a telegraphic repeater, and a telegraph line printer. He filed his harmonic telegraph patent application in February 1875, two days before Bell's similar application. In one of the most remarkable coincidences in the history of invention—which would precipitate a lengthy, bitter lawsuit—Gray filed notice of his intent to patent a telephone on February 14, 1876. Only two hours earlier Bell had filed his own telephone patent at the same office. In 1869 Gray had become a founding partner of Gray and Barton, an electric-equipment shop in Cleveland, Ohio. Three years later the company moved to Illinois and was renamed Western Electric Manufacturing of Chicago. It eventually evolved into Western Electric Company, which ironically became the largest single component of Bell Telephone Company in 1881.

Telephone Company in 1877. That same year, after refusing to buy Bell's patent for $100,000, Western Union Telegraph Company entered the telephone business by purchasing Gray's patents and using a carbon microphone designed by **Thomas Alva Edison** (see entry). Countering with improved transmitters invented by German-born American inventor Emile Berliner and Francis Blake, the Bell company sued Western Union for patent infringement. The suit was settled—in Bell's favor—in 1879.

After marrying Mabel Hubbard, the daughter of his new partner, Bell sailed to England to promote the telephone. Bell Telephone grew rapidly, making Bell a wealthy man. Upon returning to the United States in 1879, he pursued other interests but also spent much of the next several years defending hundreds of lawsuits over his patents. All of his patents were finally upheld by the United States Supreme Court in 1888.

Pursues a variety of interests

In 1880 the French government awarded Bell the Volta Prize for his achievement in sound technology. With the prize money of fifty thousand francs he established the Volta Laboratory in Washington, D.C. Among the new devices he invented were the graphophone, for recording sound on wax cylinders or disks; the photophone, for transmitting speech on a beam of light; an audiometer, an aid for the deaf; a telephone probe, used in surgery until the discovery of the X ray; and an induction balance, for detecting metal within the human body. Bell also continued his work with the deaf, founding several organizations to support education for the deaf and conducting an extensive study of the hereditary characteristics of deafness. In addition, he helped establish *Science* magazine and the National Geographic Society. Pursuing a wide range of interests, Bell worked on air conditioning, an improved strain of sheep (to bear multiple lambs), an early iron lung (an artificial respiration device), solar distillation of water, and sonar detection of icebergs.

Turns to aviation

After 1895 Bell turned his attention to aviation. He invented the tetrahedral kite, which is capable of carrying a human being. In addition to supporting the pioneering aviation experiments of American scientist Samuel Langley, he helped found the Aerial Experiment Association in 1907. He also designed a hydrofoil boat that set the world water speed record in 1918. Bell became a U.S. citizen in 1882. He died at his summer home on Cape Breton Island, Nova Scotia, in 1922.

Further Reading

Copeland, Cynthia Lewis, *Hello, Alexander Graham Bell Speaking: A Biography,* Dillon, 1991.

Farr, Naunerle C., *Thomas Edison and Alexander Graham Bell,* Pendulum Press, 1979.

Montgomery, Elizabeth Rider, *Alexander Graham Bell: Man of Sound,* Chelsea House, 1993.

Pelta, Kathy, *Alexander Graham Bell,* Silver Burdett, 1989.

Quiri, Patricia Ryon, *Alexander Graham Bell,* Franklin Watts, 1991.

St. George, Judith, *Dear Dr. Bell ... Your Friend Helen Keller,* Putnam, 1992.

Jocelyn Bell Burnell

Born July 15, 1943
Belfast, Northern Ireland

Jocelyn Bell Burnell is the astronomer who discovered pulsars while working under Antony Hewish at Cambridge University. Although Hewish was awarded the Nobel Prize in 1974 for the discovery, Bell Burnell was not included in the citation. Since 1982 Bell Burnell has been a senior research fellow at the Royal Observatory in Edinburgh, Scotland, where she has continued her work in gamma-ray, infrared, and millimeter wave astronomy.

Irish astronomer Jocelyn Bell Burnell discovered pulsars, stars that release regular bursts of radio waves.

Builds innovative telescope

Jocelyn Susan Bell Burnell was born in Belfast, Northern Ireland, on July 15, 1943. Her father was an architect who designed the Armagh Observatory, an astronomical observatory near their home, and her early interest in astronomy was encouraged by the staff there. Bell Burnell attended the Mount School in York, England, and then the University of Glasgow in Scotland. Upon earning a B.S. degree in 1965, she began work on a Ph.D. under the supervision of Hewish at Cambridge.

Bell Burnell chose to study recently discovered quasars, star formations the size of galaxies that are so distant from Earth that they appear to be single stars. She worked in radio astronomy, as opposed to optical astronomy, and spent her first two years as a graduate student building a special radio telescope designed by Hewish to detect and record rapid variations in radio signals. A radio telescope has an advantage over a visible-light telescope in that it can pick up radiation in the form of long wavelength radio waves from objects in deep space that cannot be seen through an optical telescope.

Observes curious phenomenon

In 1964 astronomers discovered that the radio signals given off by sources in space were not always steady, just as light from stars (visible wavelengths of radiation) appears to twinkle. This twinkling of radio signals, called scintillation, could be used to calculate the size of a radio source, if it were known how much the signal varied as its radio waves passed through the wispy gas between planets.

The Hewish radio telescope, with more than two thousand separate receivers spread out over four acres, was designed to receive and record signals continuously onto rolls of paper, producing some four hundred feet of charts every week. Once the telescope was operating in July 1967, Bell Burnell's job was to make sense out of the signals recorded by the instrument.

One day about a month after the receivers were in place, Bell Burnell noticed curious variations in signals that had been recorded around midnight the night before: coming from the direction opposite the Sun, they produced short, rapid bursts of energy at precise intervals. This seemed odd to Bell Burnell, because strong changes in signals from quasars occur as a result of the solar wind and thus are usually weak at night. Hewish speculated there was either electrical interference or a problem with the equipment, so he told Bell Burnell to check the instruments several more times.

Bell Burnell found no outside interference or defects in the telescope; however, this scintillating star continued to wink at her through the radio telescope. After a month of precise observation she was able to establish that the signals continued and remained fixed with respect to the stars, which meant they were coming from somewhere other than Earth or the Sun.

Considering the possibility that the source of the signals was a beacon from an extraterrestrial civilization, the research team jokingly named the source "LGM 1," for Little Green Men 1. Hewish wanted to be sure that LGM 1 was not an abnormality, so he directed Bell Burnell to search through miles and miles of charts recorded in previous months.

Finds "pulsating stars"

In the process of her search Bell Burnell discovered three other sources with similar signals, as did her fellow team members. Hewish named the sources "pulsating stars," but the term was soon shortened to "pulsars" because the stars pulsated at regular intervals. After Hewish announced the discovery on February 9, 1968, British tabloid newspapers, apparently taking the LGM 1 joke seriously, claimed the scientists had made contact with alien civilizations.

Bell Burnell and the other researchers found that the main problem with the signals from the pulsars was the short duration of the bursts and their rapid repetition. Based on the astronomers' calculations, the pulsars had to be less than ten miles in radius, when the radius of an average star is hundreds of thousands of miles. Furthermore, a star like Earth's sun could not turn on and off in less than two seconds. Hewish initially speculated that the pulsars could be white dwarf stars—stars that have contracted because their nuclear fuels have been exhausted—or neutron stars, which had been predicted but had not yet been seen by astronomers.

Prompts major discovery

The problem was solved by Thomas Gold, an astrophysicist at Cornell University in Ithaca, New York. He suggested

Frank Drake, Paul Horowitz, and the Search for Extraterrestrial Intelligence

The search for extraterrestrial intelligence, or SETI as it is commonly known, was begun in 1960 by American astronomer Frank Drake. Drake scanned the skies for radio signals from alien civilizations, arguing that any technological civilization would inevitably broadcast such signals.

Organized SETI made huge advances beginning in 1983, when the Smithsonian Institution announced plans to shut down its Harvard University radio telescope. Harvard physics professor Paul Horowitz (1942–) proposed using the observatory for SETI research. Financed by the Planetary Society, a private organization, Horowitz revamped the radio telescope and began a 24-hour-a-day sweep of the northern sky. Horowitz's META Project (Megachannel Extraterrestrial Assay) uses an 84-foot dish antenna and a bank of 128 computers to analyze some 8.4 million radio frequency bands. The project was the first operational listening station in a proposed worldwide network devoted to the search for extraterrestrial radio signals.

When the U.S. Congress cut off funds for SETI programs run by the National Aeronautic and Space Administration (NASA) in 1993, Drake established the privately financed Project Phoenix. Revitalizing NASA's original goal of examining one thousand stars before the year 2000 for signals from extraterrestrial life, Project Phoenix has thus far investigated two hundred stars from the Parkes telescope in Australia. Observation sites have now been shifted to telescopes in Puerto Rico, West Virginia, and France.

Paul Horowitz

the pulsars must be neutron stars that resulted from the explosion of a supernova. When a star is dying, the outer parts explode, causing a bright light known to astronomers as a supernova. But what happens to its inner core is a compression: rather than exploding, it implodes, causing the star to spin very fast. Gold argued that the LGM signals came from neutron stars—small, dense spheres spinning rapidly that produce an intense magnetic field. Their radio waves would thus appear through Bell Burnell's radio telescope as a beam similar to a flashing lighthouse beacon.

At first Gold's theory was almost completely ignored, so this interpretation of Bell Burnell's data obviously needed support. Verification came later in 1968. Two other astronomers, David Staelin and Edward Reifenstein at the National Radio Astronomy Observatory at Green Bank, West Virginia, found a pulsar located at the center of the Crab Nebula, the remains of an exploded supernova. The scientific community consequently acknowledged that pulsars were indeed neutron stars.

Continues work

After completing her Ph.D., Bell Burnell accepted a position in 1974 at the University of Southampton in England, where she conducted research on gamma-ray astronomy, the detection of shorter wavelengths—called gamma rays—from space. Until 1982 she also worked at the Mullard Space Science Laboratory in X-ray astronomy using signals from the British satellite *Ariel V.* That year she was appointed senior research fellow at the Royal Observatory in Edinburgh, Scotland. She has continued her research on detecting and analyzing star spectra that come from different parts of the sky using a variety of techniques, including optical astronomy, infrared astronomy, and millimeter wave astronomy.

Bell Burnell was awarded the Michelson Medal from the Franklin Institute in Philadelphia in 1973. In 1974 Hewish received the Nobel Prize in physics for his role in the discovery of pulsars; unfortunately, Bell Burnell was not recognized by the committee. She won the J. Robert Oppenheimer Memorial Prize in 1978, the Beatrice M. Tinsley Prize from the American Astronomical Society in 1987, and the Herschel Medal from the Royal Astronomical Society in 1989. Bell Burnell is a member of the Royal Astronomical Society and the International Astronomical Union. She married in 1968 and has one child.

Further Reading

Detroit Free Press, March 12, 1996.

Fisher, David E., *The Origin and Evolution of Our Own Particular Universe,* Atheneum, 1988, pp. 94–99.

Halperin, Paul, *Cosmic Wormholes: The Search for Interstellar Shortcuts,* Dutton, 1992, pp. 45–48.

Science Digest, October 1985.

Washington Post, June 11, 1983.

Paul Berg

Born June 30, 1926
Brooklyn, New York

Paul Berg is a biochemist best known for his groundbreaking work in the field of recombinant DNA technology, which is considered among the most important technical advancements in genetics in the twentieth century. He developed a technique for splicing together DNA (deoxyribonucleic acid) from different types of organisms, thus enabling scientists to study the structure of viral chromosomes and the biochemical basis of human genetic diseases. After his discovery, Berg realized the danger of gene manufacturing and took action to govern research in the new technology. In 1980 he was awarded the Nobel Prize in chemistry for his work.

Paul Berg shared the 1980 Nobel Prize in chemistry for his pioneering work in the field of genetics.

Pursues interest in microbiology

Berg was born in Brooklyn, New York, on June 30, 1926, one of three sons of Harry Berg, a clothing manufacturer, and Sarah Brodsky Berg, a homemaker. He graduated from Abraham Lincoln High School in 1943 with a keen interest in

75

microbiology. Following a tour of duty with the U.S. Navy, Berg entered The Pennsylvania State University, where he received a degree in biochemistry in 1948. His background in biochemistry and microbiology shaped his research interests during graduate school and beyond, steering him into studies of the molecular mechanisms underlying intercellular protein synthesis (the production of protein between cells). Berg received his doctoral degree from Western Reserve University (now Case Western Reserve University) in Cleveland, Ohio, in 1952.

Berg conducted postdoctoral cancer research for four years in the United States and Denmark. In 1956 he became an assistant professor of microbiology at the University of Washington School of Medicine in St. Louis, Missouri. Three years later he was appointed professor of biochemistry at Stanford University School of Medicine in Stanford, California.

Experiments with genetic engineering

During the 1950s Berg tackled the problem of how amino acids (the building blocks of proteins) are programmed to link together according to the template carried by a certain form of ribonucleic acid (RNA) called messenger RNA (mRNA). MRNA is the "decoded" form of DNA—the substance that carries the genetic information in living cells from generation to generation. A current theory, unknown to Berg at the time, held that the amino acids did not directly interact with RNA but were gathered together by special molecules in the cytoplasm of the cell to form a chain. These joiners, or adapters, called transfer RNA (tRNA), group the amino acids in a sequence set up by the mRNA.

In 1956 Berg demonstrated the action of tRNA. This discovery stimulated his interest in the structure and function of genes. It also fueled his ambition to combine genetic material from different species in order to study how these individual units of heredity worked. Berg reasoned that by recombining a gene from one species with the genes of another, he would be able to isolate and study the transferred gene in the absence of interactions that would normally take place with its natural, neighboring genes in the original organism.

Originates recombinant DNA technology

In the late 1960s, while at Stanford, Berg began studying genes of the monkey tumor virus SV40 as a model for understanding how viruses alter the function of genes from mammals. By the 1970s Berg had mapped out where on the DNA molecule the various viral genes occurred. He had also identified the specific sequences of nucleotides in the genes. (Nucleotides are the basic structures of nucleic acids like DNA.) Berg thus discovered how the SV40 genes act on the DNA of the monkeys they infect. It was this work with SV40 genes that led directly to the development of recombinant DNA technology.

Works with E. coli bacteria

While studying how genes control the production of specific proteins, Berg was also trying to understand how normal cells become cancerous. He hypothesized that cellular biochemistry (chemical reactions in organisms) and unknown genetic interactions played a part in the formation of cancers. As part of an experiment, Berg decided to combine the DNA of the SV40 virus, which was known to cause cancer in other animals as well as in monkeys, into the common intestinal bacterium *Escherichia coli* or *E. coli*. He thought it might be possible to smuggle the SV40 DNA into the bacterium by inserting it into the DNA of a bacteriophage, a type of virus that naturally infects *E. coli*.

Manufactures genes

A DNA molecule is composed of subunits called nucleotides. Each nucleotide contains a sugar, a phosphate group, and one of four nitrogenous (rich in nitrogen) bases.

▄IMPACT▄

Today, the commercial application of Paul Berg's work underlies a large and growing industry dedicated to manufacturing drugs and other chemicals. Scientists are now able to make enormous amounts of particular genes they want to study. They can also use simple organisms like bacteria to grow valuable substances like antibiotics and insulin. Moreover, the ability to recombine pieces of DNA and transfer them into cells is the basis of gene therapy, an important new medical approach to treating diseases.

Herbert W. Boyer, Biochemist, and Stanley Cohen, Geneticist

American biochemist Herbert W. Boyer (1936–) and American geneticist Stanley Cohen (1935–) made the dreams of science fiction writers everywhere come true. The two were the first to clone, or artificially construct, new and functional deoxyribonucleic acid (DNA) from two separate gene sources. Following the gene-splicing work of Paul Berg, Boyer and Cohen in 1973 managed to recombine genes from two bacteria in another cell that divided itself and produced new genetic material. It was the dawn of a new biological age, one full of great potential and fraught with ethical problems.

Boyer soon saw the commercial potential of the process he helped pioneer. By splicing segments of higher organisms—the genetic material responsible for the creation of proteins and hormones, for instance—one could turn the bacteria into factories that produce these various materials as they replicate themselves. It was this sort of vision that created the biotechnology business.

Boyer invested $500 with venture capitalist Robert Swanson, cofounding the company Genentech in 1976. A year later Genentech began producing somatostatin, a brain hormone. They were manufacturing insulin the following year and a growth hormone the next year. By 1980 Genentech was manufacturing interferon, a protein that acts as an antiviral within a cell.

Following extensive research and a 1980 Supreme Court ruling that made it legal to patent life forms, Genentech became a publicly held company. Boyer also became a millionaire many times over, but the new gene technology and its ethics began to draw sharp criticism from both laypeople and scientists who questioned the rights of humans to create new life forms. As a result of the criticism, Boyer resigned from the presidency of Genentech, but he has continued his DNA research.

Structurally, DNA resembles a twisted ladder, or helix, with each of its components arranged in a regular structure. Two long chains of alternating sugar and phosphate groups twist around each other to form the sides of the ladder. A base attaches to each sugar, and hydrogen bonding between the bases—each rung of the ladder—connects the two strands. The order or sequence of these bases determines the genetic code.

Using enzymes to unzip, or cut, the SV40 and bacterio-phage DNA into pieces, Berg successfully "recombined" the molecules, creating an interlocking chain of shared DNA—hence the term "recombinant" DNA technology.

Sees dangers of recombinant DNA technology

Berg had planned to inject the monkey virus SV40-bacteriophage DNA hybrid molecule into *E. coli.* However, he realized the potential danger of inserting a mammalian tumor gene into a bacterium that exists everywhere in the environment: if the bacterium were to spread to other *E. coli* bacteria and then infect animals or humans, the results might be catastrophic.

Berg feared that adding the tumor-causing SV40 DNA into such a common bacterium would be equivalent to planting a ticking cancer time bomb in humans who might subsequently become infected by altered bacteria that escaped from the lab. Rather than continue his groundbreaking experiment, he voluntarily halted his work at this point. He was concerned that the tools of genetic engineering might be leading researchers to perform extremely dangerous experiments.

Issues the "Berg letter"

In addition to this unusual voluntary termination of his own research, Berg led a group of ten of his colleagues from around the United States in composing and signing a letter explaining their collective concerns. Published in the July 26, 1974, issue of the journal *Science,* the statement became known as the "Berg letter." It listed a series of recommenda-tions supported by the Committee on Recombinant DNA Mol-ecules Assembly of Life Sciences (of which Berg was chairman) of the National Academy of Sciences.

"There is serious concern that some of these artificial recombinant DNA molecules could prove biologically haz-ardous," the Berg letter warned. It cited as an example the fact that *E. coli* can exchange genetic material with other types of

Paul Berg in his Stanford laboratory in 1980, after receiving the news he had been awarded the Nobel Prize for chemistry.

bacteria, some of which cause disease in humans. "Thus," according to the letter, "new DNA elements introduced into E. coli might possibly become widely disseminated among human, bacterial, plant, or animal populations with unpredictable effects." The scientists also noted certain recombinant DNA experiments that should not be conducted.

Holds international meeting

The Berg letter called for an international meeting of scientists "to further discuss appropriate ways to deal with the potential biohazards of recombinant DNA molecules." That meeting was held in Pacific Grove, California, on February 27, 1975, and brought together one hundred scientists from sixteen countries. After four days of intensive discussion, they agreed to collaborate on developing safeguards to prevent genetically engineered organisms—organisms designed only for laboratory study—from being able to survive in humans.

They also drew up professional standards that served as a blueprint for subsequent federal regulations published by the National Institutes of Health in June 1976.

Awarded Nobel Prize

In 1980 Berg was awarded the Nobel Prize in chemistry for his pioneering work on recombinant DNA technology. He shared the prize with **Walter Gilbert** (see entry) and Frederick Sanger, who determined the sequences of nucleic acids in DNA molecules. Berg also received many other awards, including the American Chemical Society's Eli Lilly Prize in biochemistry (1959); the V. D. Mattia Award of the Roche Institute of Molecular Biology (1972); the Albert Lasker Basic Medical Research Award (1980); and the National Medal of Science (1983). He is a fellow of the American Academy of Arts and Sciences and a foreign member of the Japanese Biochemistry Society and France's Académie des Sciences. Berg continues to study genetic recombinants in mammalian cells and gene therapy. He is also doing research on the molecular biology of HIV-1 (a human immunodeficiency virus believed to cause AIDS). Berg married Mildred Levy in 1947; they have a son, John Alexander.

Further Reading

Antebi, Elizabeth, and David Fishlock, *Biotechnology: Strategies for Life,* MIT Press, 1986.

Berg, Paul, and Maxine Singer, *Genes and Genomes: A Changing Perspective,* University Science Books, 1991.

Berg, Paul, and Maxine Singer, *Dealing with Genes,* University Science Books, 1992.

Magill, Frank N., ed., *The Nobel Prize Winners: Chemistry,* Volume 3: *1969–1989,* Salem Press, 1990, pp. 1027–34.

Science, July 26, 1974.

Watson, James, *Recombinant DNA,* W. H. Freeman, 1983.

Henry Bessemer

Born January 19, 1813
Charlton, England
Died May 15, 1898
London, England

British engineer Henry Bessemer is best known for inventing the converter, a steelmaking device that accelerated the Industrial Revolution.

Henry Bessemer was a nineteenth-century inventor who created the converter, a device used to make steel. During the Industrial Revolution—a period of fast-paced economic change that began in Great Britain at the end of the eighteenth century—there was a huge demand for steel, and Bessemer competed against other inventors in Europe and America to find cheaper ways to produce it. Bessemer did not "invent" steelmaking, but his invention made steelmaking more profitable and accelerated the Industrial Revolution. The converter also made Bessemer a wealthy and famous man.

Serves as apprentice

Henry Bessemer was born on January 19, 1813, in Charlton, England. His father was a French inventor who had migrated to Charlton and established the foundry (a metal-casting factory) in which his son served as an apprentice. The young Bessemer was very enthusiastic about foundry work, and he spent many hours in his father's factory modeling or designing machinery. By the time he was eighteen Bessemer had learned enough at the foundry to strike out on his own. Having earned a reputation as a hard worker, he soon found employment as a model maker and designer in London factories.

Produces first inventions

One of Bessemer's first inventions was praised and accepted by the British government because it solved the problem of document forgery, which was rampant in England at the time. The government offices had a practice of stamping important papers to identify them as legal; unfortunately, the stamps they used were easily copied. Bessemer invented a machine that would actually press the stamp into the document, making it more difficult to forge. The British government was so impressed that it immediately adopted the new machine for its offices.

Bessemer's next invention was an improved method for making bronze powder, then a widely used metal. This development was a financial success and allowed Bessemer to establish his own brass foundry in London, where he began producing weapons for the Crimean War (1853). Britain and France were allied with Turkey against the Russians in this conflict. Bessemer's foundry manufactured the weapons and missiles used by the Allies during the war. It was this work that led to his discovery of a low-cost way to make steel.

Bessemer also devised a new type of cannon shell that would revolve as it passed through the cannon to its target. The revolving shell could travel faster and hit its target more accurately than the old cannon balls. But Bessemer's invention was ahead of its time. Because cannons of that day were made of brittle cast iron and could not stand the extra pressure of the spinning shell, his invention could not be used during the war. The revolving shell did, however, prompt nineteenth-century French ruler Louis Napoléon to employ Bessemer as an engineer of better French armaments.

Henry Bessemer's work had a great impact on steelmaking in Britain and America. He continued to make improvements to the converter so that by 1860 he could produce twenty-five tons of steel from pig iron in just twenty-five minutes. Steel could be produced cheaply enough to be used in such things as railway rails. Most likely, Bessemer did not "invent" steelmaking. But he created the tools that increased the efficiency of the steelmaking process, thus greatly accelerating the Industrial Revolution.

Begins to experiment with iron

The huge demand for iron and steel arose in the 1800s because brass was not sturdy enough for some of the tasks performed in the new factories of the Industrial Revolution. Iron was much more useful, but producing good iron required a great deal of energy. In the early nineteenth century, six and one-half tons of coke or coal were needed to make a single ton of iron. In addition, iron was made in crucibles (heat-tolerant containers) that could handle only a small amount of ore at a time. As industrial mechanization increased, more and more high-quality iron was needed to make the wheels and cams (rotating or sliding parts) of mill and factory machinery. In 1850 all of Britain produced only sixty tons of iron a year. Bessemer knew he could increase iron production while decreasing cost. In his bronze foundry, he began to experiment with iron.

Makes invention profitable

The demand for tool parts encouraged extensive interest in making a form of iron that could be pressed and molded into specific shapes. This led to the discovery of the special qualities of steel—its toughness and malleability (or ability to be bent and shaped). Back in 1744 Benjamin Huntsman had produced hardened steel at temperatures of 900°C. By 1849 the famous Krupp factory in Germany had succeeded in making a steel cannon. Still, the use of steel and refined iron was not commercially profitable for most needs.

In 1851 an American named William Kelley produced steel by blasting air through molten pig iron (melted crude iron). But, as is often the case, credit for a great invention went not to the inventor but to the person who first made the invention profitable. In this case, the profiteer was Bessemer.

An 1886 engraving of Bessemer steel being forged in a Pittsburgh, Pennsylvania, mill.

Invents the converter

There is no actual evidence that Bessemer knew of the discovery made by Kelley. Soon after Kelley introduced his idea, though, Bessemer announced that he had developed a way to make steel cheaply. A preheated blast of air through molten iron resulted in steel that could be rolled on giant rollers. It may have been Kelley's idea first, but Bessemer knew what to do with it.

| Henry Bessemer

Wilhelm Siemens and Friedrich Siemens, Engineers

German-born English engineer brothers Wilhelm Siemens (1823–1883) and Friedrich Siemens (1826–1904) developed a new smelting (refining) process that would become the foremost steelmaking method of the twentieth century. To make the furnace used in steelmaking more efficient—and thereby shortening the production time—the Siemenses utilized heat regeneration, or the recapturing of heat that otherwise would have been lost to the atmosphere.

The brothers received a patent on their regenerative metal-processing chamber in 1856. This method, which became known as the open-hearth process, was applied to steelmaking two years later, with the patent awarded to Wilhelm. In the Siemens open-hearth process, a shallow hearth containing molten metal was exposed to flames from above, while a pair of chambers at either end of the furnace captured heat and returned it for more efficient processing.

In 1864 Frenchman Pierre-Émile Martin (1824-1915) took the Siemens brothers' process further by modifying the location of the chambers and also introducing scrap steel to further cheapen the steel production process. Legal battles were then waged, resulting in a compromise that recognized the contributions of both parties. The name Siemens-Martin was applied to the process that by 1900 had surpassed Henry Bessemer's technique as the most efficient method of processing steel.

Self-confident and eager to press for new wealth and glory, Bessemer designed a great crucible called a converter. Iron and other ingredients were placed in the giant juglike container and forced to interact by great heat and by the blowing up of warm air from the bottom through the melting batch inside. The converter could handle tons of material at a time, thus producing the extraordinarily useful steel at an unprecedented speed.

Becomes a publicist

Bessemer continued to reinvent and improve his steelmaking process. But he also took time to let the world know that he was the leader in this technology. In 1856 he read a paper to the British Association for the Advancement of Science on the "Manufacture of Malleable Iron and Steel Without

Fuel." Almost a decade later he presented a paper titled "On the Manufacture of Cast Steel, Its Purposes and Employment as a Substitute for Wrought Iron." By that time he had already been recognized as one of England's great engineers, winning the Telford Medal from the British Institute of Civil Engineers. Later he also received the Albert Medal from the Society of Arts. In addition to his honors, Bessemer amassed a considerable fortune.

Continues to invent in old age

Bessemer continued to experiment and invent far into his old age. He patented an invention for forcing molten metals into molds and developed improvements in methods for embossing (a form of raised ornamentation) and printing. Although his last invention, the "level cabin" (a ship cabin that would remain stable in rough weather) was a failure, he sought the challenge of new ideas until his death in London on May 15, 1898.

Further Reading

Ashton, T. S., *Iron and Steel in the Industrial Revolution,* 2nd ed., Manchester University Press, 1951.

Burn, Duncan, *The Economic History of Steelmaking, 1867–1939,* Cambridge University Press, 1961.

Derry, T. K., and Trevor L. Williams, *A Short History of Technology,* Oxford University Press, 1961.

Sisco, A., and C. S. Smith, *Memoirs on Steel and Iron,* University of Chicago Press, 1956.

Elizabeth H. Blackburn

Born November 26, 1948
Hobart, Australia

Molecular biologist and biochemist Elizabeth H. Blackburn conducted groundbreaking research on DNA and cell division.

One of the top biochemistry researchers in the world, Elizabeth H. Blackburn has made groundbreaking discoveries about deoxyribonucleic acid (DNA) that have been used in studying the behavior of chromosomes as well as certain diseases such as fungal infections and cancer. In her research she uncovered a key enzyme, telomerase, a complex protein that is necessary for chromosomes to make copies of themselves before cell division. Blackburn is the first woman to head the Department of Microbiology and Immunology at the University of California at San Francisco.

Influenced by parents

Elizabeth Helen Blackburn was born in Hobart, Australia, on November 26, 1948. Her early interest in medicine and biology was influenced by her parents, Harold and Marcia (Jack) Blackburn, both of whom were physicians. Blackburn graduated from the University of Melbourne with a bachelor of science degree in 1970 and a master of science degree the following year. She then attended Cambridge University in Cambridge, England, where she obtained her doctorate in molecular biology in 1975.

Sees opportunity in the United States

Following her graduation Blackburn moved to the United States for both professional and personal reasons. She recognized that some of the most exciting opportunities and advances in her chosen field of molecular biology were being made in the States, which also had more resources dedicated to science than most other countries. Blackburn had another incentive to come to America: while attending Cambridge she met her husband-to-be, John Sedat, an American who had earned his medical degree and was doing research in biology. They married in 1975 and later had a son.

Begins DNA research

After Blackburn arrived in the United States she was awarded a fellowship in biology at Yale University in New Haven, Connecticut. There she worked with Joseph Gall, who was conducting chromosome research. Chromosomes are threadlike structures in the nucleus of each cell that carry thousands of genes. Both chromosomes and genes are made of DNA, the hereditary material in all organisms except for some viruses. DNA is a long molecule composed of two chains of nucleotides, or organic chemicals, that contain the sugar called deoxyribose. At Yale Blackburn began her work with telomeres (natural ends of chromosomes), which help the chromosomes to remain stable and whole during the replication (duplication) cycle.

In 1978 Blackburn accepted a position as an assistant professor at the University of California at Berkeley, where she

≣IMPACT≣

Elizabeth H. Blackburn's groundbreaking research on deoxyribonucleic acid (DNA) could help determine how the earliest forms of life evolved. Her research on the enzyme telomerase—particularly how to block a chromosome's replication cycle—could be used to fight the spread of fungal diseases and cancer.

was to make her groundbreaking discoveries concerning chromosomes and DNA. Blackburn was studying the telometric DNA sequences in chromosomal structures in eukaryotes (pronounced yoo-KAR-ee-ote; one of two types of cells with a well-defined nucleus containing rodlike chromosomes). In the process of her research she observed that chromosomes appear to shrink and grow in length. Intrigued, Blackburn set out to solve this biological riddle.

Without telomeres, daughter cells (or copies of cells) have shortened versions of their parent cells' chromosomes and will eventually die. Blackburn found that, in order to survive, cells had developed a process to replace lost telomeres. Specifically, she had discovered a key enzyme, telomerase, which is necessary for chromosomes to make complete copies of themselves before cell division. Telomerase is an unusual enzyme in that it contains ribonucleic acid (RNA), which is involved in the synthesis of proteins in all organisms. It is also the hereditary material in a few viruses.

Advances fight against diseases and cancer

First studying the single-celled protozoan *Tetrahymena,* Blackburn removed its telomerase and found that the DNA progressively shortened until it died. She discovered that telomerase makes DNA from an RNA template, or pattern. Telomerase adds DNA onto the end of the *Tetrahymena* chromosomes to preserve them, thus preventing eventual cell death due to broken chromosome ends, as well as ensuring the completion of cell division.

Blackburn has used her discoveries to make artificial chromosomes for studying chromosome behavior and telomere synthesis. Such studies on the RNA of telomerase could provide information on how some of the earliest forms of life evolved. Further research into the role of telomerase in chromosome survival may even help in the development of new therapies to fight fungal diseases and in the discovery of new information on how cancer cells divide—and ultimately how to block that division.

Sidney Altman, Molecular Biologist, and Thomas R. Cech, Biochemist

In the early 1980s Sidney Altman (1939–), a Canadian-American professor of biology at Yale University, discovered that ribonucleic acid (RNA) molecules can act as enzymes, or substances that bring about specific biochemical reactions in cells. This disclosure, made independently but at the same time by American biochemist Thomas R. Cech (1947–) of the University of Colorado, broadened the understanding of the origins of life.

Before this discovery, it was believed that all enzymes were made of protein and that primitive cells, therefore, used proteins to catalyze (bring about) biochemical processes. Nucleic acids, such as RNA, only transported the genetic codes that created the proteins. Now it appears that nucleic acids may have acted as a catalyst as well. Altman and Cech thus answered the long-pondered question about the development of life: what came first, proteins or nucleic acids? They proved that nucleic acids were the building blocks of life, acting as both codes and enzymes. As a result of their findings, Altman and Cech shared the 1989 Nobel Prize for chemistry.

Achieves distinction

After twelve years at Berkeley, Blackburn joined the University of California at San Francisco as a professor of microbiology and immunology. In July 1993 she became that department's first woman chairperson. Having achieved worldwide eminence in the field of molecular biology, Blackburn was named a foreign associate to the National Academy of Sciences. This is one of the highest honors that can be given a scientist in the United States. She has also won the National Academy of Sciences Award in molecular biology and is a fellow of the Royal Society, an independent organization in the United Kingdom.

Further Reading

Science, February 2, 1990, p. 546; August 3, 1990, p. 489.

Katharine Burr Blodgett

Born January 10, 1898
Schenectady, New York
Died October 12, 1979

Industrial chemist Katharine Burr Blodgett invented invisible, or non-reflecting, glass.

Katharine Burr Blodgett, the first woman to become a General Electric (GE) scientist, made important discoveries in the study of industrial chemistry. She spent nearly all her professional life working in the GE plant in Schenectady, New York, and although her name is not well known, some of the techniques in surface chemistry that she and her supervisor and mentor, Irving Langmuir (see box), developed are still used in laboratories today. And one of her creations—nonreflecting glass—is used throughout the world.

Begins studying math and physics

Blodgett was born on January 10, 1898, in Schenectady, New York. Her father, George Bedington Blodgett, was head of the patent department at the new GE plant in town. Blodgett never knew her father because he died a few weeks before she was born. After his death, Blodgett's mother, Katharine Buchanan Burr, moved to New York City; three years later she moved the family to France so that her two children would be bilingual. While in her mid-teens, Blodgett returned with her family to New York City. She later won a scholarship to the all-women's Bryn Mawr College in Bryn Mawr, Pennsylvania, where she excelled in mathematics and physics.

Pursues graduate work

After college Blodgett decided that a career in scientific research would allow her to further pursue both of her academic interests. During Christmas vacation of her senior year, she traveled to upstate New York to explore opportunities at the Schenectady GE plant. Some of her father's former colleagues in Schenectady introduced her to research chemist Irving Langmuir. After conducting her on a tour of his laboratory, Langmuir told eighteen-year-old Blodgett that she would need to broaden her scientific education before coming to work for him.

Taking Langmuir's advice, in 1918 Blodgett enrolled at the University of Chicago to pursue a master's degree in science. Since she knew that a job awaited her in industrial research, she picked a related thesis subject: the chemical structure of gas masks. Upon graduating, Blodgett returned to GE, where Langmuir hired her as his assistant (the first female research assistant the company had ever employed). At the time, Langmuir—who had worked on vacuum pumps and light bulbs early in his GE career—had turned his attention to studying current flow under restricted conditions. Blodgett soon started working with Langmuir on these studies; the two scientists would write several papers about their work. (Blodgett's collaboration with Langmuir lasted until his death in 1957.)

Blodgett soon realized she would need a doctorate if she wanted to further her career at GE. Langmuir arranged for her to pursue doctoral studies in physics at the Cavendish Laboratory at Cambridge University in England. Though laboratory administrators hesitated to give one of their few open spots to a woman, with Langmuir's endorsement she was admitted. In 1926 Blodgett became the first woman to receive a doctorate in physics from Cambridge University.

Invents nonreflecting glass

Blodgett began working for Langmuir again when she returned to Schenectady. First he encouraged her to further some of his early research. He set her to work on perfecting tungsten filaments, the thin wires used to conduct electricity in electric lamps, for which he had received a patent in 1916. Then Langmuir asked Blodgett to concentrate her studies on surface chemistry.

In his own long-standing research on the subject, Langmuir had discovered that oily substances formed a one-molecule thin film when spread on water. Blodgett decided to see what would happen if she dipped a metal plate into stearic acid molecules; attracted to the metal, a layer of molecules formed similar to that on the water. As she inserted the plate into the solution again and again, Blodgett noticed that additional layers—all one molecule high—formed on top of one another. As the layers formed, different colors appeared on the surface, colors which could be used to gauge how many layers thick the coating was. Because this measurement was always constant, Blodgett realized that she could use the plate as a primitive gauge for measuring the thickness of film within one microinch. To measure the thickness of film a few millionths of an inch thick, the user need only compare the color of the film with the molecular grades. Not long after Blodgett's discovery, GE started marketing a more sophisticated version of her color gauge for physicists, chemists, and metallurgists (one trained in the science and technology of metals).

Blodgett continued her research in surface chemistry. Within five years she had found another practical application that resulted from Langmuir's original studies: nonreflecting, or invisible, glass. Blodgett discovered that coating sheets of ordinary glass with exactly forty-four layers of one-molecule-thick transparent liquid soap made the glass invisible. This overall layer of soap was four-millionths of an inch thick and one-quarter the wavelength of white light. It neutralized the light rays coming from the bottom of the glass with those

coming from the top so that no light was reflected. Since the transparent soap coating blocked only about 1 percent of the light coming in, invisible glass was perfect for use in optical equipment such as cameras and telescopes.

Blodgett did not hold sole credit for creating invisible glass. Two days after she announced her discovery, two physicists at the Massachusetts Institute of Technology (MIT) publicized their method of manufacturing nonreflecting glass. All three were concerned, however, that their coatings were not hard and permanent enough for industrial use. Using some of Blodgett's insights, the MIT scientists eventually found a more appropriate method of producing invisible glass.

Receives awards

During World War II, GE focused its attention on solving problems for the military. Blodgett temporarily postponed her glass research but did not move far from the field of surface

Katharine Burr Blodgett at work in her General Electric laboratory in 1938, shortly before announcing that she had invented nonreflecting glass.

Irving Langmuir, American Chemist and Physicist

Irving Langmuir (1881–1957) was a renowned chemist, physicist, and industrial researcher at the General Electric Company for more than forty years. In addition to improving the lightbulb and other devices, he made great strides in understanding the chemical forces and reactions that occur at the boundaries between different substances. For his work in this field, known as surface chemistry, Langmuir received the 1932 Nobel Prize for chemistry. He was only the second American—and the first scientist employed as an industrial researcher—to attain such an honor.

Beginning in 1938 Langmuir increasingly turned his attention to atmospheric science and meteorology. During World War II he investigated methods of aircraft deicing and invented a machine to produce smoke screens that would shield troops from enemy observation. Later, as head of Cirrus, a joint program of the U.S. Army Corps, Navy, and Air Force, Langmuir helped develop ways of seeding clouds with dry ice and silver iodide to make rain and snow.

chemistry. Her wartime experiments led to breakthroughs involving plane wing deicing, and she designed a smoke screen that saved lives during military campaigns. When the war ended, Blodgett continued doing military-related research. In 1947, for example, she worked with the Army Signal Corps, putting her thin-film knowledge to use by developing an instrument that could be placed in weather balloons to measure humidity in the upper atmosphere.

As Blodgett continued experimenting, she received praise for her research. Along with being awarded numerous honorary degrees, she won the 1945 Annual Achievement

Award from the American Association of University Women for her research in surface chemistry. In 1951 she accepted the Francis P. Garvan Medal from the American Chemical Society, and she was the only scientist honored in Boston's First Assembly of American Women in Achievement. Spending all of her adult life in her home overlooking her birthplace, she remained active in civic affairs for many years. Blodgett died at age eighty-one on October 12, 1979.

Further Reading

Clark, Alfred E., "Katharine Burr Blodgett, 81, Developer of Nonreflecting Glass," *New York Times,* October 19, 1979, p. 24.

Golemba, Beverly, *Lesser Known Women: A Biographical Dictionary,* Lynne Rienner, 1992.

O'Neill, Lois Decker, ed., *Women's Book of World Records and Achievements,* Anchor Press, 1979.

Niels Bohr

Born October 7, 1885
Copenhagen, Denmark
Died November 18, 1962
Copenhagen, Denmark

Niels Bohr won the Nobel Prize for his theory of the quantum mechanical model of the atom.

Niels Bohr received the 1922 Nobel Prize in physics for the quantum mechanical model of the atom that he had developed a decade earlier. His achievement was the most significant step forward in scientific understanding of atomic structure since English physicist **John Dalton** (see entry) first proposed the modern atomic theory in 1803. Bohr founded the Institute for Theoretical Physics at the University of Copenhagen in 1920. For over half a century the institute, which was later renamed for Bohr, was a powerful force in the shaping of atomic theory. Bohr also developed two basic concepts in quantum physics, the principles of complimentarity and correspondence. In the 1930s he became interested in problems of the atomic nucleus and contributed to the development of the liquid drop model of the nucleus, a model used in the explanation of nuclear fission.

Shows early interest in science

Niels Henrik David Bohr was born in Copenhagen, Denmark, on October 7, 1885, the second of three children of

Christian and Ellen Adler Bohr. Interested in science from an early age, he would fix the family clocks and repair other items around the house. Bohr received his primary and secondary education at the Gammelholm School in Copenhagen. In 1903 he entered the University of Copenhagen, where his father was a professor of physiology, and he would study at the university until he received his doctorate in 1911. Bohr is said to have been not only a brilliant student, but also an accomplished soccer player.

Develops revolutionary theory

After graduation Bohr traveled to England to work at the Cavendish Laboratory at Cambridge University with J. J. Thomson (see box), the discoverer of the electron (the negatively charged particle that orbits the atom's nucleus). Later he joined physicist **Ernest Rutherford** (see entry) at the University of Manchester, where he remained until 1916. While Bohr was at Manchester he developed his theory of the electronic structure of the hydrogen atom, the accomplishment for which he is most famous.

In 1911 Rutherford had proposed a new model of the atom, in which all of the atom's positive charge was concentrated in the nucleus (center). The electrons in Rutherford's model were located at relatively great distances outside the nucleus, traveling in orbits around it.

A major problem with Rutherford's model pertained to the electrons. According to the classical theory of physics (the mathematical description of nature), a moving charged particle should radiate (give off) energy. Electrons orbiting around the nucleus, therefore, should gradually give off all their energy and slowly spiral into the nucleus. Rutherford's problem was that he could not explain how this spiraling of electrons into the nucleus would not occur in his model of the atom.

Solves physics problem

Bohr saw a possible solution to Rutherford's problem in the quantum theory proposed in 1900 by German physicist **Max**

Planck (see entry), who studied black-body radiation. In theoretical physics a black body is an object that absorbs all the electromagnetic radiation that falls on it, then releases that radiation in the form of thermal (heat) energy. In his study Planck concluded that, at least in some cases, energy could be released not in continuous waves but in bundles he called quanta. The energy of a quantum depended only on the frequency of the wave.

Bohr adapted Planck's theory to Rutherford's model of the atom by suggesting that electrons could travel around the nucleus without radiating energy, provided they remained in certain restricted orbits. Further, he proposed that an electron could move from one orbit to another by gaining or losing one quantum or several quanta of energy. Bohr constructed an equation for calculating the frequency of radiation that could be expected when electrons made various possible energy-level transfers within the atom. These frequencies were known for the hydrogen atom at the time as the result of research conducted by German physicist Johann Balmer. In 1885 Balmer had developed a formula for the wavelengths (motions around an undisturbed position) of the lines in the hydrogen spectrum (electromagnetic radiation arranged according to wavelengths). However, he had worked only with experimental data and therefore had no theoretical basis for his equations.

Applies new theory to classical physics

Bohr's model of the atom provided a theoretical explanation for Balmer's equations. Yet Bohr had no reason for inventing the concept of electrons moving from one orbit to another by gaining or losing quanta. This was simply a way to account for the apparent existence of electronic orbits. Also, his model could be applied only to the hydrogen atom. Nevertheless, Bohr had successfully solved the problem of electron motion in the atom, and he had shown how quantum theory could be applied to a problem in classical physics.

Founds institute, wins Nobel Prize

In 1916 Bohr returned to the University of Copenhagen, where a chair of theoretical physics was created specifically for him. That same year he married Margrethe Nørland. The couple later had four sons: Hans, Erik, Aage, and Ernest; Aage would go on to share the 1975 Nobel Prize for his work on the structure of the atomic nucleus. In 1920 Bohr founded the Institute for Theoretical Physics at the university. During the four decades he served as director, the institute ranked as the most important center for theoretical physics in Europe, attracting young scientists from throughout the world. In 1922 Bohr was awarded the Nobel Prize for physics for his achievement in developing the quantum mechanical model of the atom.

Originates fundamental principles

Bohr continued to think, write, and speak about conflicts between classical and quantum physics. In 1927 he introduced the idea of complimentarity in dealing with physical phenomena (observable facts or events). According to this principle, a light wave sometimes demonstrates the characteristics of a wave and sometimes the characteristics of a particle. Light therefore cannot be completely understood, Bohr said, exclusively in terms of either a wave or a particle. The same could be said of electrons and particles as well as other forms of energy. He also proposed another fundamental idea, correspondence. He said that any conclusion drawn from quantum physics must not conflict with observations of the real world. Conclusions drawn from theoretical studies must correspond to the world described by classical physics.

Develops "liquid drop" model

In the 1930s Bohr turned his attention to the field of nuclear physics. Among his achievements was the development of the "liquid drop" model of the nucleus. He suggested

J. J. Thomson, English Physicist

J. J. Thomson's (1856–1940) discovery of the electron, in 1897, raised a number of fundamental questions about the structure of the atom. For nearly a century scientists had thought of the atom as an indivisible, uniform particle or mass of material. Thomson showed, however, that the atom must consist of at least two parts, one of which was the newly discovered electron. To account for his discovery, Thomson proposed a new model of the atom, sometimes referred to as the "plum pudding" atom. In this model, the atom was thought to consist of a cloud of positive charges in which discrete electrons are embedded, much as individual plums are embedded in the traditional English plum pudding. However, this model was never very successful, and, in the work of Ernest Rutherford, a better atomic picture would soon evolve. In recognition of his research in electrical discharges in gases, Thomson was awarded the 1906 Nobel Prize in physics.

that the forces that operate between protons and neutrons that make up the atomic nucleus could be compared to the forces that operate between the molecules that make up a tiny drop of liquid. Bohr suggested that the atom's nucleus should be viewed as constantly changing shape in response to the forces working inside it. This model was later of help in explaining the process of nuclear fission, the splitting of the atomic nucleus, which was discovered in 1938.

Flees war, joins Manhattan Project

World War II brought major changes in Bohr's life. For the first four years of the war he remained in Copenhagen, helping colleagues escape from Denmark. Then in 1943 he and his family fled to Sweden on a crowded fishing boat. From there, on a trip that nearly cost Bohr his life, they were flown to England aboard an airplane that had no oxygen system. Bringing with him to England news of progress in nuclear fission research in Europe, Bohr soon became an important member of the Manhattan Project in the United States. This government-sponsored, top-secret project eventually produced the world's first atomic bombs, which were dropped on Hiroshima and Nagasaki in Japan to end the war.

Works for weapons control

After World War II, Bohr became chairman of the Danish Atomic Energy Commission and a founding member of the European Center for Nuclear Research in Geneva. Throughout this period he worked to bring under control the dangers posed by nuclear weapons. For his efforts on behalf of the peaceful uses of atomic energy, in 1957 Bohr received the first Atoms for Peace Award given by the Ford Foundation. He also took part in the founding of the Nordic Institute for Theoretical Atomic Physics (Nordita) in Copenhagen. The purpose of Nordita was to promote cooperation among and provide support for physicists from Norway, Sweden, Finland, Denmark, and Iceland.

When Bohr reached the mandatory retirement age of seventy in 1955, he was required to leave his teaching position at the university; however, he continued to serve as director of the Institute for Theoretical Physics until he died on November 18, 1962. Two days before his death he conducted a meeting of the Danish Royal Academy of Sciences.

Bohr was highly respected by his colleagues in the scientific community. Among the awards he received were the Max Planck Medal of the German Physical Society (1930), the Hughes (1921) and Copley (1938) medals from the Royal Society, the Franklin Medal of the Franklin Institute (1926), and the Faraday Medal of the Chemical Society of London (1930). He was elected to numerous scientific societies around the world and was awarded honorary doctorates by several universities, including Cambridge, Oxford, Manchester, Edinburgh, the Sorbonne, Harvard, and Princeton.

Further Reading

Bethe, Hans A., and others, "Did Bohr Share Nuclear Secrets?" *Scientific American,* May 1995.

Boxer, Sarah, "Being Geniuses Together (Niels Bohr and Albert Einstein)," *New York Times Book Review,* January 26, 1992, p. 3.

Breindel, Eric, "A Case of Book Burning," *National Review,* August 29, 1994.

Dictionary of Scientific Biography, Volume 2, Scribner, 1975.

French, A. P., and P. J. Kennedy, *Niels Bohr: A Centenary Volume,* Harvard University Press, 1985.

Norman Borlaug

Born March 25, 1914
Cresco, Iowa

Norman Borlaug began his career as a plant pathologist and became a force in international politics through his position as an agronomy consultant to the Mexican government. While working in Mexico he created a system of plant breeding and crop management that was then exported throughout the world. The movement that resulted, called the Green Revolution, took entire countries from starvation to self-sufficiency in the span of a few years. Borlaug was aware, however, that his innovations were no final answer to the world's population explosion; he realized they only bought time to deal with this essential ecological problem. In 1970 Borlaug became the first agricultural scientist and the fifteenth American, after Martin Luther King, Jr., in 1964, to win the Nobel Peace Prize for service to humanity.

Norman Borlaug initiated the Green Revolution, a transformation in farming practices that has dramatically increased world food production.

Influenced by immigrant community

Norman Ernest Borlaug was born on March 25, 1914, to Henry O. and Clara Vaala Borlaug, Norwegian immigrants who owned a farm near Cresco, Iowa. With his two sisters Borlaug grew up on the family farm in an area populated by Norwegian immigrants whose lives reflected experiences with hunger and hardship that led them to emigrate to America. At an early age Borlaug learned that careful planning and hard work were important to survival. In Cresco he attended grade school and high school, where he was the captain of the football team. In his agricultural classes he showed considerable interest in crop and soil management.

In 1932, instead of becoming a farmer, Borlaug entered the University of Minnesota to honor his grandmother's wish that he go to college. He worked his way through college, earning a bachelor of science degree in forestry in 1937. During his freshman year he had attended a lecture by Elvin Charles Stakman, an authority on crop research who headed the department of plant pathology (the study of diseases in plants) at the school. The lecture had made such an impact on Borlaug that he decided to pursue the study of plant pathology under Stakman's direction. At Stakman's urging Borlaug remained at the university for postgraduate work. Earning money from a part-time job as a forester, he completed a master's degree in 1939 and a doctorate in 1942, both in plant pathology. For his doctoral thesis he studied a fungus rot found in the flax plant. In 1937 Borlaug married Margaret G. Gibson. They would later have a daughter, Norma Jean, and a son, William Gibson.

Studies effects of pesticides on plant life

Before Borlaug left graduate school, widespread use of chemical pesticides had begun. Swiss chemist Paul Müller had already developed dichlorodiphenyltrichloroethane (DDT) in 1939. During World War II the United States military had made extensive use of DDT, using it to combat typhus (carried by body lice) in Italy. It had also proven effective in killing other insects. The government was also making a concerted effort to industrialize agriculture by developing new chemicals to control plant diseases and insects. In 1942 Borlaug joined E. I. du Pont de Nemours and Company in Wilmington,

Delaware, to study the effects of chemicals on plants and plant diseases. He stayed with du Pont for two years, researching ways to use chemicals to counteract fungus and bacteria that attack plants.

Appointed agricultural consultant in Mexico

In 1944 Mexico had a succession of wheat crop failures. In an effort to control the problem the Mexican Ministry of Agriculture asked the Rockefeller Foundation in the United States to send a team of agricultural scientists to share technological advances with the people of Mexico. George Harrar, a plant pathologist and future head of the Rockefeller Foundation, chose a group that included Borlaug, whom he appointed director of the Cooperative Wheat Research and Production Program. Except for modernization programs in the northwest area of the country, most wheat production in Mexico had not changed since conquering Spaniards had introduced the crop in the sixteenth century. The fields were prepared with wooden plows pulled by animals, and harvesting and winnowing (separating the grain from the husk) were done by hand. Only one scientist was available to conduct wheat-breeding experiments for the entire country, and the government had no soil management or disease and insect control programs.

Develops high-yield, disease-resistant wheat

Borlaug began by improving the variety of wheat that was commonly grown in Mexico, a tall, thin-stemmed breed that had resulted from centuries of competition with weeds for sunlight. Working with Mexican agricultural scientists, Borlaug's team of researchers began breeding the native wheat to develop a high-yield, disease-resistant species that would

With his unique combination of technological innovation, idealism, and impatience with bureaucratic inefficiency, Norman Borlaug started the Green Revolution. This international agricultural improvement program took entire countries from starvation to self-sufficiency within only a few years. Some countries were even able to export their surplus grain, which contributed to peace and prosperity within the countries.

Gurdev S. Khush, Indian Plant Geneticist

Gurdev S. Khush (1935–) is principle plant breeder and a division head with the International Rice Research Institute (IRRI) in Manila, Philippines. He has developed over two hundred high-yielding varieties of rice that have contributed to a doubling of world rice production between 1966 and 1990. Since beginning his involvement in the IRRI, Khush has succeeded in modifying various strains of rice, allowing them to grow more rapidly and respond more readily to chemical fertilizers. In addition, his work in genetics has led to the identification of genes that improve disease and insect resistance. His research is considered a cornerstone of the Green Revolution.

thrive in its natural environment. Borlaug showed it was possible to speed up crop production by harvesting two generations of the new wheat every year, one in Sonora in the northwest and the other in the mountains near Mexico City. By 1948 wheat production had improved so dramatically that Mexico became self-sufficient, no longer needing to import half of its wheat for food.

Problems with the new strain of wheat soon surfaced, however, and in the 1950s wheat yields decreased dramatically. Crop losses occurred when the heads of plants, enlarged by fertilizer and irrigation, grew too heavy for their thin stalks and fell over (lodged). Borlaug realized he would have to breed a wheat plant with a shorter, thicker stem to support the larger heads. In 1954 he and his assistants created a hybrid strain. It consisted of the improved Mexican grain and a Japanese dwarf variety, called Gaines, that had been perfected by agronomist Orville A. Vogel of Washington State University.

Not only did Borlaug's Mexican-Gaines hybrid prove effective at preventing lodging, it also used fertilizer more efficiently by concentrating growth in the grain head rather than the stalk. This strain was twice as productive as Borlaug's initial improvement and ten times as productive as the original Mexican strain. In 1961 Mexican farmers began growing the new dwarf variety.

Leads Green Revolution

By the late 1950s Borlaug, as director of the International Center for Maize and Wheat Improvement, was expanding agricultural improvements to other countries. He visited Pakistan in 1959 and India in 1963. As the result of his experiences in these countries, he began speaking out against bureaucratic red tape that prevented agricultural progress. He insisted that his agrarian reforms could not take place without a government that was willing to support his proposals and that had the ability to provide chemicals and machinery necessary for modern agriculture. Borlaug also required a commitment to training young scientists in agronomy (field crop production and management).

Borlaug's desire to see immediate results led him to inaugurate his Green Revolution program in the mid-1960s. His aim was to double wheat yields in the first year of his agricultural improvements. His purpose was to reduce a country's reliance on food imports and to break through the skepticism of government officials. Borlaug's programs ultimately benefited nations in Latin America, the Middle East, and Asia. In the 1960s scientists at the International Rice Research Institute in the Philippines succeeded in breeding strains of dwarf rice using techniques similar to those Borlaug had perfected with dwarf wheat in Mexico. The new rice strains extended the Green Revolution to Southeast Asia, a region of the world where the staple grain is rice.

Awarded Nobel Prize

In 1970 Borlaug was awarded the Nobel Peace Prize for starting the Green Revolution, which contributed to peace and prosperity throughout the less-developed world. In his Nobel Prize speech he stressed that an adequate food supply, while essential to a stable world order, was only a first step. He identified population growth as the greatest problem facing humanity.

During the 1970s, however, environmentalists began to criticize Borlaug's techniques for relying on pollution-causing

M. S. Swaminathan, Indian Geneticist and Agricultural Scientist

M. S. Swaminathan (1925–) was the first recipient of the World Food Prize, the equivalent of a Nobel Prize for agriculture. At the Indian Agricultural Research Institute in New Delhi, Swaminathan carried out some of his most vital research in increasing Indian wheat production by introducing various hybrid strains of wheat, including the dwarf Mexican, into the agricultural system.

Swaminathan and his students at the institute carried out genetic research into rice varieties, transferring the gene for dwarfing into the popular basmati variety of Indian rice. He also adapted strains of rice for both drought and deep water conditions and instituted a gene bank for rice plants now comprising seventy-five thousand varieties. Swaminathan became internationally known in 1982 when he was named director general of the International Rice Research Institute (IRRI) in Manila, Philippines. In 1989 he left the IRRI to found the Center for Research on Sustainable Agricultural and Rural Development in Madras, India.

industrial products such as fertilizers and insecticides. Borlaug countered by reiterating his view that the greatest danger to the environment came not from industrialization but from the population explosion. While admitting the Green Revolution involved problems of food distribution, he asserted that these difficulties were an improvement over those caused by famine.

Remains active after retirement

In 1979 Borlaug retired from the International Center for Maize and Wheat Improvement in Mexico but continued, as associate director of the Rockefeller Foundation, to participate in research projects sponsored by the Mexican Ministry of Agriculture. He became a professor of international agriculture at Texas A&M University in 1984. After receiving the Nobel Prize he also consulted with the Renewable Resources Foundation and the United States Citizens' Commission of Science, Law, and Food Supply, among other organizations. He has coauthored several books and written numerous articles. Borlaug has received honors from the governments of

Mexico, Pakistan, and the United States and from agricultural societies throughout the world.

Further Reading

Borlaug, Norman, and Paul F. Bente, Jr., *Land Use, Food, Energy, and Recreation,* University of Colorado Press, 1983.

Borlaug, Norman, R. Glen Anderson, and Haldore Hanson, *Wheat in the Third World,* Westview, 1982.

Critchfield, Richard, "Bring the Green Revolution to Africa," *New York Times,* September 14, 1992.

"Crop Genetics International Corp.," *Wall Street Journal,* January 12, 1990.

Current Biography Yearbook, H. W. Wilson, 1971.

Wasson, Tyler, ed., *Nobel Prize Winners,* H. W. Wilson, 1987, pp. 118–21.

Luther Burbank

Born March 7, 1849
Lancaster, Massachusetts

Died April 11, 1926
Santa Rosa, California

Luther Burbank was an American horticulturalist who developed more than eight hundred new varieties of fruits, flowers, grains, grasses, and other plants.

Luther Burbank developed an early interest in gardening, which he continued to explore throughout his life. Although he did not participate in the developing science of plant genetics, he began his work thirty years before the rediscovery of the techniques perfected by the Austrian biologist **Gregor Mendel** (see entry), who developed the laws of heredity in the 1860s. A horticultural genius, Burbank had great success in extensively applying the techniques of hybridization and selection to plant varieties.

Influenced by Darwin

Luther Burbank was born the thirteenth of fifteen children on March 7, 1849, in Lancaster, Massachusetts. He was educated in the local schools, where he obtained a high school diploma. He did not go on to college, but his natural talents with botany (a branch of biology dealing with plant life) more than made up for his lack of a formal education. During his youth Burbank worked continuously to understand the details of plant breeding. He paid attention to the small differences between plants, gaining knowledge he later used to perform advanced techniques such as hybridization (cross-pollination of plants of different varieties to produce seed) and grafting (connecting the sprout of one plant to the stock of another). A strong influence on Burbank was the book *Variation of Animals and Plants Under Domestication* by **Charles Darwin** (see entry). In the book Darwin proposed that new species originate through natural selection (the process whereby better adapted forms of a species spontaneously develop from a preexisting population). Burbank thought this idea could be applied to producing superior varieties of plants.

Develops the Burbank potato

At age twenty-one Burbank purchased a seventeen-acre farm in Lunenberg, Massachusetts. Beginning his botanical work, he set out to test Darwin's theory. In less than a year he had achieved success by developing a new variety of high-yield potato seedling—the Burbank potato. Usually potatoes are not grown from seed but rather are bred by replanting parts of the tuber (underground stem). There are few varieties of potatoes because any variations in potatoes result from the recombination of genes, which takes place only during sexual reproduction in the tuber, not during the asexual, vegetative growth of above-ground stems and leaves.

One day, while inspecting his potatoes, Burbank found a seedball containing twenty seeds. He planted the seeds, and after they had grown he found each had produced a plant that was different from the others. Applying Darwin's principle of selection, he saved only four plants that produced better potatoes than could then be found on the market. One of Burbank's potatoes was so superior that he called it a new "creation," and it eventually became the famous Burbank potato. Now known as the Idaho potato, the Burbank was the preferred variety throughout the world within fifty years.

Luther Burbank made a lasting contribution to plant breeding. His first achievement was the Burbank potato—now known as the Idaho potato—which has become a preferred variety throughout the world. He developed new varieties of fruit, including at least sixty varieties of plums and ten new commercial varieties of berries. He also worked with nuts (including almonds and walnuts), as well as flowers (the Fire poppy, the Burbank rose, the Shasta daisy, and the Ostrich-plume clematis). Altogether, Burbank produced over eight hundred new varieties of fruits, vegetables, grains, grasses, and ornamental plants.

Develops plant hybridization and selection

Five years later, in 1875, Burbank moved to California. Using the money he had earned by selling the rights to his potato, he settled on a four-acre plot of land near Santa Rosa. He established a nursery and greenhouse, then bought an eight-acre tract nearby for growing plants on a larger scale. As he embarked on his adventure in horticulture (the science of growing fruits, vegetables, flowers, and ornamental plants), Burbank shaped his own ideas about plant breeding and genetics. He was especially observant of soil conditions and other factors that promoted vigorous and healthy growth. Burbank also became aware of the importance of variation (differences in traits of a particular species), which would allow a plant strain (variety) to retain survival characteristics, such as the ability to resist disease. Modifying the hereditary characteristics of plants, he experimented with hybridization to produce numerous varieties. Next he applied Darwin's principle of selection by sorting out the plants and keeping only the best hybrids.

Supports theory of inheritance

While various genetic theories were taking shape during the late nineteenth century, Burbank supported the idea of inheritance of acquired characteristics. That is, he believed plants passed on traits that came exclusively from parent plants, and that genes did not have any role in determining those traits. Genetic theory eventually emerged as being more accurate than inheritance of acquired characteristics, but Burbank never fully understood how genetic principles worked. The main reason was that he did not have the resources or the

environment for wider genetic experimentation. For instance, he worked only with plants, whose form and structure are less uniform and more changeable than those found in animals. In addition, when Burbank noted his observations of differences in plant varieties, he concluded that he—not genetic activity—was creating the changes himself by favorably adjusting the environment.

Luther Burbank studying his plants in his Santa Rosa garden in 1924.

Establishes foundation for plant breeding

In spite of the limitations of his work, Burbank used his natural intelligence to make major contributions to the development of plant breeding. He conducted his hybridization and selection process on an impressive scale, maintaining as many as three thousand experiments involving more than one million plants at one time. To improve upon plums, for instance, he tested more than 30,000 varieties through hybridization to produce 113 new varieties. The resulting plums were better than any that had previously been available. By the time of his death he had developed over eight hundred new varieties of fruits, flowers, grains, grasses, and other plants. Burbank died in Santa Rosa on April 11, 1926.

Further Reading

Faber, Doris, *Luther Burbank: Partner of Nature,* Garrard Publishing, 1963.

Quackenbush, Robert M., *Here A Plant, There A Plant, Everywhere a Plant, Plant! A Story of Luther Burbank,* Prentice-Hall, 1982.

E. Margaret Burbidge

Born August 12, 1919
Davenport, England

Geoffrey Burbidge

Born September 24, 1925
Chipping Norton, England

Margaret Burbidge and Geoffrey Burbidge are astrophysicists who study the manner in which stars synthesize heavy elements; they also analyze quasars and active galaxies. Geoffrey Burbidge is among a small group of scientists who are challenging the big bang theory, which states that all matter in the universe was created by a huge explosion. Margaret Burbidge played a part in the development of the Hubble Space Telescope.

Margaret Burbidge becomes an astronomer

Eleanor Margaret Peachey was born in Davenport, England, on August 12, 1919, the daughter of Stanley John and Marjorie Stott Peachey. Her father was a lecturer in chemistry at the Manchester School of Technology, where her mother was a chemistry student. When Burbidge was a year and a half old her father obtained patents in rubber chemistry and moved the family to London, where he set up a laboratory. Burbidge's

E. Margaret Burbidge

Magaret and Geoffrey Burbidge's investigations into quasars led them to challenge the validity of the widely accepted big bang theory.

117

A team of astrophysicists headed by Margaret and Geoffrey Burbidge conducted a study that showed how a massive star lives out its life through the process of nuclear fusion. They also demonstrated how elements heavier than iron could be synthesized under the high-energy conditions of a supernova. One of the most important results of these findings was the discovery that heavier elements such as carbon, nitrogen, and oxygen, which are found in all living organisms, were ultimately forged in the interiors of ancient, long-dead stars. Indeed, all life on Earth is made of "star-stuff."

parents encouraged her curiosity about astronomy from an early age.

After Burbidge earned a bachelor's degree in science from University College, London, in 1939, she remained at the University Observatory for her graduate education. World War II was raging across Europe at the time. Burbidge cared for the observatory's telescope and would repair shrapnel damage to the instrument. At night she used the telescope for her research. In 1943 Burbidge earned a Ph.D. for her studies of the physics of hot stars. In the late 1940s she served as assistant director and acting director of the observatory. She met Geoffrey Burbidge, a graduate student at University College, in 1947.

Geoffrey Burbidge starts as physicist

Geoffrey Burbidge was born on September 24, 1925, in Chipping Norton, England, to Leslie and Eveline Burbidge. He attended Bristol University in Bristol, England, as a physics student, receiving a bachelor's degree in 1946. Shortly thereafter he began graduate studies at University College, where he met Margaret Peachey. They were married in 1948 and would later have a daughter. Margaret Burbidge's influence extended not only to her husband's personal life but to his professional career as well, for he ultimately decided to pursue astronomy as his life's work. He received his Ph.D. in 1951.

Burbidges study content of stars

In 1951 the Burbidges were awarded fellowships at Harvard University in Cambridge, Massachusetts. Two years later they returned to England, where Geoffrey took a job with the Cavendish Laboratory at Cambridge University. The following year the couple returned to Cambridge to join English astronomer Fred Hoyle and American physicist William A. Fowler in a study of the content of stars.

Although the Burbidges were appointed to academic positions at the University of Chicago in 1957, they continued their research with Hoyle and Fowler. Their work was spurred by the discovery, in 1952, of the relatively new element technetium among the spectral lines (the characteristic pattern of colored lines emitted by each element within a light source) of red giant stars. Technetium is an unstable element that could not possibly have been present at the time of the formation of the giant stars in which it was found. Researchers concluded that the stars therefore must have synthesized (produced) the element comparatively recently.

The Burbidges, Fowler, and Hoyle showed how a massive star lives out its life through nuclear fusion by synthesizing helium from hydrogen, then carbon, nitrogen, and oxygen. They further demonstrated how elements heavier than iron—iodine, platinum, gold, and uranium—could be synthesized under the high-energy conditions of a supernova (a catastrophic explosion in which a large portion of a star's mass is blown out into space, or the star is entirely destroyed). One of the most important results of their study was the discovery that heavier elements such as carbon, nitrogen, and oxygen, which are found in all living organisms, are also present in the interiors of ancient, long-dead stars.

Conduct research on quasars

Further explorations into even more exciting mysteries awaited the Burbidge team. Their research would lead them to ponder the evolution of the entire universe. In 1963 Geoffrey Burbidge became professor of physics at the University of California at San Diego. In 1964 Margaret Burbidge was appointed full professor of astronomy at the same university. During the late 1950s and early 1960s she had conducted pioneering work on the rotation of galaxies. In the late 1960s she turned her attention to quasars (celestial objects more distant than stars that emit large amounts of radiation). Her discoveries also led Geoffrey to investigate quasars.

First discovered from their intense radio emission and then identified with a radio telescope (see **Jocelyn Bell Burnell** entry), quasars exhibit a curious property. The lines of their spectra are all drastically shifted toward the red end of the spectrum (the range of colors produced by individual elements within a light source). The simplest explanation for the quasar redshifts is that the quasars are receding away from Earth. This motion causes their light to redden due to the Doppler effect (see box), which states that light received from objects moving away from Earth shifts toward the red end of the spectrum.

Similar Doppler redshifting of the light of distant galaxies was the principal evidence presented in the 1920s and 1930s that the universe is expanding. Everything in the universe appears to be moving away from everything else. If the Doppler effect applies to quasars, then the huge redshifts displayed by quasars indicate that they are exceedingly distant from Earth's galaxy, at the very "edge" of the observable universe. The farther from Earth an object resides in space, the longer it takes for its light to reach this planet. For that reason the distant quasars appear as a kind of "fossil" from earlier periods of the expanding universe. In 1967 the Burbidges published *Quasi-Stellar Objects,* one of the first surveys of quasars.

Geoffrey Burbidge disputes the big bang

For quasars to be visible at such remote distances meant that they were extremely energetic and luminous. But quasars also appeared to be quite small. No one could propose a suitable explanation or theory that could completely account for the discrepancy between the small size of the quasars and their intense energy output. Further research seemed only to compound the mystery. The Burbidges, along with other astronomers, also found that seemingly distant quasars were grouped with supposedly nearby, bright galaxies.

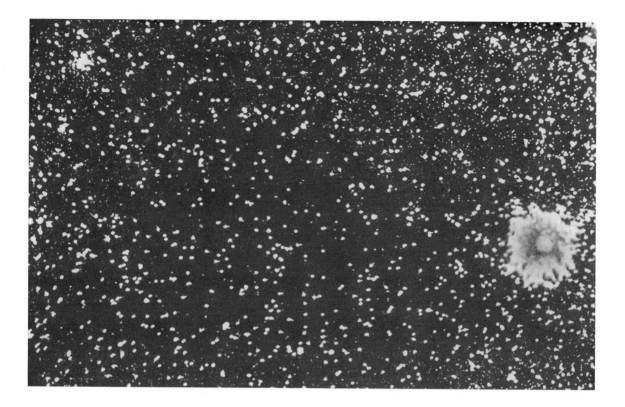

Finally Geoffrey Burbidge and others astronomers proposed a solution to the mystery: quasars were not distant objects after all, but were smaller, closer objects that were being energetically ejected (pushed away) from nearby galaxies. This explanation was highly controversial, for it implied that Doppler shifts could not be relied upon as an indicator of the expansion of the universe. For if quasars received their large redshifts from some cause other than the supposed universal expansion, then perhaps the redshift observed in distant galaxies also resulted from another cause. Under these conditions, there would be no strong basis to assume that the universe was expanding and that the big bang ever took place.

Geoffrey Burbidge's explanation for the redshifts of quasars put him at odds with the established acceptance of the big bang theory of the creation of the universe. He was not alone, however, in his reluctance to accept the big bang theory. Other astronomers such as Hoyle and Halton Arp have joined him in focusing attention on its flaws.

This X-ray picture taken by NASA's High Energy Astronomy Observatory II (HEAO II) in 1979 shows two quasars; the one in the upper left corner was discovered in the late 1970s and is believed to be more than ten billion years old, and the one in the lower right corner was discovered in the mid-1960s.

| E. M. and G. Burbidge

Christian Johann Doppler, Austrian Physicist

Christian Johann Doppler (1803–1853) discovered the Doppler effect when he tried to find out why the pitch of a sound varies as the source moves toward or away from the listener. The most familiar example is a train whistle: when the train is approaching, the whistle is high pitched; when it moves away, the whistle sounds deeper. In 1842 Doppler worked out a mathematical formula, now called the Doppler effect, that states that the distance and force of a sound can be found by measuring the acoustical shift of a bounced signal. This effect forms the basis for modern sonar and radar, as well as for speed guns used by traffic police.

Doppler predicted that his formula could also be applied to light waves. In 1901 an experiment showed that when starlight is receding from the observer it is shifted toward the red end of the visible spectrum, while light approaching the observer is shifted toward the blue end. Scientists determined that many stars are moving away from a central point in the universe, forming the foundation for the big bang theory.

Continue work in astronomy

From 1971 to 1974 Geoffrey Burbidge served on the Board of Directors of the Associated Universities for Research in Astronomy. In 1978 he became Director of Kitt Peak National Observatory in Arizona, one the most productive astronomy facilities in the world. Margaret Burbidge was director of the Center for Astrophysics and Space Sciences at the University of California at San Diego from 1979 to 1988. She continues her work in spectroscopy and the ultraviolet spectrum of quasars. She served on the committees that planned and outfitted the Hubble Space Telescope, an instrument designed to provide the clearest snapshots of distant galaxies yet produced. She became professor emeritus in 1990.

The Burbidges shared the Warner Prize from the American Astronomical Society in 1959. Margaret Burbidge has also received a number of awards, including the National Medal of Science, several honorary doctoral degrees, and the Albert Einstein World of Science Medal. During her tenure as president of the American Astronomical Society in the late 1970s she obtained U.S. citizenship.

Further Reading

Abbott, David, ed., *Biographical Dictionary of Scientists: Astronomers,* Peter Bedrick Books, 1984.

Beichman, Arnold, "The Big Bang Censorship," *Insight on the News,* April 13, 1992.

Burbidge, Geoffrey, "The Cult of the Missing Mass," *Sky and Telescope,* June 1990, p. 580.

Burbidge, Geoffrey, and Adelaide Hewitt, "A Catalog of Quasars Near and Far," *Sky and Telescope,* December 1994.

Cowen, R., "Enigmas of the Sky: Partners or Strangers?" *Science News,* March 24, 1990, p. 181.

"3C 273: The Quasar Next Door?" *Sky and Telescope,* June 1990.

Helen Caldicott

Born August 7, 1938
Melbourne, Australia

"I've ... planted 400 eucalyptus and rain-forest trees on my land. It was like having a baby, the joy it gave me because I'm replenishing the land."

Helen Caldicott is a pediatrician and an antinuclear activist who opposes both nuclear weapons and nuclear power. In the early 1970s she organized an antinuclear movement in her native Australia. As the result of these efforts France was forced to end nuclear testing in the South Pacific for a time, and Australian uranium exports were halted from 1974 to 1982. In the late 1970s and early 1980s Caldicott became a leader in the antinuclear movement in the United States through her role in reviving the organization Physicians for Social Responsibility. She helped found several other groups that have worked to abolish controlled nuclear fission. A passionate public speaker who has a thorough knowledge of the medical effects of exposure to radiation, Caldicott has been instrumental in increasing public awareness of nuclear issues.

Becomes a physician

Helen Caldicott was born on August 7, 1938, in Melbourne, Australia, the daughter of Philip Broinowski, a factory manager, and Mary Mona Enyd Coffey Broinowski, an interior designer. Caldicott received a public primary school education, then attended the Fintona Girls School, a private secondary school in Adelaide. Today she recalls having been strongly affected as an adolescent by reading *On the Beach* by Nevil Shute, a novel about nuclear devastation set in Australia. At the age of seventeen she enrolled at the University of Adelaide Medical School.

Caldicott graduated from medical school in 1961 with a bachelor's degree in surgery and a master's degree in medicine (the equivalent of a medical degree in the United States). The following year she married William Caldicott, a pediatric radiologist (a physician who specializes in using X rays and radium in the treatment of diseases in children). In 1966 they moved to Boston, Massachusetts, where Caldicott had obtained a three-year fellowship in nutrition at Harvard Medical School. Returning to Adelaide in 1969, she accepted a position in the renal unit (for the treatment of kidney disease) of Queen Elizabeth Hospital. In the early 1970s she completed a one-year residency and a two-year internship in pediatrics (the treatment of childhood diseases) at the same hospital. She also established a clinic for cystic fibrosis (an incurable children's disease).

Reveals radiation threat to Australians

In 1971 Caldicott discovered that France had been conducting nuclear tests over its South Pacific colony of Mururoa for five years, in violation of the International Atmospheric Test Ban Treaty of 1962. Nuclear fallout (the drifting of radioactive particles into the atmosphere as the result of nuclear explosions) from the tests had moved toward Australia and entered the food chain in that country. A confidential South Australian government report, for instance, confirmed that higher than normal levels of radiation had been found in drinking water in 1971 and in rain in 1972.

Caldicott organized opposition to nuclear testing at a time when few Australians were aware of either the testing or

In her speeches and books, Helen Caldicott presents detailed medical descriptions of the potentially devastating results of nuclear radiation. Through witness accounts of people's personal experiences, Caldicott successfully demonstrates that nuclear danger is not merely an abstract possibility, but instead an actual threat to individual human lives. Although she often argues that women, as nurturers, are particularly suited to saving the earth from warmongers and transnational corporations, she also has a strong following among men.

the resulting radioactive fallout. She began by sending a letter of protest to a local newspaper, then she appeared on radio and television to comment on the medical risks of radiation. Because of her work in pediatrics she was acutely aware that children are more sensitive to radiation than adults. Emphasizing this fact, Caldicott appealed to parents to become responsible for the well-being of their children. She then made public the confidential report about elevated levels of radiation in drinking water and rain, which had been passed on to her by a sympathizer within the state government.

Organizes movement against nuclear testing

Caldicott's speeches began a mass movement against the French tests. Thousands of people took part in protest marches that resulted in the boycotting of French products. In December 1972 the Australian government undertook legal action against France in the International Court of Justice. Although the court issued an ambiguous ruling, the French ceased atmospheric testing in the face of widespread organized opposition.

Caldicott was less successful in her efforts to bring about a ban on the commercial exploitation of uranium, a relatively rare raw material necessary for most nuclear technology. Australia has rich uranium deposits and exported the material to several countries. Stressing the connection between radiation and birth defects—radiation exposure can produce deformed sperm cells and thus cause a rise in the rate of birth defects—Caldicott gained union backing for an export ban by organizing workers. In 1975 the Australian Council of Trade Unions passed a resolution against the mining, transport, and sale of uranium. Later that year the government imposed an export ban. After continued international pressure, however, the ban was lifted in 1982.

Revitalizes Physicians for Social Responsibility

Caldicott returned to Boston in 1975, having been appointed a fellow in cystic fibrosis at the Children's Hospital Medical Center. Although she and her family moved back to Australia briefly the following year, they returned to the United States in 1977. Caldicott was appointed associate in medicine at the Children's Hospital Medical Center and an instructor in pediatrics at Harvard Medical School. In 1978 she became active in Physicians for Social Responsibility, which had been formed in 1962. At the time of Caldicott's involvement the group's membership and impact had dwindled. The organization remained small until March 28, 1979, when the Three Mile Island nuclear reactor in Pennsylvania came within sixty minutes of a possible meltdown (the accidental melting of the reactor core that could cause a nuclear explosion, endangering many lives as well as the environment).

Immediately more than five hundred physicians joined Physicians for Social Responsibility in protest against the potential nuclear disaster at Three Mile Island. From that point onward the membership, budget, and staff of the organization continued to grow. With Caldicott heading their efforts, Physicians for Social Responsibility fought the nuclear industry,

A 5,000-foot water column rises into a mushroom cloud after the U.S. government exploded an underwater atomic bomb at Bikini Atoll in the Marshall Islands on July 25, 1946.

Benjamin Spock, American Pediatrician

Like Helen Caldicott, pediatrician Benjamin Spock (1903–) was led by his experience in treating children to campaign for a safer world for children. Hailed as the grandfather of pediatrics, Spock is known as the leading authority on child rearing. With his first book, the renowned *Baby and Child Care*, he single-handedly broke the tradition of cold and rigid discipline, radically changing popular ideas on rearing children.

Spock's involvement in politics began in 1962, when he was convinced by a Unitarian minister that children were being hurt by the fallout from nuclear testing. Joining forces with the antinuclear National Committee for a Sane Nuclear Policy (SANE), he became a chairperson of the group later that year. In 1994 he wrote about the relationship between child rearing and politics in the book *A Better World for Our Children*. Spock advises parents to worry more about politics, less about their own children, and more about issues that impact the well-being of children throughout the world.

conducted research on the results of nuclear war, worked politically for nuclear disarmament, and presented public seminars and lectures.

Leaves medicine to be full-time activist

By 1980 Caldicott had given up the practice of medicine to devote herself to full-time leadership of the organization. In addition to giving speeches to audiences at churches, labor unions, and universities, she wrote *Nuclear Madness: What You Can Do!* (1980) with Nancy Herrington and Nahum Stiskin. The book provides detailed descriptions of the medical and environmental effects of nuclear war and outlines political action that can be taken to prevent nuclear disaster. In 1982 Physicians for Social Responsibility produced a documentary film titled *Eight Minutes to Midnight*, which was nominated for an Academy Award.

The growth of Physicians for Social Responsibility brought a more diverse membership. Many physicians who were unwilling to support Caldicott in her opposition to nuclear power as well as nuclear weapons began pushing for the organization to take a more mainstream position. In 1983 Caldicott resigned as president but continued to serve on the board of directors. She also helped found the Medical Campaign Against Nuclear War, Women's Action for Nuclear Disarmament, the Women's Party for Survival, and other organizations pertaining to nuclear and environmental issues. Her second book, *Missile Envy: The Arms Race and Nuclear War,* was published in 1984.

Continues environmental campaign

After returning to Australia, in 1990 Caldicott ran for a seat in parliament and lost by only a narrow margin. Since then she has published a third book, *If You Love This Planet: A Plan to Heal the Earth* (1992), which expands her treatment of environmental issues. Caldicott lives with her family in Canberra. She and her husband, who has been actively involved in her campaigns, have three children, Philip, Penny, and William, Jr.

Caldicott has received numerous honors, including the Humanist of the Year Award from the American Association of Humanist Psychology in 1982, and the International Year of Peace Award from the Australian government in 1986. She was nominated for the Nobel Peace Prize in 1985 and holds several honorary degrees.

Further Reading

Caldicott, Helen, *If You Love This Planet: A Plan to Heal the Earth,* Norton, 1992.

Caldicott, Helen, *Missile Envy: The Arms Race and Nuclear War,* Morrow, 1984.

Caldicott, Helen, Nancy Herrington, and Nahum Stiskin, *Nuclear Madness: What You Can Do!* Bantam, 1980.

McGuinness, Elizabeth Anne, *People Waging Peace: Stories of Americans Striving for Peace and Justice in the World Today,* Alberti Press, 1988.

Nixon, Will, "Helen Caldicott: Practicing Global Preventive Medicine," *E Magazine,* Volume 3, September/October 1992, pp. 12–15.

Annie Jump Cannon

Born December 11, 1863
Dover, Delaware
Died April 13, 1941
Cambridge, Massachusetts

Annie Jump Cannon observed, classified, and analyzed 400,000 stars, carefully placing them in groups based on their spectra (or emission of radiation in waves). The best-known American woman astronomer of her time, she also gave lectures, wrote papers, and cataloged many variable stars. Although spectral classification was not new at the end of the 1890s, no one prior to Cannon had made a detailed survey of the stars according to their temperature and composition. Her method, which was adopted by the astronomical community in 1910, became known as the "Harvard system."

Annie Jump Cannon compiled the first detailed catalog of the spectra of stars.

Mother influences early interest in astronomy

Annie Jump Cannon was born on December 11, 1863, in Dover, Delaware. She was the eldest of three children of Wilson Lee Cannon (who also had four children by a previous marriage), a shipbuilder, farm owner, and state senator, and his second wife, the former Mary Elizabeth Jump. Cannon's

131

mother had been interested in astronomy since her own childhood, and together mother and daughter studied the sky from the attic of their house, where they had set up a simple observatory.

Cannon received her early education at local schools. In 1880 she graduated from the Wilmington Conference Academy (a Methodist institution), then continued her education at Wellesley College in Massachusetts. At Wellesley she studied with Sarah Frances Whiting, a professor of physics and astronomy. Cannon also delved into research on stellar spectroscopy, a process that breaks a star's light into component colors so that the various elements of the star can be observed.

Pursues interest in stellar spectroscopy

After earning a bachelor's degree at Wellesley in 1884, Cannon returned to her family home in Dover, where she lived for ten years. Continuing her involvement in astronomy, she visited Italy and Spain to observe a solar eclipse. She also became interested in photography. In 1894, following her mother's death, Cannon returned to Wellesley for postgraduate studies. There she worked as a teaching assistant in physics for Whiting and participated in experiments to confirm **Wilhelm Röntgen**'s (see entry) discovery of X rays. She soon turned to her attention to stellar spectroscopy, however, and in 1895 enrolled at Radcliffe College as a special student in astronomy.

Creates new system

The following year Cannon became an assistant at the Harvard College Observatory through the support of Edward Pickering, director of the observatory and a leader in the field of spectroscopy. She began a study of variable stars (stars whose light output varies because of internal fluctuations or because they are eclipsed by another star) and stellar spectra (the distinctive mix of radiation emitted by every star). She worked for a time at the Harvard astronomical station in Arequipa, Peru, which had been established by Pickering and his brother, William.

Using a method that combined the classification systems developed by American astronomers Antonia Maury and Williamina P. Fleming, Cannon classified 1,122 bright stars whose spectra had been photographed at Arequipa. Cannon's system arranged stars according to the color of the light they emit, which is determined by their temperature. She classified the hot, white or blue stars as types O, B, and A. Type F and G stars, like Earth's sun, are yellow; type K stars are orange; and type M, R, N, and S are reddish and therefore relatively cool. Known as the Harvard system, Cannon's method made possible the easy classification of all stars in relatively few, rationally related categories.

Catalogs stellar spectra

In 1911, the year after the Harvard system was adopted by other astronomers, Cannon was promoted to curator (superintendent) of astronomical photographs at the observatory. At this time she began one of the most extensive collections of astronomical data ever achieved by a single observer—the Henry Draper Catalogue of stellar spectra. Published by the Harvard College Observatory in ten volumes from 1918 to 1924, the catalog lists the spectral types of 225,300 stars, their positions in the sky, and their visual and photographic magnitudes; it also includes notes on the eccentricities of particular stars. As soon as Cannon finished this survey, she began enlarging the catalog to include fainter stars in the Milky Way, the Large Magellanic Cloud, and other selected regions of the cosmos. In all, Cannon classified the spectra of some 400,000 stars in her lifetime.

During the same period Cannon pursued her interest in variable stars (stars whose brightness changes, usually in more or less regular periods). In 1903 she issued a catalog of the

1,227 variable stars known at the time. Four years later she published a second catalog of variable stars, presenting precise data and notes on two thousand stars. In the course of her work she discovered three hundred previously unknown variables and five novae. (Novae are stars that suddenly increase in light output and then fade away within a few months or years.)

Achieves international reputation

Cannon was active in professional activities such as the annual meeting of astronomical societies. Astronomers from all over the world visited her at Star Cottage, her home in Cambridge, Massachusetts. She received a number of honorary degrees and awards, including election to the American Philosophical Society in 1925. Cannon was the first woman to be presented the Henry Draper Gold Medal of the National Academy of Sciences (NAS; 1931), the first woman granted an honorary doctoral degree from Oxford University in Cambridge,

Tycho Brahe, Danish Astronomer

Known as the "reformer of observational astronomy," Tycho Brahe (1546–1601) recorded celestial observations that greatly advanced the knowledge of the universe. He was the first to realize that continuous and systematic observations of celestial bodies were crucial to understanding the true motion of stars and planets. In Brahe's day, planets were commonly believed to be controlled by health, destiny, and other factors such as weather and natural disasters. Brahe himself was interested in "judicial astrology" and made horoscopes for his friends and the nobility based on celestial movements. Some of his predictions were apparently correct: he is said to have predicted mathematician Caspar Peucer's imprisonment and eventual freedom, and he was noted for his accuracy in predicting rain. However, when one of his predictions—the death of a Turkish sultan—was made after the ruler had already died, Brahe became the subject of many jokes.

England, and the first woman elected to an office of the prestigious American Astronomical Society. In 1929 the National League of Woman Voters listed her as one of the twelve greatest living American women. She was later appointed William Cranch Bond Astronomer at Harvard University.

Faces discrimination

Cannon's achievements came at a time in the history of science when the roles for women in male-dominated disciplines were severely limited. Backward social attitudes and deep-seated gender prejudices blinded the scientific community to the outstanding contributions of women in the field. In

1923 two prominent members of the NAS discussed the possibility of electing Cannon to the ranks of the academy, an honor no woman had yet received. Despite the support of several distinguished fellow astronomers and Cannon's recognized contributions to science, she was not elected to the academy.

Cannon held her position at Harvard University until her retirement in 1940. She continued observing the stars until shortly before her death in Cambridge on April 13, 1941, at the age of seventy-seven.

Further Reading

Lankford, John, and Rickey L. Slavings, "Gender and Science: Women in American Astronomy, 1859–1940," *Physics Today,* March 1990, pp. 58–65.

Rossiter, Margaret W., *Women Scientists in America: Struggles and Strategies to 1940,* Johns Hopkins University Press, 1982.

Rachel Carson

Born May 27, 1907
Springdale, Pennsylvania
Died April 14, 1964
Silver Spring, Maryland

During the late 1940s and throughout the 1950s, worldwide use of chemical pesticides on crops and in pest control programs grew rapidly. The most popular pesticide was dichlorodiphenyltrichloroethane (DDT), which was promoted as the "savior of mankind" after being used successfully against typhus epidemics in Italy and proven effective in killing insects. It was not yet known that DDT and several other widely used chemicals were highly toxic, and they were aggressively promoted for use on crops by the petrochemical and agricultural industries. However, Rachel Carson, the National Book Award-winning author of environmental best-sellers, had researched DDT and discovered the threat it posed to the environment. Her book *Silent Spring* unleashed a heated controversy and led to the banning of DDT and other toxic chemicals. President Jimmy Carter recognized her service to the environment and human health in 1980 when he posthumously awarded her the President's Medal of Freedom.

"I can remember no time when I wasn't interested in the out-of-doors and the whole world of nature."

Despite criticisms from some sectors of government and business, Rachel Carson and *Silent Spring* raised the consciousness of the general public. Suddenly everyone began to realize how dangerous pesticides really were. She never argued that all pesticides should be banned; she maintained that their use should be carefully regulated and monitored. By the end of 1962 state legislators had introduced over forty bills calling for pesticide regulation, and in 1972 the government finally banned DDT use. The influence Carson generated was powerful. *Silent Spring* not only led to the creation of the Environmental Protection Agency (EPA) in 1970 but helped spark an environmental movement that continues to shape our way of thinking today.

Becomes interested in nature

The youngest of three children, Rachel Louise Carson grew up in Springdale, Pennsylvania, a small town twenty miles north of Pittsburgh. Her parents, Robert Warden and Maria McLean Carson, lived on a farm and kept cows, chickens, and horses. The surrounding countryside, near the shores of the Allegheny River, was where Carson first learned about water, land, and animals. Her mother was the daughter of a Presbyterian minister and instilled in her own daughter a love of nature, music, art, and literature. A solitary child, Carson had few friends besides her cats, and she spent most of her time reading and pursuing the study of nature.

Begins career in science

In 1925 Carson received a scholarship to the Pennsylvania College for Women (now Chatham College) in Pittsburgh. Her freshman biology course had a profound effect on her, leading her to change her major from English to zoology in the middle of her junior year. After Carson graduated with high honors in 1928, her biology teacher helped her obtain a summer fellowship at the Marine Biology Laboratory at Woods Hole on Cape Cod in Massachusetts. There she saw the ocean for the first time and such exotic sea creatures as anemones and urchins. She then received a scholarship to Johns Hopkins University in Baltimore, Maryland, where she studied zoology and genetics.

Takes government job

Following graduation in 1932 Carson taught zoology at various universities. Three years later, when her father died and left her with the responsibility of supporting her mother, Carson applied for a job at the Bureau of Fisheries. Although women were discouraged from taking the required civil service exam, Carson did well on the test and outscored all the other applicants. She was the second woman ever hired by the bureau for a permanent professional post.

Carson wrote and edited government publications at the Bureau of Fisheries and earned a reputation as a ruthless editor. She submitted an essay to the *Atlantic Monthly* and, to her surprise, it was published as "Undersea" in 1937. That same year her older sister, Marian, died at the age of forty; Carson then raised her nieces. "Undersea" was later expanded into the book *Under the Sea-Wind.* Despite favorable reviews, it sold few copies.

The Bureau of Fisheries was merged with the Biological Survey in 1940 and renamed the Fish and Wildlife Service. Carson quickly moved up in the professional ranks, eventually reaching the position of biologist and chief editor. She wrote a small book about national wildlife refuges, *Conservation in Action,* that took her back into the field. As part of her research she visited the Florida Everglades, Parker River in Massachusetts, and Chincoteague Island in Chesapeake Bay.

Becomes successful writer

Then Carson began work on a new book that focused on oceanography. With World War II over, she could now use previously classified government research data on oceanography, which included a number of technical and scientific breakthroughs. During the summer of 1949 Carson did undersea diving off the Florida coast. Then she battled skeptical administrators to arrange a deep-sea cruise to Georges Bank near Nova Scotia aboard the Fish and Wildlife Service research vessel *Albatross III.* Her book on oceanography, *The Sea Around Us,* was published in 1951, becoming an unexpected success and remaining on the *New York Times* bestseller list for eighty-six weeks. Carson won the National Book Award and several other honors for it. She retired from government service and devoted her time to writing.

Carson began work on another book, focusing this time on life along the shoreline. She took excursions to the coasts of Florida and returned to one of her favorite locations, the rocky shores of Maine. *The Edge of the Sea* was published in 1955 and earned her more awards. It was on the bestseller list for twenty weeks, and RKO Studios bought the film rights, making a movie version that sensationalized the material and ignored scientific fact. Although Carson corrected some of the more serious errors, she was never satisfied with the film, even after it won an Oscar as the best documentary of the year.

In 1956 one of Carson's nieces died, leaving her son in Carson's care. After legally adopting the boy, Carson built a new winter home in Silver Spring, Maryland.

Writes Silent Spring

Carson's next book grew out of her long-held concern about the overuse of pesticides. She had received a letter from a woman named Olga Owens Huckins, who described how aerial spraying of the toxic pesticide DDT had destroyed her bird sanctuary in Massachusetts. DDT was considered a good pest control because it resulted in higher crop yields. Carson discovered, however, that the chemical had destructive long-term effects on the environment.

Although she initially thought that the most effective tactic to stop the use of DDT would be to write an article for a popular magazine, Carson ultimately wrote a book instead. Consulting with biologists, chemists, entomologists (scientists who study insects), and pathologists (specialists who interpret and diagnose the changes caused by disease in tissues and body fluids), Carson spent four years gathering data for *Silent Spring*. In the book she showed that once DDT is introduced into the food chain it is transferred to living organisms that are not intended targets, such as birds and fish. Consequently, the chemical virtually exterminated the American falcon, and in high concentrations it was found to be dangerous to humans.

Book draws hostile response

When an excerpt of *Silent Spring* first appeared in the *New Yorker* magazine in June 1962, it drew a hostile response from the chemical industry. They questioned Carson's credentials and called her a "hysterical woman." Carson argued that chemical efforts to control nature upset the environment's delicate balance. Although her message is no longer controversial, the book caused near panic in some circles. Chemical companies tried unsuccessfully to pressure the publisher, Houghton Mifflin, to suppress the book.

Becomes powerful public figure

In spite of a negative response from government and industry, *Silent Spring* soon attracted a large, concerned audience in the United States and around the world. A 1963 special CBS television broadcast, *The Silent Spring of Rachel Carson,* featured a debate between Carson and a chemical company

Rachel Carson birding outside her Silver Spring, Maryland, home in 1963.

George M. Woodwell, American Ecologist

From the 1960s controversy over the insecticide dichlorodiphenyltrichloroethane (DDT) through the debate in the 1990s over global warming, ecologist George M. Woodwell (1928–) has been involved in nearly every environmental issue of the late twentieth century. In the 1950s Woodwell was asked by the Conservation Foundation to study the effects of DDT on Maine forests. At first, he supported the use of the popular pesticide. He changed his mind a short time later, however, when he discovered that only about one-half of the DDT sprayed on crops and forests actually settled on the soil—the rest was scattered by the wind. The drifting pesticide made its way into the food chain as eagles, pelicans, ospreys, and other birds ate contaminated fish, then laid eggs with shells that were too fragile to survive. In 1966 Woodwell and some of his colleagues filed the first of a series of lawsuits calling for a ban on the use of DDT. Their efforts led the Environmental Protection Agency to outlaw the insecticide in 1972.

spokesperson. Her cool-headed approach won her many fans and brought national attention to the problems associated with pesticide use. Although Carson's poor health prevented her from giving speeches, she did appear before the Ribicoff Committee, the U.S. Senate committee on environmental hazards.

In 1963, the year after *Silent Spring* was published, Carson received numerous honors, including an award from the Izaak Walton League of America, the Audubon Medal, and the Cullen Medal of the American Geographical Society. She was also elected to the American Academy of Arts and Sciences. Carson died of heart failure on April 14, 1964, at the age of fifty-six.

Further Reading

Accorsi, William, *Rachel Carson,* Holiday House, 1993.

Carson, Rachel, and Dorothy Freeman, *Always Rachel: The Letters of Rachel Carson and Dorothy Freeman,* Beacon Press, 1995.

Foster, Leila Merrell, *The Story of Rachel Carson and the Environmental Movement,* Childrens Press, 1990.

Greene, Carol, *Rachel Carson: Friend of Nature,* Childrens Press, 1992.

Hendricksson, John, *Rachel Carson: The Environmental Movement,* Millbrook Press, 1991.

McKay, Mary A., *Rachel Carson,* Twayne Publishers, 1993.

Wadsworth, Ginger, *Rachel Carson: Voice of the Earth,* Lerner, 1992.

George Washington Carver

Born c. 1864
Diamond, Missouri
Died January 5, 1943

"It has always been the one great ideal of my life to be of the greatest good to the greatest number of my people."

George Washington Carver was an agricultural scientist who gained acclaim for his discovery of alternative farming methods. A widely talented man who was born into slavery and orphaned in infancy, Carver became an almost mythical American folk hero. He was a faculty member at the all-black Tuskegee Institute, where he worked to improve the lives of impoverished local farmers. Carver is best known for his discovery of uses for the peanut. His testimony in 1921 before the House Ways and Means Committee in support of a tariff to protect the U.S. peanut industry helped earn him the nickname the "peanut wizard."

Known as the "plant doctor"

George Washington Carver was born near the end of the Civil War in Diamond, Missouri. His mother, Mary, was a slave owned by Moses and Susan Carver, who were struggling homesteaders. His father, who is believed to have been a slave on a nearby plantation, was killed in an accident soon after Carver was born. Carver's mother disappeared following a kidnapping by bushwhackers, and he and his brother were then brought up by Moses and Susan. The Carvers were stern but kindly people who did their best for the brothers, despite their limited means.

As a young man Carver was too frail to do heavy farm work like his brother, so he helped his foster mother with household chores such as cleaning and sewing. He also spent considerable time indulging his deep curiosity for nature. He built a pond for his frog collection and kept a little plant nursery in the woods. Because of his talent with plants, Carver became known as the neighborhood "plant doctor."

Encounters discrimination

Carver desperately wanted to learn to read and write, but the local school did not accept black children. Consequently he left his foster parents when he was ten to attend the black school in the county seat of Neosho. This marked the beginning of his long journey through three states in pursuit of a basic education. During these years Carver supported himself with odd jobs, working for and living with various families along the way. He was over twenty years old when he finally graduated from high school in 1885. That same year he was accepted as a student at Highland College in northeastern Kansas. When he arrived there ready to start classes, however, he was told that Highland did not accept students of color. Disillusioned and poor, Carver found work in a nearby fruit farm, mending fences and picking fruit.

Pursues higher education

In 1890 Carver began attending Simpson College at Indianola, Iowa. He had planned to study painting, but the art teacher, who recognized Carver's talent, also foresaw the difficulty a black man would have pursuing a career as a painter at the time. She suggested he consider a career in botany; her father was a professor at Iowa Agricultural College at Ames. Carver was admitted to that college the following year.

Although George Washington Carver did not come up with the idea for peanut butter himself, this popular product and many others are common today largely because of his genius. Through his painstaking research and innovative thinking, he found ways of making more than three hundred peanut-based products and concocted dozens of delicious recipes and useful medicinal preparations. Carver received worldwide fame for his discoveries. Even people like Mohandas Gandhi—the eminent pacifist from India who sought independence from Britain through antiviolent means—consulted him about the Indian diet.

At Iowa, Carver was a popular student and became active in a variety of campus affairs. Because of his wide-ranging abilities he was affectionately called "doctor" by the other students. Carver's academic record was excellent, and his skills in raising, cross-fertilizing, and grafting plants were lauded by his professors. His bachelor's degree thesis, "Plants as Modified by Man," described the positive aspects of hybridization (interbreeding). Carver stayed on at Iowa for graduate work and was soon appointed an assistant in botany (the branch of biology that deals with plant life).

Joins Tuskegee administration

After Carver received his master's degree from Iowa in 1896, he was invited by respected African American educator and leader Booker T. Washington to become director of agriculture at Tuskegee Institute in Tuskegee, Alabama. The institute had been established by Washington in the 1880s as an industrial and agricultural school for black students, and Carver felt that this was where he was most needed.

Carver had many responsibilities at Tuskegee. In addition to heading the agriculture department, he directed the newly established Agricultural Experiment Station. He also assisted local farmers, who were desperately poor, by writing instructional pamphlets on farming. He even set up a movable school that traveled around the South to instruct farmers in agricultural methods.

When Carver started the movable school in 1906, it was no more than a mule-drawn cart. Soon he was driving a large truck, traveling from place to place with tools and exhibits to enhance his lessons. One of his aims was to persuade farmers to give up growing cotton (which was depleting the soil and bringing in very little money) and to diversify by growing vegetables, peanuts, and soybeans.

Contributes to "scientific agriculture"

In 1910 Washington transferred Carver from the agriculture department, appointing him director of a new research department and giving him the title "consulting chemist." Experimental work was more to Carver's liking. At the time, however, the resources at Tuskegee were limited. Carver had no proper laboratory, and he had to make his own equipment out of bits of wire, old bottles, and whatever else he could lay his hands on. He apparently enjoyed these challenges to his ingenuity; indeed, the lack of proper resources led to many of his inventions, for it forced him to find ways of improving the local agriculture in practical and inexpensive ways.

Carver was at the forefront of the new discipline of scientific agriculture, a field dedicated to the exploration of alternative farming methods. He focused his experimental research on finding ways to improve the lives of local farmers. He analyzed water, feed, and soil; experimented with paints that could be made with clay; worked with organic fertilizers; demonstrated uses for cheap and locally available materials, such as swamp muck; and searched for new, inexpensive foodstuffs to supplement the farmers' diets. In addition to human food items, Carver developed stock feeds, cosmetics, dyes, stains, medicines, and ink from peanuts and sweet potatoes.

The most important resource Carver researched was the peanut. He recognized the plant's value in restoring nitrogen to depleted southern soil—cotton crops exhausted the farmers' land—and publicized its high protein and nutritional value. Among the products Carver developed from peanuts were soap, face powder, mayonnaise, shampoo, metal polish, and adhesives—but he was not the one to invent peanut butter.

Gains recognition

In 1916 Carver received two prestigious invitations: to serve on the advisory board of the U.S. National Agricultural

Society and to become a fellow of the Royal Society for the Arts in London. In 1919 he received his first salary increase in twenty years. He had become increasingly popular as a lecturer, and his testimony before the House Ways and Means Committee in 1921 concerning the importance of the peanut industry thrust him into the national limelight. Two years later Carver was awarded the prestigious Spingarn Medal from the National Association for the Advancement of Colored People (NAACP) for his contributions to agricultural chemistry. He was also honored for his lectures to religious, educational, and farming audiences—lectures that had "increased inter-racial knowledge and respect."

Becomes a spokesperson for "chemurgy"

In the mid-1930s Carver became an advocate of "chemurgy," the process of putting chemistry to work in industry for the farmer. In 1937 he met industrialist Henry Ford at a chemurgy conference Ford had sponsored. A long friendship developed between the two men. Three years later, when Carver established the Carver Museum in Tuskegee (a foundation to continue and preserve his work), it was dedicated by Ford. The museum contains seventy-one of Carver's pictures as well as handicrafts, case studies, and results of his research.

Receives numerous awards and honors

In addition to the Spingarn Medal, Carver received numerous other awards and honors for his contributions to the field of scientific agriculture. Noteworthy among them are the Roosevelt Medal in 1939, an honorary doctorate from the University of Rochester, and the first award for "outstanding service to the welfare of the South" from the Catholic Conference of the South. In 1942 Ford erected a Carver memorial cabin and a nutritional laboratory in Carver's honor at Dearborn, Michigan's Greenfield Village.

Carver's health had begun to fail in the 1930s. When he died on January 5, 1943, Tuskegee Institute was flooded with letters of sympathy. Carver was buried in the Tuskegee Institute cemetery near the grave of Booker T. Washington. On January

9, 1943, President Franklin D. Roosevelt paid tribute to Carver in an address before Congress. Later that year Roosevelt signed legislation making Carver's birthplace a national monument.

George Washington Carver in 1940, shortly after announcing he was donating $33,000 to the Tuskegee Institute to carry on the work he had begun there.

Further Reading

Adair, Gene, *George Washington Carver,* Chelsea House, 1989.

Elliott, Lawrence, *George Washington Carver: The Man Who Overcame,* Prentice-Hall, 1966.

Greene, Carol, *George Washington Carver, Scientist and Teacher,* Childrens Press, 1992.

Kremer, Gary R., *George Washington Carver: In His Own Words,* University of Missouri Press, 1987.

McMurray, Linda O., *George Washington Carver: Scientist and Symbol,* Oxford University Press, 1981.

Moore, Eva, *The Story of George Washington Carver,* Scholastic, 1990.

Subrahmanyan Chandrasekhar

Born October 19, 1910
Lahore, India

Subrahmanyan Chandrasekhar turned the astronomical world upside down by challenging previously held theories of stellar evolution.

Subrahmanyan Chandrasekhar is an Indian-born American astrophysicist and applied mathematician who proposed radical new theories of stellar evolution. His most celebrated work concerns the radiation of energy from stars, particularly white dwarfs, which are the dying fragments of stars. Though at first disputed by the prominent British astronomer and physicist Sir Arthur Stanley Eddington, his theory was later shown to be correct. Chandrasekhar has made numerous other contributions to astrophysics in such areas as the system of energy transfer within stars, stellar structure, and theories of planetary and stellar atmospheres. Throughout the course of his career, he has received numerous awards and distinctions, most notably the 1983 Nobel Prize for physics for his research into the depths of aged stars.

Undertakes independent study

Subrahmanyan Chandrasekhar, better known as Chandra, was born on October 19, 1910, in Lahore, India (now part of

Pakistan). He was the first son of C. Subrahmanyan Ayyar and Sitalakshmi nee Balakrishnan. Chandra received his early education at home, beginning when he was five. He learned Tamil (the language spoken in his native region of India) from his mother and English and arithmetic from his father. Influenced by his uncle, the physicist Sir Chandrasekhar V. Raman, who was awarded the Nobel Prize in 1930, Chandra set his sights on the field of science at an early age. To this end he undertook, at his own initiative, an independent study of calculus and physics.

Attends college

In 1918 Chandra's family moved south to Madras. Chandra was taught by private tutors until 1921, when he enrolled in the Hindu High School in Triplicane. With typical drive and motivation, he studied on his own, moving ahead of the class and completing school by the age of fifteen. After high school Chandra attended Presidency College in Madras, where he studied physics, chemistry, English, and Sanskrit (the classical language of India and Hinduism). He wanted to study pure mathematics but his father insisted that he take physics. Chandra resolved this conflict by registering as an honors physics student but attending mathematics lectures. A highlight of his college years was the publication of his paper "The Compton Scattering and the New Statistics," a discussion of the recently discovered Compton effect relating to X-ray and gamma-ray wavelengths. This and other early successes–achieved while Chandra was still an eighteen-year-old undergraduate–only strengthened his resolve to pursue a career in scientific research.

Goes to Cambridge

Upon earning a master's degree in 1930, Chandra entered Trinity College in Cambridge, England, with a research scholarship from the Indian government. At Cambridge, Chandra turned to astrophysics, having been inspired by a theory of stellar evolution that occurred to him on the long boat journey from India to England. This theory would preoccupy him for

While his contribution to astrophysics has been immense, Subrahmanyan Chandrasekhar has always preferred to remain outside the mainstream of research. His reputation as a loner was no doubt fostered by the treatment he received from other scientists over the years. When the prominent astronomer and physicist Sir Arthur Stanley Eddington publicly ridiculed Chandra's theory on white dwarfs, Chandra was deeply upset. The quarrel led not only to the fifty-year-long postponement of his receiving the Nobel Prize but also to a delay in the discovery of black holes and neutron stars. The ramifications of the debate echoed throughout the entire field of astronomy.

the next ten years. In 1933, after Chandra took his doctoral exams, he was awarded a fellowship at Cambridge. He returned to his study of astrophysics, focusing on researching white dwarfs.

Introduces theory on white dwarf stars

As a member of the Royal Astronomical Society since 1932, Chandra was entitled to present papers at its twice-monthly meetings. At one of these meetings in 1935, he announced the results of the work that would later earn him the Nobel Prize. As stars evolve, he told the assembled audience, they emit energy generated primarily by their conversion of hydrogen into helium. As they reach the end of their lives, stars have progressively less hydrogen left to convert and thus emit less energy in the form of radiation. They eventually reach a stage when they are no longer able to generate the pressure needed to sustain their size against their own gravitational pull. At this point stars begin to contract.

As their density increases during the contraction process, stars build up sufficient internal energy to collapse their atomic structure into a degenerate state: they begin to collapse into themselves. Their electrons become so tightly packed that they turn into tiny objects of enormous density—so-called white dwarfs. According to Chandra, the greater the mass of a white dwarf, the smaller its radius. Chandra rocked the scientific community with his radical proposal that not all stars end their lives as stable white dwarfs. If the mass of evolving stars increases beyond a certain limit (eventually named the Chandrasekhar limit and calculated as 1.4 times the mass of the Sun), stars cannot become stable white dwarfs.

A star with a mass above the limit has to either lose mass to form a white dwarf or take an alternative evolutionary path and become a supernova, which releases its excess energy in the form of an explosion. Any mass that remains after this spectacular event may become a white dwarf but more likely will form a neutron star. (In a neutron star, protons and electrons are packed together to form neutrons, the components of the atomic nucleus.) Neutron stars have even greater density than white dwarfs and are observed as pulsars, which emit bursts of radio waves.

Mocked for his theory

Although Chandra's theory would later be validated, his ideas were unexpectedly undermined and ridiculed by a prominent astronomer and physicist, Sir Arthur Stanley Eddington. Eddington thought Chandra's notion that stars can evolve into anything other than white dwarfs was absurd. Since Chandra did not carry the status and authority of Eddington, he was not given the benefit of the doubt by the researchers in his field. Twenty years passed before his theory gained general acceptance among astrophysicists, although it was quickly recognized as valid by physicists as noteworthy as Wolfgang Pauli, **Niels Bohr** (see entry), Ralph H. Fowler, and Paul Dirac.

Rather than continue sparring with Eddington, Chandra collected his thoughts on the matter in his first book, *An Introduction to the Study of Stellar Structure*. He then took up new research on stellar dynamics. An unfortunate result of the scientific quarrel, however, was the postponement of the discovery of black holes and neutron stars by at least twenty years. In addition, fifty years went by before Chandra received a Nobel Prize for his white dwarf work.

Immigrates to America

Following his theoretical dispute with England's greatest astronomer, Chandra felt he had few academic options left in

England. As a result, he moved to the United States in 1935 and became a visiting lecturer in cosmic physics at Harvard University in Cambridge, Massachusetts. While at Harvard, Chandra was offered a research associate position at the Yerkes Observatory (operated by the University of Chicago) at Williams Bay, Wisconsin.

After returning to India briefly to marry Lalitha Doraiswamy, Chandra took up his post at Yerkes in January 1937. His main job was to develop a graduate program in astronomy and astrophysics, but he also taught some courses. Chandra's reputation as an outstanding teacher soon attracted top students to the graduate school. He continued researching stellar evolution, stellar structure, and the transfer of energy within stars, and in 1938 he was promoted to assistant professor of astrophysics. During this time Chandra revealed his conclusions regarding the life paths of stars.

Advances at University of Chicago

During World War II, Chandra was employed at the Aberdeen Proving Grounds in Maryland, working on ballistics testing (the motion of projectiles in flight), the theory of shock waves, the Mach effect (high speed in relation to the speed of sound), and transport problems related to neutron diffusion (for instance, after an atomic bomb was dropped). In 1942 he was promoted to associate professor of astrophysics at the University of Chicago; he became a full professor the following year. Around 1944 Chandra switched his research from stellar dynamics to radiative transfer, or the transfer of energy within stars. That year he also realized a lifelong ambition when he was elected to the Royal Society of London.

In 1952 Chandra became Morton D. Hull Distinguished Service Professor of Astrophysics in Chicago's departments of astronomy and physics, as well as at the Institute for Nuclear Physics at Yerkes Observatory. Later that same year he was appointed managing editor of the *Astrophysical Journal,* a position he held until 1971. He transformed the journal from a private publication of the University of Chicago to the national journal of the American Astronomical Society.

Subrahmanyan Chandrasekhar pauses briefly at the base of the Henry Moore sculpture Nuclear Energy *on the University of Chicago campus in 1983.*

Publishes work on black holes

Chandra became a citizen of the United States in 1953. Despite receiving numerous offers from other universities in the United States and abroad, he never left the University of Chicago. As the result of a disagreement with the head of Yerkes, however, Chandra stopped teaching astrophysics and astronomy and began lecturing in mathematical physics at the

Fritz Zwicky, Swiss astronomer

Swiss astronomer Fritz Zwicky (1898–1974) was puzzled by stars that appeared suddenly in the sky, like a nova (an exploding star), but were far more intense than a nova. Around the turn of the seventeenth century, astronomers Tycho Brahe (1546–1601) and Johannes Kepler (1571–1630) had both seen extremely bright novas, which must have been supernovas, which are many times brighter than novas, within our own galaxy. Unfortunately, no supernovas had appeared since Kepler's time, so Zwicky had to be content with searching other galaxies for supernovas.

Zwicky's research showed that only two or three supernovas occur in a galaxy every thousand years! (In 1987 a supernova erupted in the Large Magellanic Cloud, the Milky Way's closest neighbor.) He had a faint idea of what a supernova was, and he even speculated, correctly, that neutron stars were the remains of exploded supernovas. But an explanation for the existence of supernovas had to wait until Subrahmanyan Chandrasekhar worked out the mechanics of stellar combustion in 1939.

University of Chicago campus in Chicago. He voluntarily retired from the university in 1980, although he stayed on as a postretirement researcher. In 1983 he published a classic work on the mathematical theory of black holes. That same year he won the Nobel Prize in physics for his research on aging stars.

Receives numerous awards and honors

Throughout his long career Chandrasekhar has been recognized for his achievements with numerous awards and honors in the United States, Europe, and India. In 1984, the year after he won the Nobel Prize, he received the Copley Prize from the Royal Society of London and the R. D. Birla Memorial Award of the Indian Physics Association, among other honors. In 1985 the Vainu Bappu Memorial Award was bestowed upon him by the Indian National Science Academy. In May 1993 Chandrasekhar was awarded the highest honor in the state of Illinois, the Lincoln Academy Award, for his outstanding contributions to science.

Further Reading

Chandrasekhar, Subrahmanyan, *The Mathematical Theory of Black Holes,* Clarendon Press, 1983.

Goldsmith, Donald, *The Astronomers,* St. Martin's, 1991.

Hammond, Allen L., ed., *A Passion to Know,* Scribner, 1984.

Wali, Kameshwar C., *Chandra: A Biography of S. Chandrasekhar,* University of Chicago Press, 1991.

Lynn Conway

Born January 2, 1938
Mount Vernon, New York

American electrical engineer Lynn Conway simplified computer chip design.

Lynn Conway is an American electrical engineer who performed pioneering work in very large scale integrated (VLSI) circuit and system design methodology. She helped simplify the way integrated (unified) computer circuit chips are designed. She also developed a rapid means of prototype fabrication (new model production) that fundamentally changed the method of computer design and contributed to the explosion of the development of new hardware and software. A professor of electrical engineering and computer sciences and associate dean of the College of Engineering at the University of Michigan, Conway includes computer architecture, artificial intelligence, and collaboration technology among her research interests.

Begins impressive career

Born in Mount Vernon, New York, on January 2, 1938, Lynn Ann Conway received an M.S. degree in electrical engineering from Columbia University in 1963 and worked as a staff researcher at IBM Corporation from 1964 to 1969. She then served as senior staff engineer at Memorex Corporation from 1969 to 1973, when she accepted a research position with Xerox Corporation at its Palo Alto Research Center in California. Conway founded the VLSI systems and Knowledge Systems research departments at Xerox and remained resident fellow and manager there until 1983. At that time she began two years of service as chief scientist and assistant director of Strategic Computing at the Defense Advisory Research Projects Agency (DARPA). In 1985 Conway accepted a position in the College of Engineering at the University of Michigan.

IMPACT

Because Lynn Conway simplified the way computer chips are designed, specialists are no longer necessary to do the work. Now computer engineers with only general backgrounds can design chips. This development has fundamentally changed the way computers are designed and opened the field to the new ideas of nonspecialists, resulting in an explosion in the development of new computer hardware and software.

Makes major advances in circuitry

Conway is renowned for two major developments in circuitry. The first, a joint effort with several colleagues, was the invention of a new approach to the design of integrated computer circuit chips. (An integrated circuit is a tiny complex of electronic components and their connections that is produced on a small slice, or chip, of material such as silicon. Computer chips allow modern computers to perform complex calculations and run programs rapidly.) Previously, many designers, each with specialized skills, were needed in the laborious process of circuitry development. Conway helped create a unified structural methodology that allowed computer engineers with general backgrounds to design chips.

Conway's second achievement, which was published in the textbook *Introduction to VLSI Systems,* was a new method of chip fabrication (production), whereby designers could very rapidly obtain prototypes (original models) with which to test their hardware and software inventions. This quick way of fabrication as well as Conway's earlier contribution to the design of integrated circuitry have increased the sharing of information among both specialists and nonspecialists working in the computer industry.

Receives awards and honors

Conway has received extensive recognition for her work, including the John Price Wetherill Medal from the Franklin Institute in 1985; the Meritorious Civilian Service Award, given by the Secretary of Defense in 1985; and the Harold Pender Award, bestowed by the University of Pennsylvania in 1984. She was honored in 1990 with an achievement award of the Society of Women Engineers. She also received the Major Educational Innovation Award from the Institute of Electrical and Electronics Engineers, and the Electronics Magazine Achievement Award.

Conway has held numerous consulting positions and was visiting associate professor of electrical engineering and computer sciences at the Massachusetts Institute of Technology (MIT) in Cambridge, Massachusetts, for academic year 1978–79. She has served on such advisory panels as the United States Air Force Scientific Advisory Board, the Executive Council of the American Association for Artificial Intelligence, and the Technical Council Society for Machine Intelligence. Her love of adventure has led her to the hobby of motocross racing.

Further Reading

Conway, Lynn, "Haunted by the Metaphor of the PC," *Electronics,* August 1990, p. 62.

Conway, Lynn, *Introduction to VLSI Systems,* Addison-Wesley, 1980.

Carl Ferdinand Cori

Born December 5, 1896
Prague, Czechoslovakia
Died October 20, 1984
Cambridge, Massachusetts

Gerty T. Cori

Born August 15, 1896
Prague, Czechoslovakia
Died October 26, 1957

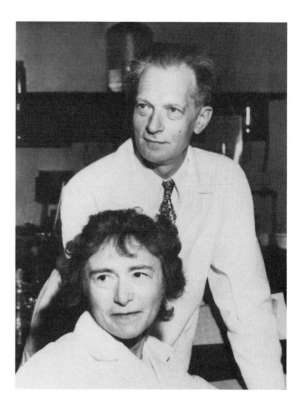

Carl Ferdinand Cori and Gerty T. Cori made important contributions to science in the area of biochemistry. They specialized in the action of glucose, carbohydrate metabolism in tumors, phosphate processes in the muscles, and glucose-glycogen interconversion. In 1947 they received the Nobel Prize for physiology or medicine for their research on sugar metabolism. They shared the award with Bernardo A. Houssay, an Argentinean physiologist who discovered how the pituitary gland, which sits at the base of the cranium, functions in the metabolism of carbohydrates. The Coris' contributions broadened the field of biochemistry for future research.

For their pioneering research on sugar metabolism, Carl Ferdinand Cori and Gerty T. Cori shared the 1947 Nobel Prize for physiology or medicine.

Influenced by families

Carl Ferdinand Cori was born on December 5, 1896, in Prague, which was then part of the Austro-Hungarian empire. His parents were Marie Lippich Cori and Carl Isidor Cori, a professor of zoology at the German University of Prague.

When Cori was still young the family moved to Trieste, Italy, where his father had been appointed director of a marine biology station. Cori studied at the gymnasium (high school) in Trieste from 1906 to 1914, then returned to Prague to study medicine at the German University. His education was interrupted by World War I, during which he served in the Austrian army working in hospitals for infectious diseases on the Italian front.

Gerty T. Cori, also a native of Prague, was born on August 15, 1896, the first of three daughters of Otto and Martha Neustadt Radnitz. Her career was influenced by her family background. Her father was a manager of sugar refineries; her maternal uncle, a professor of pediatrics (medical care of children), encouraged her to pursue her interest in science. At that time girls did not usually attend a university, so in order to follow her dream of becoming a chemist she first studied at a special high school. Then, in 1914, she entered medical school at the German University.

Meet in college

The Coris met at the German University, where they attended the same classes. Together they studied human complement, a substance in blood that plays a key role in immune responses by combining with antibodies. This was the first in a series of lifelong collaborations; eventually they would publish more than two hundred research articles together. In 1920, after receiving their doctor of medicine (M.D.) degrees, the couple moved to Vienna, where they were married. Carl worked at the University of Vienna and the University of Graz while Gerty served as an assistant at the Karolinen Children's Hospital. Around this time she became particularly interested in how the thyroid gland regulates body temperature.

Seek better life in United States

In the early 1920s, after World War I had ended, Europe was in the midst of great social and economic unrest. Because of these circumstances the Coris moved to the United States in 1922. They took positions at the New York State Institute for the Study of Malignant Diseases (later the Roswell Park Memorial Institute) in Buffalo, New York. Carl worked as a biochemist and Gerty was an assistant pathologist.

The Coris continued conducting research together, although colleagues cautioned that collaboration would hurt Carl's career. They ignored these warnings, nevertheless, and started a study of carbohydrate metabolism, or the breakdown of compounds like glucose and starch and their uses in the body. During their years in Buffalo they jointly published a number of influential papers on sugar metabolism, or how sugars supply energy to the body.

IMPACT

Carl Ferdinand Cori and Gerty T. Cori made a significant impact on the field of biochemistry with their studies of sugar metabolism, the process by which the body stores and uses sugars and other carbohydrates. Gerty also opened new areas of study to other scientists with her research on glycogen storage disorders.

Discover important compound

When the Coris began to study carbohydrate metabolism, it was generally believed that the sugar called glucose (a type of carbohydrate) was formed when another carbohydrate, glycogen, was broken down by the action of water molecules in a process known as hydrolysis. Glucose circulates in the blood and is used by the body's cells in virtually all cellular processes that require energy. Glycogen is a natural polymer (a large molecule consisting of many similar smaller molecules) formed by combining large numbers of individual sugar molecules for storage in the body. Glycogen is like a stored form of energy: it allows the body to function normally on a continual basis by providing a store from which glucose can be broken down and released as needed.

Hydrolysis is a chemical process that does not require enzymes. If, as was believed to be the case in the 1920s, glycogen were broken down to glucose by simple hydrolysis, carbohydrate metabolism would be a simple, straightforward process. However, in the course of their work the Coris discovered a chemical compound, glucose-1-phosphate, made up of glucose and a phosphate group (one phosphorous atom combined with three oxygen atoms). Glucose-1-phosphate is derived from glycogen by the action of an enzyme called phosphorylase (pronounced fos-FOR-uh-laze). Now known as the Cori ester, this finding was the basis for later research on how carbohydrates are used, stored, and converted in the body.

Study insulin

In 1924 the Coris wrote about their comparison of sugar levels in the blood of arteries and veins under the influence of insulin. Gerty had been interested in hormones (chemicals released in the body that produce a specific effect on targeted cells and organs) since her early thyroid research in Vienna. The discovery of the hormone insulin in 1921 had stimulated her to examine the role of sugar in metabolism. The capacity of insulin to control diabetes (the absence or inadequate secretion of insulin naturally by the body) lent greater importance to the Coris' investigations. At the same time, inspired by the earlier work of other scientists, they examined the reason that tumors (abnormal overgrowths of tissue) store large amounts of glucose.

As a result of their studies of glucose in tumors, the Coris became convinced that extensive research on carbohydrate metabolism still needed to be done. They began this task by examining the rate of absorption of various sugars from the intestine. They also measured levels of several products of sugar metabolism, particularly glycogen and lactic acid (the result of sugar combining with oxygen), in the muscles and the liver. From these studies they proposed a cycle, now called the Cori cycle in their honor, that linked glucose with glycogen and lactic acid.

The Coris' suggestion generated excitement among medical researchers. As they continued their work the couple unraveled more steps in the complex process of carbohydrate metabolism: they found a second intermediate compound, glucose-6-phosphate, which is formed from glucose-1-phosphate. (The two compounds differ in where the phosphate

group is attached to the sugar.) They also found phosphoglu-comutase (fos-foe-GLOO-koe-MYOO-taze), the enzyme that accomplishes this conversion.

Carl Ferdinand Cori and Gerty T. Cori at a Washington University lab.

Win Nobel Prize

In 1928 the Coris became naturalized citizens of the United States. Three years later they moved to St. Louis, Missouri, where they took research positions at Washington University School of Medicine. By the early 1940s they had gained a fairly complete picture of carbohydrate metabolism. Their work changed the way scientists thought about reactions in the human body, and it suggested that specific, enzyme-driven reactions existed for many biological conversions that constitute life. In 1944 Carl was appointed professor of biochemistry at Washington University; Gerty became a full professor three years later. Their laboratory had acquired an international reputation as an important center of biochemical breakthroughs. For their pivotal studies in sugar metabolism the Coris were awarded the Nobel Prize for physiology or medicine in 1947, an honor they shared with Bernardo A. Houssay. Gerty was only the third woman to receive a Nobel Prize in science, following **Marie Curie** (see entry) and Curie's daughter, Irène Joloit-Curie.

Gerty Cori works independently

Working alone, Gerty turned her attention to a group of inherited childhood diseases known collectively as glycogen storage disorders. In 1952 she determined the structure of the highly branched glycogen molecule. She found that diseases of glycogen storage fall into two general groups, one involving too much glycogen and the other involving abnormal glycogen. Showing that both types of diseases originated in the enzymes that control glycogen metabolism, she opened new fields of study to other scientists. Later, Gerty was instrumental in the discovery of a number of other intermediate chemical compounds and enzymes that play key roles in biological processes.

Awarded other prizes

At the time the Coris won the Nobel Prize, Gerty was diagnosed as having myelosclerosis, a disease of the blood. She died on October 26, 1957. During her lifetime Gerty was honored for her achievements with the prestigious Garvan Medal for women chemists from the American Chemical

Society as well as membership in the National Academy of Sciences. Three years after Gerty's death Carl married Anne Fitzgerald Jones; in 1966, after retiring from Washington University, he served as a visiting professor at the Harvard University School of Medicine in Cambridge, Massachusetts. Throughout his life Carl had received numerous honorary degrees and awards; among them were the Isaac Adler Award from Harvard in 1944 and the 1947 Squibb Award of the Society of Endocrinologists, which he shared with Gerty. Carl died on October 20, 1984, in Cambridge. The Coris had one son, Carl Thomas Cori.

Further Reading

Magill, Frank N., ed., *The Nobel Prize Winners: Physiology or Medicine,* Volume 2, *1944–1969,* Salem Press, 1991, pp. 550–59.

Opfell, Olga S., *The Lady Laureates,* Scarecrow, 1986, pp. 213–23.

Wasson, Tyler, ed., *Nobel Prize Winners,* H. W. Wilson, 1987, pp. 216–20.

Jacques Cousteau

Born June 11, 1910
Saint-André-de-Cubzac, France

> *"Sometimes we are lucky enough to know that our lives have been changed .... It happened to me ... when my eyes were opened on the sea."*

While some critics have challenged Jacques Cousteau's scientific credentials, he has never claimed to be an expert in any area. His talents seem to be more "poetic" than scientific; his films and books—which include the television series *The Undersea World of Jacques Cousteau* and the popular book *The Silent World*—convey his great love of nature. Known worldwide for his concern about conservation issues, Cousteau claims that irreversible damage has been done to both land and sea by so-called industrial progress.

Becomes interested in photography

Jacques-Yves Cousteau was born in Saint-André-de-Cubzac, France, on June 11, 1910, to Elizabeth Duranthon and Daniel Cousteau. For the first seven years of his life he suffered from chronic enteritis, a painful intestinal condition. Later, the family traveled extensively because of Daniel's job as a lawyer representing American businesspeople in Europe and the United States. As a result Cousteau spent his youth traveling between Paris and New York City. He recorded few memories from his childhood; his earliest impressions, however, involved water and ships.

At the age of thirteen Cousteau became interested in photography when he purchased one of the first home movie cameras sold in France and started to make his own films. An indifferent student, he was expelled from a Paris secondary school, or lycée, for throwing rocks at the school windows. As punishment, his parents sent him to a boarding school in Alsace, where his grades improved. Cousteau was then admitted to the French Naval Academy in 1930, graduating second in his class two years later with a degree in engineering. The military won out over filmmaking simply because it offered Cousteau the opportunity for extended travel.

Accident changes life

Cousteau entered the pilot training program at the French naval aviation school. He had made his first solo flight and was close to graduation when an accident dashed his hopes for a flying career. While he was driving at night on a deserted mountain road, his car spun out of control and crashed. Cousteau was seriously hurt, his right arm paralyzed. Forced to drop out of aviation school, he underwent several years of physical therapy before he regained full use of his arm.

After he had recovered sufficiently, Cousteau was assigned to the cruiser *Dupleix,* which was stationed at Toulon, a French port on the Mediterranean. In Toulon a fellow officer suggested that Cousteau take up swimming to help rehabilitate his arm. This advice redirected Cousteau's life in ways neither man could then see. In the summer of 1936 he began to spend all his free time at the beach. He started using goggles as a way of seeing underwater and adapted his camera so he could film fish. The next year he married his first wife, Simone Melchoir, who later became his partner on most of his sea voyages. Their two sons, Jean-Michel and Philippe, were born shortly thereafter.

Invents aqualung

Although Cousteau loved diving, he was impatient with the limitations of goggle diving, which did not permit him enough time for extended underwater exploration. The standard helmet and heavy suit apparatus had similar drawbacks: the diver was helplessly tethered by an air line to the ship, which greatly restricted underwater mobility. After much hard work Cousteau and an engineer friend, Emile Bagnan, eventually developed a breathing device they called the aqualung. The aqualung consists of a canister of compressed air, a regulator that supplies a constant flow of oxygen (at the same pressure as the water the diver is in), and a mouthpiece that enables the diver to breathe.

At the end of World War II, Cousteau convinced the French navy that his new invention could be put to an immediate practical use. He organized diving crews to remove mines, placed by the German occupying force during the war, that were blocking southern French ports. Cousteau remained in the French navy until 1956 and continued experimentation with underwater photography. He improved his equipment in order to make increasingly deeper dives. In the process he developed an underwater camera that could operate up to 600 meters (1,970 feet) below the surface of the water, making some of the first photographs and films of life undersea.

Explores with the Calypso

On July 19, 1950, Cousteau bought *Calypso,* a converted U.S. minesweeper. Sixteen months later, after undergoing significant renovations, the ship sailed for the Red Sea. The *Calypso* Red Sea Expedition (1951–52) yielded numerous discoveries, including the identification of previously unknown plant and animal species and the discovery of volcanic basins beneath the Red Sea. In February 1952 *Calypso* sailed toward Toulon. On the way home, the crew investigated an uncharted

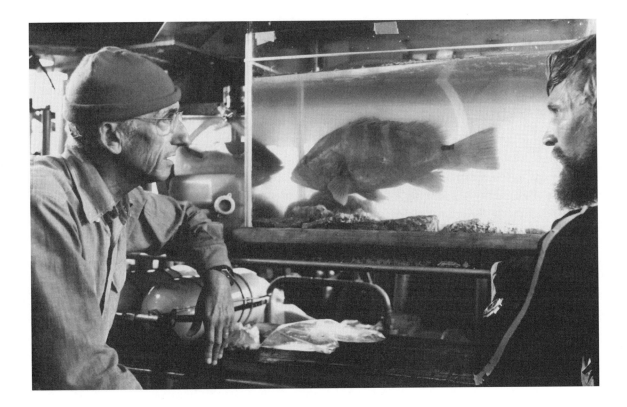

wreck near the southern coast of Grand Congloué and discovered a large Roman ship filled with treasures.

The discovery of the ancient ship made Cousteau famous in France. In 1953 the publication of *The Silent World,* drawn from Cousteau's daily logs and including many startling underwater photographs, brought him international fame. Released in more than twenty languages, *The Silent World* eventually sold more than five million copies worldwide; it was later made into a film that won an Academy Award in 1957.

Invents the "Conshelf"

In the 1950s Cousteau and his team invented a small, easily maneuverable submarine that he called the diving saucer, which made more than one thousand dives. By the 1960s, though, Cousteau was looking for ways to actually live beneath the sea. With the Conshelf Saturation Dive program, he devel-

Jacques Cousteau and diver Bernard Delemotte examine a small grouper in a segment of "The Fish That Swallowed Jonah," a 1976 program in the series The Undersea World of Jacques Cousteau.

Harold Edgerton, American Inventor and Electrical Engineer

Harold Edgerton (1903–1990), an inventor who came to be known as "Papa Flash," developed the strobe light and high-speed flash photography. He held over forty patents for inventions related to seeing the unseen, including high-speed camera equipment, sonar probes, and underwater lighting devices. While his inventions earned him the respect and admiration of his engineering colleagues, he is perhaps best known to the public for his photographs. The high-speed filming techniques he developed made it possible for him to freeze the action of such things as a bullet passing through an apple and a drop of milk as it splashes and forms a coronet (crown shape). By the time of his death in 1990, Edgerton had made ten voyages aboard Jacques Cousteau's research vessel *Calypso*.

oped a number of Conshelf stations, the first underwater living environments where divers lived and worked for weeks at a time. Cousteau's underwater stations predated the U.S. Navy Sealab experiments. In the first Conshelf project in 1962, two men stayed for a week in a small chamber 33 feet below the surface of the Mediterranean Sea. Conshelf 2, which followed in 1963 in the Red Sea off the coast of Egypt, involved more complicated experiments. This time five men lived in a complex underwater settlement for one month, again at a depth of 33 feet. Conshelf 3 followed in 1965, by which time Cousteau was thinking of setting up semipermanent stations, similar to space stations, where people could live indefinitely.

Founds Cousteau Society

Beginning in 1960, when he opposed the French government's decision to dump nuclear waste in the Mediterranean, Cousteau became a spokesperson for environmental causes. In 1970 he founded the Cousteau Society, which is based in Bridgeport, Connecticut. He uses his fame as an underwater explorer to lobby for greater awareness of the environmental dangers in the oceans of the world. Cousteau speaks with passion about his belief that the fate of the planet and the human species is being jeopardized by pollution and the lack of population control. According to Cousteau, whatever is dumped into the seas will remain there indefinitely, affecting the earth's ecological balance.

Cousteau effectively uses television to educate people throughout the world. *The Undersea World of Jacques Cousteau* premiered in 1968, featuring Cousteau, his sons, and sea creatures from around the globe. The documentary ran for eight seasons. In 1970 he produced twelve one-hour programs in a series titled *The Undersea Odyssey of the "Calypso,"* followed by six more programs in 1973. He also produced a 1984 series on the underwater exploration of the Amazon River and then, starting in 1985, twenty-two one-hour-long programs on oceans. In all, Cousteau has made more than one hundred documentaries and has won ten Emmys and three Oscars. He has also written more than two dozen books on undersea life such as whales, squid, octopuses, and sharks.

In honor of his achievements Cousteau received the Grand Croix dans l'Orde National du Merite from the French government in 1985. That same year he was also awarded the U.S. Presidential Medal of Freedom. In 1987 he was inducted into the Television Academy Hall of Fame and later received the founder's award from the International Council of the National Academy of Television Arts and Sciences. In 1988 the National Geographic Society honored him with its Centennial Award for "special contributions to mankind throughout the years."

Further Reading

Cousteau, Jacques, *A Bill of Rights for Future Generations,* Myrin Institute, 1980.

Cousteau, Jacques, *Cousteau's Calypso,* Abrams, 1980.

Cousteau Society, *An Adventure in the Amazon,* Simon & Schuster Books for Young Readers, 1992.

Iverson, Genie, *Jacques Cousteau,* Putnam, 1976.

Madsen, Axel, *Cousteau: An Unauthorized Biography,* Beaufort Books, 1986.

Munson, Richard, *Cousteau: The Captain and His World,* Morrow, 1989.

Sinnot, Susan, *Jacques-Yves Cousteau,* Childrens Press, 1992.

Francis Crick

Born June 8, 1916
Northampton, England

Francis Crick,
along with
James D. Watson,
unraveled the
mystery surrounding
the structure
of DNA.

Francis Crick is one half of the famous pair of molecular biologists—the other is **James D. Watson** (see entry)—who unraveled the mystery of the structure of deoxyribonucleic acid (DNA), carrier of genetic information. Crick and Watson are credited with ushering in the modern era of molecular biology. Since this fundamental discovery, Crick has made significant contributions to the understanding of the genetic code and gene action as well as molecular neurobiology. Crick shared the Nobel Prize in medicine in 1962 with Watson and Maurice Wilkins for their work on DNA.

Enjoys experimental science

The eldest of two sons, Francis Harry Compton Crick was born to Harry Crick and Anne Elizabeth Wilkins on June 8, 1916, in Northampton, England. His father and uncle ran a shoe and boot factory. Crick attended grammar school in Northampton, and was an enthusiastic experimental scientist at an early age, producing the customary number of youthful chemical explosions. As a schoolboy, he won a prize for collecting wild-flowers. At the age of fourteen, he obtained a scholarship to Mill Hill School in North London. Four years later he entered University College and the University of London, where he earned a second-class honors degree in physics in three years.

Following his undergraduate studies, Crick conducted research on the viscosity (resistance to flow) of water under pressure at high temperatures at University College. In 1940, during World War II, he took a civilian job with the admiralty (British naval office), eventually working on the design of mines used to destroy ships. Shortly thereafter Crick married Ruth Doreen Dodd; their son Michael was born during an air raid on London. By the end of the war Crick was assigned to scientific intelligence at the admiralty headquarters in White-hall to design weapons.

Studies X-ray diffraction

Realizing he would need additional education to satisfy his desire to do research, Crick decided to pursue an advanced degree. After preliminary inquiries at University College, Crick settled on a program at the Strangeways Laboratory at Cambridge University to work on the physical properties of cytoplasm (the substances surrounding the nucleus of a cell) in chick fibroblast (connective tissue) cells grown in a laboratory. Two years later he joined the Medical Research Council Unit at the Cavendish Laboratory to work on protein structure with British chemists Max Perutz and John Kendrew.

In 1947 Crick divorced his wife, then in 1949 married Odile Speed, an art student whom he had met during the war. Their marriage coincided with the start of Crick's Ph.D. thesis work on the X-ray diffraction of proteins. X-ray diffraction is a technique for studying the crystalline structure of molecules, permitting investigators to examine their three-dimensional structure. In this technique, X rays are directed at a compound, and the subsequent scattering of the X-ray beam reflects the configuration of the molecule on a photographic plate.

Works with Watson on DNA structure

In 1951 Crick was joined at the Cavendish by James Watson, a visiting American who was a member of the "phage group," scientists who studied bacterial viruses (known as bacteriophages, or simply phages). Like his phage colleagues, Watson was interested in discovering the substance that composes genes and thought that unraveling the structure of DNA was the most promising solution. The informal partnership between Crick and Watson developed, according to Crick, because of their "youthful arrogance" and similar thought processes. It was also clear that their experiences complemented one another. By the time of their first meeting, Crick had gained substantial knowledge of X-ray diffraction and protein structure, while Watson had become well informed about phage and bacterial genetics.

Both Crick and Watson were aware of the work of biochemists Maurice Wilkins and **Rosalind Franklin** (see entry) at King's College of London University, who were using X-ray diffraction to study the structure of DNA. Crick, in particular, urged the London group to build models, much as American chemist **Linus Pauling** (see entry) had done to solve the problem of the alpha-helix (coiled structure) of proteins. The originator of the concept of the chemical bond, Pauling had demonstrated that proteins have a three-dimensional structure and are not simply linear strings of amino acids (the chief components of proteins). Wilkins and Franklin, working independently, preferred a more deliberate experimental approach over the theoretical model-building method. Finding the King's College group unresponsive to their suggestions, Crick and Watson thus devoted portions of a two-year period discussing and arguing about the problem.

Builds DNA model

Crick and Watson were certain the answer lay in model building, so they began to build their DNA model in 1953. Watson in particular was impressed by the method used by Pauling who, employing the rules of chemistry, fit together "Tinkertoy" pieces that stood for the atoms known to be present in a given molecule. Crick and Watson worked with Tinkertoy-like models and determined that DNA is shaped like a spiral staircase, or "double helix." They also used data published by Austrian-born American biochemist Erwin Chargaff on the four nucleotides (or "bases") of DNA molecules, concluding that these building blocks had to be arranged in pairs. In 1950 Chargaff had demonstrated that the relative amounts of the four nucleotides that make up DNA conformed to certain rules. One rule states that the amount of adenine (A) was always equal to the amount of thymine (T), and the amount of guanine (G) was always equal to the amount of cytosine (C). Such a relationship suggests pairings of A and T, and G and C, and refutes the idea that DNA is nothing more than a "tetranucleotide," that is, a simple molecule consisting of all four bases.

After extensive experimentation, during which they used X-ray crystallography to take pictures of crystallized forms of DNA, Crick and Watson found that the double-helix structure corresponded to the theoretical data produced by Wilkins, Franklin, and their colleagues. Watson and Crick were also engaged in a "race" with Pauling, whom they feared was building his own model of DNA. In early 1953 they wrote four papers about the structure and the supposed function of DNA, the first of which appeared in the journal *Nature* on April 25. The paper was accompanied by papers by Wilkins, Franklin, and their colleagues that presented experimental evidence supporting the Watson-Crick model. Since Watson won a coin toss that placed his name first in authorship, this scientific accomplishment became known as the "Watson-Crick" discovery. Within a year, the Watson-Crick model began to generate a broad range of important

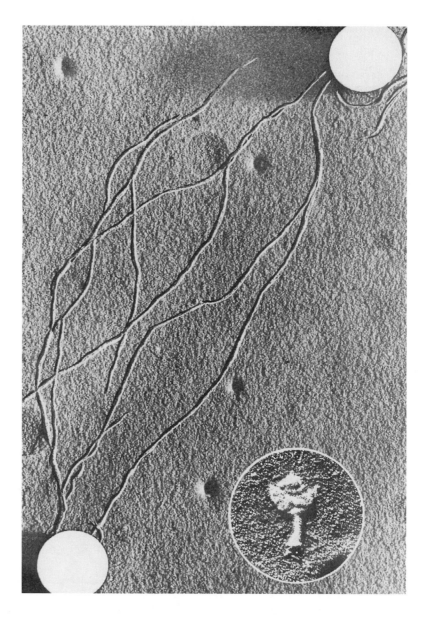

A 1954 photograph of DNA magnified 100,000 times; in the circle at bottom right is the virus from which DNA had been extracted.

research in genetics. In 1962 Crick, Watson, and Wilkins received the Nobel Prize in medicine for their work on DNA.

Investigates genetic code

Over the next several years Crick examined the relationship between DNA and the genetic code. One of his first efforts was a collaboration with Vernon Ingram, which led to

Ingram's 1956 demonstration that sickle-cell hemoglobin (abnormal hemoglobin that occurs in red blood cells of crescent shape) differs from normal hemoglobin by a single amino acid. Ingram's research presented evidence that sickle-cell anemia—a "molecular genetic disease"—could be connected to a DNA-protein relationship. The importance of this work to Crick's thinking about the function of DNA cannot be underestimated. It established the first function of "the genetic substance" in determining the specific nature of proteins.

About this time, South African-born English geneticist and molecular biologist Sydney Brenner joined Crick at the Cavendish Laboratory. They began to work on "the coding problem," that is, how the sequence of DNA bases would specify the amino acid sequence in a protein. Crick presented the results of their work in 1957 to the Symposium of the Society for Experimental Biology in a paper titled "On Protein Synthesis." In the paper Crick established not only the basis of the genetic code but predicted the mechanism for protein synthesis (production). The first step, transcription, would be the transfer of information in DNA to ribonucleic acid (RNA), and the second step, translation, would be the transfer of information from RNA to the protein. Hence, to use the language of molecular biologists, the genetic message is "transcribed" to a messenger, and that message is eventually "translated" into action in the synthesis of a protein.

Joins Salk Institute

In 1976, while on sabbatical from the Cavendish, Crick was offered a permanent position at the Salk Institute for Biological Studies in La Jolla, California. He accepted an endowed chair as Kieckhefer Professor and has been at the institute since that time. One of his projects has been a study of the workings of the brain, a subject that had interested him from the beginning of his scientific career. While his primary focus was consciousness, he attempted to approach the question of how the brain works through the study of vision. He published several speculative papers on the mechanisms of dreams and attention, but, as he stated in his autobiography,

What Mad Pursuit, "I have yet to produce any theory that is both novel and also explains many disconnected experimental facts in a convincing way." In 1993 Crick reunited with Watson for the fortieth anniversary celebration of their discovery of the DNA molecular structure.

Further Reading

Breo, Dennis L., "The Double Helix," *Journal of the American Medical Association,* February 24, 1993, pp. 1040–46.

Crick, Francis, *The Astonishing Hypothesis: The Scientific Search for the Soul,* Scribner, 1994.

Crick, Francis, and Leslie Orgel, *Life Itself,* Simon & Schuster, 1981.

Crick, Francis, *What Mad Pursuit: A Personal View of Scientific Discovery,* Basic Books, 1988.

Jacob, François, *The Statue Within,* Basic Books, 1988.

Jaroff, Leon, "A Few Words From the Pioneers," *Time,* March 15, 1993.

Johnson, George, "Two Sides to Every Science Story," *New York Times Book Review,* April 9, 1989.

Sherron, Victoria, *James Watson and Francis Crick: Decoding the Secrets of DNA,* Blackbirch Press, 1995.

Watson, James D., *The Double Helix: A Personal Account of the Discovery of the Structure of DNA,* Norton, 1968.

Marie Curie

Born November 7, 1867
Warsaw, Poland
Died July 4, 1934
Sallanches, France

Pierre Curie

Born May 15, 1859
Paris, France
Died April 19, 1906
Paris, France

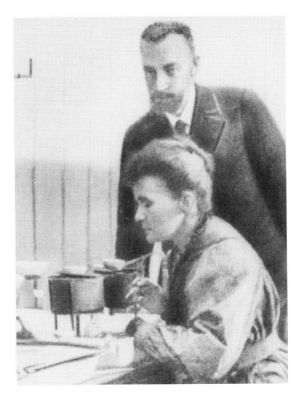

Marie Curie and her husband, Pierre Curie, developed and introduced the concept of radioactivity to the world. Working under primitive laboratory conditions, they investigated the nature of high energy rays that are spontaneously produced by certain elements. They also collaborated on the isolation of two new radioactive elements, polonium and radium. When the Curies shared the Nobel Prize for physics in 1903, Marie Curie became its first female recipient; she was later one of the few scientists to win the award twice. Before Pierre Curie joined his wife in the study of radioactivity, he had codiscovered piezo-electricity (producing an electrical field by applying stress to crystals) and invented the quartz balance.

"A scientist in his laboratory is not a mere technician: he is also a child confronting natural phenomena that impress him as though they were fairy tales."

—Marie Curie

Marie Curie's early years

Marie Curie was born Marya Sklodowska in Warsaw, Poland, the fifth and youngest child of Bronsitwa Boguska Sklodowska, a pianist, singer, and teacher, and Ladislas

Sklodowski, a professor of mathematics and physics. Bronsitwa died of tuberculosis when Marya was not quite eleven, leaving Ladislas as his daughter's chief role model. Even as a very young girl Marya was fascinated by her father's physics equipment, and like him she was quiet and studious.

An outstanding student, Marya graduated at the top of her high school class when she was only fifteen. She then spent eight years working as a tutor and a governess to earn enough money to attend the Sorbonne in Paris, France. In her spare time she studied mathematics and physics on her own and attended a so-called "floating" university. A loosely organized, secret program, the floating university was run by Polish professors in defiance of the Russians then in charge of the Polish educational system. Finally, in November 1891, Marya left Poland and registered at the Sorbonne under the French version of her first name, "Marie."

Moves to Paris

Despite living under less than comfortable conditions and becoming ill on several occasions from lack of food and sleep, Marie graduated first in her class in the spring of 1893. A year later she obtained her master's degree in mathematics, then remained in Paris to conduct experiments for a French industrial society. Finding the Sorbonne's facilities inadequate, Marie began looking for other laboratory space and equipment. Her search led her to Pierre Curie, a highly acclaimed professor at the Municipal School of Industrial Physics and Chemistry in Paris. The two scientists shared many of the same beliefs and habits and were immediately drawn to each other.

Pierre Curie's early years

Pierre Curie was born in Paris on May 15, 1859, the son of Sophie-Claire Depouilly Curie and Eugène Curie, a physician. Pierre was a dreamer whose style of learning clashed with the restraints of formal schooling. He received his pre-university education entirely at home, taught first by his mother, then by his father and older brother, Jacques. At the age of fourteen Pierre studied with a mathematics professor who helped him develop his natural ability in the subject. With his knowledge of physics and mathematics he gained a bachelor of science degree in 1875 at the age of sixteen. Curie went on to earn the equivalent of a master's degree in physical sciences from the Sorbonne in 1877.

Studies electricity in crystals

The following year Curie became a laboratory assistant at the Sorbonne. At the time Jacques was already working in the university's mineralogy laboratory, and the two brothers began a productive five-year collaboration. They investigated pyroelectricity, the way different faces of certain types of crystals receive electrical charges when heated. Led by their knowledge of symmetry (balance and proportion) in crystals, the Curie brothers discovered the previously unknown phenomenon of piezoelectricity, the property of certain crystals that results in voltages being generated across them when a mechanical force is applied to them.

After publishing papers about their discovery in 1880, the Curie brothers studied the opposite effect—the compression of piezoelectric crystal by an electric field. In order to measure the very small amounts of electricity involved, they invented a new laboratory instrument, the piezoelectric quartz electrometer, or balance. This device became useful for electrical researchers and would prove highly valuable to Marie Curie in her studies of radioactivity.

Formulates Curie's law and Curie's point

In 1882 Pierre Curie was appointed head of the laboratory at the newly created Municipal School of Industrial Physics and Chemistry in Paris. Although the position was poorly paid, he stayed at the school for twenty-two years. In 1883 Jacques left Paris to become a lecturer in mineralogy at

the University of Montpellier in southern France. After the brothers' collaboration ended, Pierre conducted theoretical and experimental research on crystal symmetry.

From 1890 to 1895 Curie performed a series of investigations that formed the basis of his doctoral dissertation: a study of the magnetic properties of substances of different temperatures. Hampered by overwork, lack of funds, and poor laboratory facilities, he was forced to conduct his research in a corridor. Despite these limitations, Pierre's work was valuable to other scientists. His expression of the results of his findings about the relationship between temperature and magnetism became known as Curie's law. The temperature above which magnetic properties disappear is called the Curie point.

The Curies meet and marry

During this period Pierre Curie also constructed a periodic precision balance with direct reading that provided a

great advantage over older balance systems and was especially valuable for chemical analysis. He was by this time becoming well known among physicists. His work came to the attention of the noted Scottish mathematician and physicist **William Thomson, Lord Kelvin** (see entry). Partly through Thomson's influence Curie was named to a newly created chair of physics at the school. Although his status was improved, he still did not have an adequate laboratory.

In early 1894, at the age of thirty-five, Curie met Marie. They were married in July 1895. Marie used a cash wedding gift to buy two bicycles, which they used for transportation on their honeymoon in the French countryside. After the Curies returned to Paris they were inseparable, working side by side in the laboratory during the day and studying together in the evening. Even the birth of their daughter Irène in 1897 barely interrupted their routine. Around this time, Marie decided to pursue her doctorate in physics, and for her thesis she chose to focus on the source of the mysterious rays given off by the extremely heavy element uranium—a phenomenon scientist Henri Becquerel (see box) had first observed in 1896.

Search for new chemical element

Marie Curie set up her equipment in a small, glass-walled shed at the Municipal School. Despite the primitive conditions—a dirt floor, drafty windows, and perpetual dampness—within two months she had made two important discoveries: the intensity of the rays was in direct proportion to the amount of uranium in her sample, and nothing she did to alter the uranium (such as combining it with other elements or subjecting it to light, heat, or cold) affected the rays. This led her to formulate the theory that the rays were the result of something happening within each atom of the element itself, a property she called *radioactivity.* Subsequent tests she performed on the minerals chalcocite, uranite, and pitchblende (the chief ore of uranium) revealed higher than expected levels of radioactivity; she therefore concluded that a new, more powerful element had to be present in the samples.

Recognizing the significance of his wife's findings, Pierre Curie set aside his work on crystals to join Marie in the search for the new element. Confining their study to pitchblende because it emitted the strongest rays, they developed a painstaking refining method that required them to process tons of the mineral ore to obtain just a tiny sample of radioactive material. Marie acted as the chemist, separating the pitchblende in the yard adjoining the shed-laboratory. Pierre was the physicist, analyzing the physical properties of the substances yielded by Marie's separations. At last they uncovered a new radioactive element they named polonium in honor of Marie's native Poland. They then identified an even stronger radioactive element, which they named radium.

Make numerous scientific contributions

The Curies' research produced a wealth of information about radioactivity, which they shared in a series of papers published between 1898 and 1904. They wrote about the luminous (light emission) and chemical effects of radioactive rays and their chemical charge. Pierre studied the action of a magnetic field on radium rays, then he investigated the persistence of radioactivity. He also developed a standard for measuring time on the basis of radioactivity, an important contribution to geologic and archaeological dating techniques.

Pierre even used himself as a human guinea pig, deliberately exposing his arm to radium for several hours and recording the progressive, slowly healing burns that resulted. He collaborated with physicians in animal experiments that led to the use of radium therapy—then called "Curie therapie"—to treat cancer and lupus, a disease of the connective tissue. In 1904 he published a paper on the liberation of heat by radium salts.

Win Nobel Prize

Through all this intensive research the Curies struggled to keep up with their teaching, household, and financial obligations. It was March 1902 before they were able to isolate enough radium to confirm its existence and thus enable Marie to earn her doctorate (the first awarded to a woman in Europe). By this time Pierre had begun to suffer from extreme fatigue and sharp pains throughout his body. Although the Curies attributed these symptoms to overwork, they were most certainly a sign of radiation poisoning, an unrecognized illness at the time.

In 1902 Pierre Curie's candidacy for election to the French Academy of Sciences failed, and the next year his application for the chair of mineralogy at the Sorbonne was rejected. These setbacks increased his bitterness toward the French academic establishment. But Recognition in France finally came through international awards. In 1903 the Royal Society, a prestigious scientific institution in London, England, presented the Davy Medal to the Curies. Shortly thereafter they were awarded the 1903 Nobel Prize in physics—which they shared with Becquerel—for their work on radioac-

Henri Becquerel, French Physicist

One of the many scientists fascinated by Wilhelm Röntgen's discovery of X rays, French physicist Henri Becquerel (1852–1908) wondered if these "penetrating rays" were related to the luminescence he had studied for many years. He experimented in a darkroom with a sample of potassium uranyl sulfate crystal and a photographic plate. Though the plate showed developed streaks, indicating the presence of penetrating rays, Becquerel soon noticed that the penetrating rays were present whether the crystal had been exposed to light or not. He realized he had discovered a new type of penetrating ray.

Becquerel presented his findings in 1896, labeling these new emissions Becquerel rays. Soon Pierre and Marie Curie found that thorium also emitted Becquerel rays, and they later discovered why: the presence of a radioactive element. Becquerel continued his own research, isolating electrons in radiation in 1900 and noting the first evidence of radioactive transformation in 1902. From this point the Curies took the leading role in radiation research. For his discovery of radioactivity, Becquerel shared the Nobel Prize for physics with the Curies.

tivity. Because of illness, Pierre delayed delivery of his Nobel lecture until 1905. He concluded his speech by musing whether the knowledge of radium and radioactivity would be harmful for humanity, adding that personally he felt more good than harm would result from the new discoveries.

Pierre Curie's life cut short

With the Nobel Prize came immediate international fame that disrupted the two scientists' personal and professional lives for quite some time. They were inundated by journalists, photographers, curiosity-seekers, visitors, and mail. Nevertheless the cash award provided enough money to ease some of their financial burdens. (They had supported the radium research with their own money.) Then came news in early 1904 that the French parliament had created a new professorship in physics at the Sorbonne for Pierre. He said he would take the position only if it included a fully funded laboratory, complete with assistants. His demand was met, and Marie became his new laboratory chief. After their second daughter, Eve, was born in December 1904, they continued with their work, taking brief vacations to the countryside. They had just returned from one of their vacations on April 19, 1906, when Pierre was killed as he stepped into the path of a horse-drawn wagon on a Paris street.

Marie Curie wins second Nobel

After Pierre's death, Marie assumed his physics professorship at the invitation of the Sorbonne, becoming the university's first female faculty member. In addition to teaching, Curie continued to spend time in the laboratory, determined to isolate pure polonium and pure radium to remove any remaining doubts about the existence of the two new elements. Her success resulted in her winning the Nobel Prize for chemistry in 1911. Within three years Curie was heading two laboratories, one in her native Warsaw and one at the Sorbonne, known as the Radium Institute. Unable to continue her experiments after the outbreak of World War I and eager to be of service, she received approval to operate X-ray machines on the battlefield so that the wounded could receive immediate treatment. It was exhausting and dangerous work, but within two years she had established two hundred permanent X-ray units throughout France and Belgium.

Becomes successful fund-raiser

After the war ended Curie campaigned to raise funds for a hospital and laboratory devoted to radiology, the branch of medicine that uses X rays and radium to diagnose and treat disease. An American journalist named Marie Meloney heard about Curie's efforts and invited her to tour the United States to publicize the project. Although she dreaded the thought, Curie eventually accepted and sailed for America in 1921. An overwhelming reception left her frightened and exhausted, but she did manage to return to France with enough radium, money, and equipment to outfit her new laboratory.

Realizing that her status as a celebrity gave her the power to have an impact on causes she favored, Curie began speaking at meetings and conferences throughout the world, gradually becoming more comfortable in the spotlight. People were eager to support her work, and she had great success as a fundraiser for the Radium Institute. Curie also lent her name to the cause for world peace by serving on the council of the League of Nations and on its international committee on intellectual cooperation.

Death linked to work

As the 1920s drew to a close, Curie began to suffer almost constantly from fatigue, dizziness, and a low-grade fever. She also experienced a continuous humming in her ears and a gradual loss of eyesight that was helped only partially by a series of cataract operations. Even though a number of her colleagues who had worked with radium were displaying many of the same symptoms and others had died at relatively young ages of cancer, for a long time Curie could not bring herself to admit that the element she and her husband had discovered could possibly be at fault. Even after accepting the fact that radium was dangerous, she continued to work with it anyway.

In the early 1930s, however, Curie's health had worsened noticeably, and doctors finally discovered the cause: pernicious anemia, a severe blood disorder caused by the cumulative effects of radiation exposure. The news was kept from the public as well as from Curie herself, and on July 4, 1934, she died at a sanitorium in the French Alps. She was buried next to her husband in Sceaux, France. In 1995 the Curies' remains were enshrined in the Pantheon in Paris.

Further Reading

Birch, Beverly, *Marie Curie,* Gareth Stevens Publishing, 1988.

Detroit Free Press, April 21, 1995, p. 4A.

Keller, Mollie, *Marie Curie,* F. Watts, 1982.

Parker, Steve, *Marie Curie and Radium,* HarperCollins, 1992.

Pflaum, Rosalynd, *Grand Obsession: Madame Curie and Her World,* Doubleday, 1989.

Pflaum, Rosalynd, *Marie Curie and Her Daughter Irène,* Lerner, 1993.

Poynter, Margaret, *Marie Curie: Discoverer of Uranium,* Enslow Publishers, 1994.

Francisco Dallmeier

Born February 15, 1953
Caracas, Venezuela

Hispanic American wildlife biologist Francisco Dallmeier specializes in issues relating to biodiversity.

Francisco Dallmeier, a Venezuelan-born American wildlife biologist, specializes in issues relating to biodiversity, or the numbers of different species of plants and animals in an environment. His work in developing countries, particularly in Latin America, helped form strategies for sustainable use of their natural resources. He also refined the use of long-term research plots to evaluate and monitor changes in the ecological balance of tropical forests.

Begins professional career

Francisco Gómez-Dallmeier was born on February 15, 1953, in Caracas, Venezuela. He began his professional career while still a student, becoming the Curator of Mammals at the LaSalle Museum of Natural History in Caracas at the age of eighteen. He served as the museum director from 1973 until 1977, when he received his licentiate (degree) in biology from the Central University of Venezuela. During this period,

Dallmeier served as a research assistant with Central University's Institute of Tropical Zoology, studying the flora (plant life) and fauna (animal life) of southern Venezuela. His work in this field led to the banding of more than three thousand birds for study. At the institute he also collaborated in a number of ecological efforts with Polish scientists Kazimierz Dobrolowski and Jan Pinowski. After earning his licentiate, Dallmeier worked independently until 1981, coordinating the ecological program for INELMECA, a Venezuelan environmental engineering company. He also helped prepare Venezuela's first environmental impact statement for the Morón Power Plant.

Dallmeier earned a master's degree in 1984 and a doctorate two years later from Colorado State University in Fort Collins, Colorado, specializing in wildlife ecology. He then joined the staff of the Smithsonian Institution, becoming program manager of its Man and the Biosphere (SI/MAB) Biological Diversity Program, a joint project with the United Nations Educational, Scientific, and Cultural Organization (UNESCO).

Encourages sustainable development

Dallmeier is concerned about the profound effects of human economic development on tropical ecosystems (the complex of a community of organisms and its environment functioning as an ecological unit in nature). In the late 1980s biologists estimated that more than one million species of plants and animals would become extinct before the middle of the twenty-first century. In an effort to encourage sustainable (ongoing) development, Dallmeier began an intensive research and education program to train ecologists from developing countries in methods of assessing the biodiversity status of their natural resources. By 1989 the SI/MAB program had conducted field research and training workshops in nine Latin American countries as well as China and four sites in the United States. During the early 1990s Dallmeier coordinated long-term biodiversity research in more than ten countries.

Francisco Dallmeier refined the use of long-term research plots to evaluate and monitor changes in the ecological balance of tropical forests. He developed a technique that provided standardized information so that research from many different sites could be compared accurately. His methodology emphasized the use of personal computers, enabling ecologists for the first time to accumulate and make widely available large amounts of data.

Develops research plots

Long-term biodiversity research is accomplished primarily by establishing forest inventory plots that can be observed in great detail and monitored for changes over time. Dallmeier helped develop a plot research technique that would provide standardized information so that research from many different sites could be compared accurately. A research plot is laid out in a grid, and a census is taken of every species (usually trees) within the plot. The density, variety, and dominance of each species is recorded. Standard methods of measuring tree and branch size are used for living stands of trees, snags, and fallen trees. Researchers note geological, topographical (land surface), and climatic factors as well as land use history in the area. Over time, shifts in the survival rate and health of each species can be noted. Dallmeier helped establish this research methodology that enabled ecologists to accumulate large amounts of data and make it widely available for the first time. This method emphasized the use of personal computers to record data in the field and to apply new analytic techniques to the resulting databases.

Holds prominent positions

Dallmeier is especially interested in tropical birds, holding memberships in the Audubon Society of Venezuela, the Wildfowl Trust, the American Ornithologists Union, and many other ecological organizations. As an author or editor he has published more than seventy scholarly reports. In addition to his formal scientific training, Dallmeier studied management communication, including neuro-linguistic programming and transactional analysis (a system of psychotherapy that involves analysis of social interaction to aid communication), as well as

computer programming and database management. He is a certified open water diver and private pilot. Dallmeier married Nancy Joy Parton, with whom he has two children.

Further Reading

Biodiversity, Winter 1992, p. 2.

BioScience, Volume 43, Number 11, p. 762.

Dallmeier, Francisco, "Forest Biodiversity in Latin America: Reversing the Losses?" *Journal of Tropical Forest Science,* Volume 5, Number 2, 1992, pp. 232–70.

Dallmeier, Francisco, "Tracking Biodiversity for Practical Applications," *Global Biodiversity,* Volume 3, Number 1, 1993, pp. 24–27.

Dallmeier, Francisco, and A. T. Cringan, *Biology, Conservation and Management of Waterfowl in Venezuela,* Editorial Ex Libris, 1990.

Wemmer, Chris, and others, "Training Developing-Country Nationals Is the Critical Ingredient to Conserving Global Diversity," *BioScience,* December 1993, p. 762.

John Dalton

Born c. September 6, 1766
Eaglesfield, Cumberland, England
Died July 27, 1844
Manchester, England

When English scientist and teacher John Dalton began studying the weather as a young man, little did he know that his theories would lead to the creation of the study of chemistry. But his work in meteorology led him to speculate about the behavior of gases, and he eventually arrived at the idea that all elements, including gases, are made up of tiny particles that have the same weight and are in fact identical in each element. The theory of the atom dated back to Greek times, but Dalton was the first to think of defining the atom by its "atomic weight" and thus formulated the basis of modern chemistry.

British chemist John Dalton revolutionized the field of chemistry with his atomic theory of matter.

Inspired by mentor

John Dalton was born around September 6, 1766, in the small northern English village of Eaglesfield. Like many Eaglesfield residents, Dalton's parents, Joseph, a weaver by trade, and Deborah Greenup Dalton, were Quakers. Dalton, his older brother Jonathan, and their sister Mary went to a

Quaker school near their home. Dalton's education was strongly influenced by Elihu Robinson, a wealthy neighbor and amateur scientist who took an interest in the young boy. Robinson explained the latest scientific advances to Dalton and often gave him difficult math problems to solve.

Becomes a teacher

Although Dalton wanted a formal education, his family was so poor that by the time he was about ten it was clear that he and Jonathan would soon have to help support the household. Taking a practical approach, Dalton decided that if he could not attend school as a student, he would do so as a teacher and learn that way. Luckily the local school had recently lost its teacher, and, at the age of twelve, Dalton began teaching children only slightly younger than himself. After a year, however, he had made so little money teaching that he was forced to seek work on local farms. Although two years of physical labor made his body strong, it offered little stimulation for his mind.

Influenced by famous scientist

Meanwhile Jonathan Dalton had landed a teaching job at a Quaker school in the town of Kendal in the nearby Lake District; he was able to find a job there for his younger brother, too. So in 1781, at the age of fifteen, Dalton became an elementary school teacher. Soon he and Jonathan were running the school, and their sister Mary was keeping house for them. The following twelve years proved to be a time of growth and self-education for Dalton.

Since Kendal was a larger and busier town than Eaglesfield, it offered opportunities for Dalton to explore and broaden his interests. Leading figures in science and mathematics, such as the scientist John Gough, gave public lectures. Gough, who was also a Quaker, recognized Dalton's intellectual talent and, like Robinson, became his mentor. Gough taught Dalton Latin, Greek, French, and mathematics and offered insights on various branches of science, including chemistry and meteorology.

Dalton was particularly intrigued by meteorology. Following Gough's example, he began keeping a daily weather record in which he noted barometric pressure, wind direction and velocity, rainfall, and other details. He recorded these data faithfully every day for the rest of his life; by the time he died, his weather diary filled eleven volumes.

Becomes science lecturer

By his early twenties Dalton was presenting lectures on scientific topics. In 1792 he accepted a teaching post at a Quaker university that had been established in Manchester, the largest city in northern England. For more than ten years he taught mathematics and science there while continuing to lecture occasionally at Kendal. He also took the important step of joining several scientific organizations, among them the Manchester Literary and Philosophical Society. The society would later become one of the most prominent in England.

In 1793 Dalton published his first major work, *Meteorological Observations and Essays*. While it is primarily a summary of meteorological techniques, parts of the book show an original mind at work. For instance, Dalton discusses the aurora borealis—also called the northern lights—concluding correctly that the strange glow of the aurora is caused by Earth's magnetic forces.

Identifies color blindness

A few weeks after joining the Manchester Literary and Philosophical Society, Dalton presented his first paper, a piece on color blindness, which earned him a place in science history. He himself was color blind, as was his brother. It was

≡IMPACT≡

John Dalton's atomic theory could not be proved until the development of better scientific instruments, yet he made a revolutionary contribution to the scientific community. Through extensive experimentation over the course of twenty-five years, Dalton compiled a table of known atomic weights. This table has become the basic tool of modern chemistry, the science of how substances interact.

Democritus, Greek Philosopher

Atomic theory was widely accepted among the ancient Greeks. The most highly developed theory was formulated by Democritus of Abdera (c. 460–c. 370 B.C.), who argued that all matter consists of tiny, physically invisible particles. The Greek word *atomos,* in fact, means "indivisible." Democritus taught that an infinite number of atoms exist, they are in constant motion, and the space between them is occupied by a void. Atoms were never created, according to Democritus, but have always existed, and they can never be destroyed. They have physical properties that explain the properties of matter. Atoms of water, for example, are round and smooth, permitting them to slide over each other; conversely, atoms of fire have jagged edges.

Democritus's atomic theory was disputed by many of his contemporaries, particularly the followers of Socrates. Plato and Aristotle, for example, rejected the notion of a void and the possibility of particles being able to move by themselves. Because of the influence of Aristotle on later philosophers, Democritus's ideas eventually fell into decline.

already known that some people had difficulty telling certain colors apart, yet, up to this time, no one had ever thought about the problem scientifically. Although most Europeans call color blindness "Daltonism," British scientists link Dalton's name to his other discoveries.

Originates Dalton's law

Dalton spent the remainder of the 1790s developing his ideas about meteorology. In 1800 he quit his teaching job and went into business for himself as a private instructor. In the meantime he continued to write papers, most of which he read to the society or to similar groups in London. He discussed, among other subjects, the behavior of gases, an issue he had also raised in his *Observations*. Dalton suggested that air is simply a mixture of gases that keep their own identities although mixed together, not a chemical compound, as was commonly believed.

In 1801 Dalton published several articles that developed this idea further and supported it with experiments. This time the scientific world paid more attention. The theory he put forth later became known as Dalton's law, or the law of partial pressures. According to Dalton's law, the total pressure of a mixture of gases equals the sum of the pressures of each individual gas in the mixture. Each gas in the mixture can be thought of as acting independently, with a pressure the same as if the other gases were absent. All the separate pressures can be added up to get the total pressure of the mixture as a whole.

Proposes atomic theory

While some scientists supported Dalton's idea, many—including his old friend Gough—attacked it. They still preferred to think of gases as a single substance rather than as a mixture. In defending his theory, Dalton was forced to look more closely at some of the details in his own work by pursuing the study of chemistry. In 1801 and 1802 Dalton casually put a new twist on an old idea that in the end changed science forever. The idea of the atom—the "uncuttable" (*atomos*), the smallest possible bit of matter—had come from the ancient Greek philosophers. Dalton was the first chemist to describe how atoms behaved in terms of the central concept of modern science—the measurement of weight.

Finds new system

As Dalton slowly developed his new theory with repeated experimentation, he became increasingly aware of its revolutionary possibilities. By 1808, when he published Part I of his book *A New System of Chemical Philosophy,* his basic theory was in place; with Part II, published two years later, he worked out some of the remaining details.

Dalton's theory was that the atoms in each element are identical in size and weight. Since hydrogen is the lightest known element, he assigned it an "atomic weight" of one. "Compound atoms" (later called molecules) were formed when the atoms of one or more elements combined. Dalton also showed in his experiments that the atoms always combined in simple ratios: one to one, or two to one, or two to three, for example. That is, molecules are composed of predictable proportions that will always be the same. Ironically, he was mistaken about the proportion of water: he thought it was one atom of hydrogen and one of oxygen, whereas it was eventually proven to be two atoms of hydrogen and one of oxygen.

Gains national fame

As Dalton's theory gained acceptance, he became the best-known scientist of his day in England. Remaining modest about his fame, however, he continued to teach. Dalton died on July 27, 1844, at his home in Manchester. Further advances in atomic theory would have to wait until decades after his death.

Further Reading

Greenaway, Frank, *John Dalton and the Atom,* Heinemann, 1966.

Thackray, Arnold, *John Dalton: Critical Assessments of His Life and Science,* Harvard University Press, 1972.

Charles Darwin

Born February 12, 1809
Shrewsbury, England
Died April 19, 1882
Kent, England

nglish naturalist Charles Darwin was not the first scientist to argue that life evolved (changed form) over generations. He was, however, the first to offer a detailed theory suggesting how evolution might take place. In 1859 he presented his theory, which he called natural selection, in his book *The Origin of Species by Means of Natural Selection.* It is considered one of the most influential scientific works of all time.

"Animals ... may partake of our origin in one common ancestor—we may be all netted together."

A distaste for formal education

Charles Robert Darwin was born in Shrewsbury, England, on February 12, 1809. His mother was Susannah Wedgwood, the daughter of Josiah Wedgwood, the founder of the famous pottery firm. His father, Robert Waring Darwin, was a physician and the son of Erasmus Darwin, a well-known physician, poet, and botanist. Darwin's mother died when he was a child, and his older sisters provided his early education. Showing an interest in science, he began collecting specimens

Charles Darwin first proposed a theory of evolution based on natural selection in his book *The Origin of Species by Means of Natural Selection*. Publication of the work ushered in a new era of thinking about the nature of human beings. The intellectual revolution it caused and the impact it produced were far greater than the effects of the work of Isaac Newton, who discovered gravity. *The Origin of Species* has been referred to as "the book that shook the world." Discussion of such modern issues as the purpose of human life in the universe, the population explosion, and the relation of human beings to nature can be traced directly to Darwin.

and conducting scientific experiments when he was still quite young.

Darwin was a less than enthusiastic student. In 1817 he was sent to a day school, but he did not do well. A year later he went to the Shrewsbury School, where he studied the classics, which he did not especially like. Although he went on to Edinburgh University to study medicine, he left college because the mandatory observation of operations on unanesthetized patients deeply troubled him. Darwin's father finally sent him to Cambridge University to prepare for a career as a clergyman in the Church of England. At Cambridge Darwin had his first rewarding experience with education when he met John Henslow, a botanist, who became his mentor and encouraged his interest in natural history.

Teaches himself scientific method

After Darwin earned a bachelor's degree in 1831, Henslow recommended him for the position of unpaid naturalist (a biologist who studies nature) on board the H.M.S. *Beagle.* The expedition had been chartered to establish a number of chronometric (time-keeping) stations and to survey the southern coasts of South America as well as several Pacific islands. Darwin's father initially opposed the trip because it was dangerous and would delay his son's entry into the church, but he finally relented.

Although Darwin had no formal scientific training, over the course of the trip—which began in December 1831 and lasted nearly five years—he turned himself into an expert scientist. Since he was often seasick, he would spend as much time ashore as possible and travel overland to meet the *Beagle* at the nearest port. During his excursions he taught himself the scientific method, which involved meticulously collecting evidence and carefully formulating theories based on that evidence.

Notices evolutionary changes

While in Brazil, Darwin found his first fossil, the skull of an extinct giant sloth (a slow-moving tropical mammal). For the next three years he made geological and biological observations, took records, and collected specimens of every kind as the ship cruised back and forth along the coast of South America. Darwin had begun to notice that animals and plants had undergone indisputable evolutionary changes. In some areas certain species had become extinct, like the gigantic fossil armadillos of South America; but Darwin noticed similar, though not identical, armadillos in other areas nearby.

Darwin was also perplexed by the fact that existing species had demonstrated characteristics similar to those of extinct species. He observed, too, that clearly different species of animals found in some locations were completely lacking in other areas. Moreover, the fledgling naturalist was intrigued by the fact that plants and animals of oceanic islands were likely to resemble the same plant and animal species existing on neighboring continents. Yet it was peculiar, he thought, that islands with the same geological features could each contain completely different animal species.

Suggests common ancestor

Four years after setting sail, the *Beagle* landed in the Galápagos Islands, where Darwin would make the most significant observations of the expedition. He documented fourteen different types of finch birds on the various islands, yet he observed that each type of finch appeared to have adapted completely to the island on which it lived. For instance, insect-eating finches had sharp, fine beaks that they used to stab their prey. Seed-eating finches, however, had more powerful, parrot-like bills for breaking seed shells.

Another curiosity were giant tortoises that appeared to be similar to one another but possessed distinctive features. Local

Aristotle, Carl Linnaeus, Georges Cuvier, and Taxonomy

Taxonomy, the science of classifying animals and plants, has been practiced since the ancient Greek philosopher Aristotle (384–322 B.C.) devised the first system over two thousand years ago. Because only about one thousand species were then known, Aristotle grouped them into simple categories of animals with and without vertebrae (bony segments that make up the spinal column). Aristotle's system was finally replaced in the late 1700s by a more comprehensive and systematic method developed by Swiss naturalist Carl Linnaeus (1707–1778). Linnaeus created a hierarchical system in which living things were grouped according to their similarities, with each succeeding level possessing a larger number of shared traits. He named these levels class, order, genus, and species. Linnaeus also popularized binomial nomenclature, giving each living thing a Latin name consisting of its genus and species, which distinguished it from all other organisms.

Carl Linnaeus

The Linnaen system has remained intact except for one important modification. In the early 1800s the French naturalist Georges Cuvier (1769–1832) contributed a fourth category based on his research in anatomy and fossilized evidence. He identified four major groups called phyla within the animal kingdom. These included mollusca (such as snails and cuttlefish), radiata (with starfish and jellyfish), articulata (with worms and insects), and verbrata (all the higher animals). Cuvier interpreted his vast body of fossilized evidence in the book *The Animal Kingdom, Distributed According to Its Organization* (1817). Cuvier's contributions to anatomy and paleontology inevitably helped Darwin shape many of his own theories.

Georges Cuvier

island inhabitants could tell by sight from which island any of the giant creatures had come. As he continued to observe specimens Darwin began to wonder whether this biological diversity occurred at random or if in fact a pattern could be detected. Eventually he arrived at a possible explanation: differences between species had to be the result of change over a long period of time.

Originates theory of natural selection

After Darwin returned to Britain in 1836 his ideas came into focus, and he formulated a theory to support his premise about a common ancestor. He began by asserting that if species had changed over time, the issue of diversity was resolved. However, numerous other questions arose. For instance, he asked why a human's arm and leg bones are basically similar to those of a dog and a horse. He also questioned why lizards and rabbits are similar in embryo form but are distinctly different in their adult forms. He noticed that many animals, including humans, have organs that have no vital function, such as the appendix. And he wondered why many different organisms behave in similar ways. Darwin concluded the bulk of these questions could be answered—but only if species were connected by descent from common ancestors.

Publishes revolutionary work

As a result of the *Beagle* voyage, Darwin had a lifetime of data upon which to base his theory–and he had not yet reached the age of thirty. He never went abroad again. His most important work, *The Origin of Species by Means of Natural Selection,* was published in 1859. All copies sold in one day. Using comparative anatomy as evidence, Darwin formulated the theory of evolution that has guided scientists ever since: in the struggle for survival, successive generations of a species pass on to their offspring the characteristics that enable the species to survive. Darwin named this process natural selection. For example, the whitish fur of a polar bear blends in with the bear's snowy environment, strongly contrasting

Jean Baptiste Lamarck, French Botanist

When French botanist Jean Baptiste Lamarck (1744-1829) went about classifying invertebrates, he categorized them according to their anatomic similarities, much as Swiss naturalist Carl Linnaeus (1707–1778; see previous box) had done, but with greater specificity. Lamarck eventually published the results of his efforts in a seven-volume work, *Natural History of Invertebrates* (1815–22), perhaps his greatest contribution to botany.

While creating his classification system, Lamarck, who had previously believed in the fixity (the quality or state of being fixed or stable) of species, gradually developed an evolutionary theory to explain the differences between living animals and fossils. He proposed that species gradually change over time. He also theorized that living creatures fit into a linear, hierarchical scheme that began with the simplest life form and progressed to the most complex—humans. In his 1809 work *Zoological Philosophy,* Lamarck stated four laws: organisms possess an innate (inborn) drive toward perfection; they can adapt to the environment; spontaneous generation occurs frequently; and acquired characteristics can be passed from one generation to the next. Lamarck is best known for his last law, which has since been disproved. Although Lamarck's belief in acquired characteristics was incorrect, he remains the first scientist to acknowledge the adaptability of organisms and develop a consistent evolutionary theory.

with the brown and black fur of bears living in the forest. Different traits among similar animals thus represent genetic adaptations to specific environments.

Causes scientific controversy

In 1871 Darwin applied his theory to the evolution of human beings in *The Descent of Man*. Many people were repulsed by the suggestion that humans could somehow be related to earlier, nonhuman life forms. Yet Darwin's ideas were so convincing that he succeeded in persuading most of the scientific community that natural selection and evolution were a real possibility. Toward the end of the nineteenth century, however, he lost some of his followers because he lacked an explanation for how evolutionary variations were produced or passed on. Without knowing how such variations occurred, critics argued, scientists could reach no workable conclusions through the theory of natural selection.

But Darwin's ideas were later confirmed by the work of **Gregor Mendel** (see entry), the Austrian biologist who identified the gene as the basic unit of heredity. Although Mendel's theory was not formally acknowledged until the early 1900s, he demonstrated that genes are the molecular "blueprints"—called the genetic code—that are passed on to succeeding generations. Evolutionists known as neo-Darwinists were therefore able to validate Darwin's theory: natural selection involves the evolution not only of physical and behavioral traits but also the genes that carry those traits.

Offends religious leaders

Following his return to England, Darwin lived for a while as a bachelor in London. In January 1839 he married Emma Wedgwood, his cousin, and later that month he was elected to the Royal Society, a prestigious scientific organization. The Darwins first settled in London, but because of Darwin's poor health they moved to the county of Kent, where they spent the rest of their lives. They had ten children, three of whom died in childhood.

Since no organic cause could ever be found for Darwin's ill health, he was suspected of being a hypochondriac, a person who worries abnormally about personal health and often creates imaginary illnesses. A strong possibility is that he actually suffered from Chagas' disease (a tropical American disease): he had been bitten by the Benchuca, the "black bug of the pampas," which is a carrier, and he had all the symptoms of the disease. Darwin died at the age of seventy-three on April 19, 1882. He received no recognition from the British government during his lifetime because his ideas about evolution offended leaders of the Church of England, who espoused the doctrine of divine creation of humanity. At the request of Parliament, however, Darwin was accorded the honor of burial in Westminster Abbey.

Further Reading

Anderson, Margaret Jean, *Charles Darwin, Naturalist,* Enslow Publishers, 1994.

Bowlby, John, *Charles Darwin: A New Life,* Norton, 1990.

Browne, E. Janet, *Charles Darwin: A Biography,* Knopf, 1995.

Darwin, Charles, *The Origin of Species by Means of Natural Selection,* originally published in 1859, reprinted, Random House, 1993.

Evans, J. Edward, *Charles Darwin: Revolutionary Biologist,* Lerner, 1993.

Moorehead, Alan, *Darwin and the Beagle,* Harper & Row, 1969, reprinted, Crescent Books, 1983.

Nardo, Don, *Charles Darwin,* Chelsea House, 1993.

Twist, Clint, *Charles Darwin: On the Trail of Evolution,* Raintree/Steck-Vaughn, 1994.

Humphry Davy

Born in 1778
Cornwall, England
Died in 1829

During his brief lifetime Humphry Davy made many major contributions to the fields of chemistry and invention. A pioneer in the study of electrochemistry, he used electrolytic methods to discover the elements sodium, potassium, magnesium, calcium, strontium, and barium. He also identified the elements in chlorine and gave the gas its name. At first ignored by the medical profession, Davy's discovery of nitrous oxide led to the use of the first chemical anesthetic. Davy's invention of the carbon arc lamp kicked off the era of the electric light, and his miner's safety lamp (known as the Davy lamp) made the coal-mining industry safer by reducing the number of explosions in mines.

English chemist and inventor Humphry Davy pioneered the study of electrochemistry.

Educates himself

Davy was born in 1778 in Cornwall, England, where he grew up poor. His deceased father, who had been a woodcarver, had lost money in unwise investments, so Davy had to help his

One of Humphry Davy's last inventions was a method for protecting metal from corrosion. Called cathodic protection, it was used to prevent the corrosion of copper-bottomed ships by seawater. Although only partially successful, Davy's method represents the first application of cathodic protection in scientific history. Today similar methods are used to protect metal pipelines and other equipment from corrosion.

mother pay off the debts. As a result, his education was haphazard, and he disliked being a student. At the time, the schools in Cornwall, in the remote southwest area of England, were academically weak. Nevertheless, Davy managed to absorb knowledge of classic literature and science. In later life he said he was happy he did not have to study too hard in school because he had more time to think on his own.

With no money for further education, Davy began at age seventeen to serve as an apprentice to a surgeon-pharmacist. During this time he started to learn on his own more about other subjects that interested him, such as geography, languages, and philosophy. He also wrote poems that later earned him the respect and friendship of William Wordsworth, Samuel Coleridge, and other leading English poets of his time.

When he was nineteen years old Davy read a book on chemistry by the famous French scientist **Antoine-Laurent Lavoisier** (see entry) that convinced him to concentrate on that subject. For the rest of his life, Davy's career was marked by brilliant and impulsive scientific explorations in chemistry and electrochemistry, the science that deals with the relation of electricity to chemical changes and with chemical and electrical energy.

Discovers effects of nitrous oxide

One of Davy's scientific trademarks was his willingness, and even eagerness, to use himself as a guinea pig. In early tests with hydrogen, for instance, he breathed four quarts of the gas and nearly suffocated. He also tried to breathe pure carbon dioxide, which is actually a product of human respiration (the act of breathing). Davy conducted these experiments while he was director of the laboratory of the Pneumatic Institute at Clifton, which was devoted to the study of the therapeutic properties of various gases. (The term "therapeutic" means having a capacity for use in treating disease or disorders.)

In one case Davy's fondness for risk paid off. While studying nitrous oxide gas, he discovered that it made him feel giddy and intoxicated. When Davy encouraged his friends to inhale the gas with him, he found their inhibitions were lowered and their feelings of happiness or sadness intensified. Davy's poet friend Robert Southey referred to his own experience as being "turned on," and thus nitrous oxide became known as laughing gas. Soon nitrous oxide parties became a fad among wealthy people.

Davy recognized, however, that the gas could be used for a more constructive purpose: to dull physical pain during minor surgery. Although the medical profession ignored his discovery for nearly half a century, nitrous oxide eventually became the first chemical anesthetic. In an 1844 experiment, for example, a dentist had one of his teeth extracted successfully while under the influence of nitrous oxide (having first taken the precaution of writing his will). Dentists still use the gas today for apprehensive patients.

Invents carbon arc lamp

After working briefly in agricultural chemistry, Davy entered his most productive period of discovery. His style in the laboratory was to work quickly and intensely, pursuing one new idea after another. He liked making new and creative discoveries better than repeating tests and confirming results. Stimulated by the Italian physicist Alessandro Volta's (see box) invention of the electric battery, Davy rushed into the new field of electrochemistry and, in 1808, invented the carbon arc lamp. Scientists knew that sparks were created between electrodes (conductors used to establish electrical contact with a nonmetallic part of a circuit) in a battery. However, Davy proposed using carbon as the electrode material instead of metal. With carbon electrodes he made a strong electric current leap from one electrode to the other, creating an intense white light that was practical for illumination.

Alessandro Volta, Italian physicist

In 1775 Alessandro Volta (1745–1827) invented the electrophorus, a device that could store significant electrical charges. It replaced the Leyden jar, which until that time had been used for storing similar, smaller charges. Volta's discovery actually began with the work of French physicist Charles Augustin Coulomb (1736–1806). Coulomb had found that electrical charges are located on the surface of a charged body, not in its body.

In the 1790s Volta experimented with different types of metal to create an electric current. After stacking discs of copper, discs of tin or zinc, and cardboard soaked in a saline solution on top of one another, he connected a wire to each end of the pile to produce a current. The result was the Voltaic pile, the earliest form of an electrical battery. In Volta's honor, the unit of force that moves an electric current is called the "volt."

Davy's invention gave birth to the entire science of electric lighting. Arc lamps are still used today, as is arc welding, another practical outcome of Davy's electric arc research.

Becomes popular speaker

In 1801 Davy was hired to lecture for the Royal Institution, a new scientific organization that was having financial problems. Davy's charm as a speaker and his spectacular demonstrations of electric arc lighting drew enthusiastic crowds from London's high society and soon reversed the institution's fortunes. (Some historians have also referred to Davy's attractive appearance, which probably contributed to his popularity among the fashionable women in the audience.) Davy was a professor at the Royal Institution from 1802 until 1813.

Identifies new elements

Greatly excited with the new tool of electricity, Davy went on to build his own large battery—the strongest one at the time—and used it to break down substances most scientists thought were pure elements. According to many sources, Davy exuberantly danced around the room when, in 1807, he discovered the element potassium, which he created by electrolyzing (subjecting to electrolysis) potash. (Electrolysis involves producing chemical changes by passage of an electric current through an electrolyte, a nonmetallic electric conductor.) Within a week he had isolated sodium from soda in a similar way. Then in 1808, using a slightly modified method, he isolated the elements calcium, magnesium, barium, and strontium.

Shares field with other scientists

By now other scientists, spurred by Davy's triumphs, had begun to compete with him. Although Davy discovered boron in 1808, French chemists Joseph Gay-Lussac and Louis Thenard had identified the element nine days earlier. Indeed, Gay-Lussac and Davy mined the same fields for metals for their experiments for a time. Davy proved that hydrochloric acid did not contain oxygen—thus contradicting the current theory—and Gay-Lussac did the same for prussic acid. Both scientists showed that iodine, discovered by French chemist Bernard Courtois, was an element. In his analysis of hydrochloric acid, Davy identified a greenish-colored gas and named it chlorine, after the Greek word for *green*. This study led to his proof that chlorine also was an element. In addition, Davy was the first to notice that platinum could catalyze (speed up) chemical reactions.

Invents lamp for mining safety

Davy was knighted in 1812, when he was in his early thirties. He then married a wealthy Scottish widow and began to travel extensively, enjoying his fame wherever he went. Using a great microscopic lens in Florence, Italy, he studied diamonds and concluded that they are a form of carbon. Davy was accompanied on some of these trips by his assistant-valet

Michael Faraday (see entry), who was destined to eclipse his mentor's reputation in the realm of science.

Upon his return to England, Davy was asked to study coal-mine explosions, which in those days killed hundreds of miners each year. In less than three months, he invented the miner's safety lamp, also called the Davy lamp. When Davy tested samples of the fire-damp gas (combustible mine gas) that caused the explosions, he confirmed that it was mainly methane and that it would ignite only at high temperatures. In the safety lamp he designed, the flame is surrounded by wire gauze that reduces heat and prevents ignition of flammable gases. This invention was the first major step toward safety in the coal-mining industry.

Honored for discoveries and inventions

Davy's work was rewarded by many honors and medals. In addition to his knighthood, he was made a baronet in 1818 for his service to the mining industry and was elected president of the prestigious Royal Society in 1820. As a result of his conflicts with other scientists, however, Davy made some enemies who thought he was arrogant, as he well may have been. He even tried to prevent his associate Faraday from being elected to the Royal Society.

Ill health began to plague Davy while he was still in his thirties. The same curiosity that had driven him to discover and invent with such success had also taken its toll on his body. By sniffing and tasting unknown chemicals, he had poisoned his system, and his eyes had been damaged in a laboratory explosion. Although Davy continued to pursue scientific interests, he suffered a stroke when he was only forty-nine and died two years later while traveling abroad.

Further Reading

Davy, Humphry, *Sir Humphry Davy's Published Works,* edited by June Z. Fullmer, Harvard University Press, 1969.

Knight, David M., *Humphry Davy: Science and Power,* Cambridge University Press, 1996.

Lee De Forest

Born August 26, 1873
Council Bluffs, Iowa
Died June 30, 1961
Hollywood, California

Lee De Forest invented the triode, or three-electrode vacuum tube, which he called the audion. An important step in the early development of the radio, the audion eventually led to radio signals being received through airwaves, without wires. During the course of his often controversial career, De Forest secured more than three hundred patents for inventions related to communications.

"I must be brilliant, win fame, show the greatness of genius and to no small degree."

Builds locomotive at age ten

Lee De Forest was born in Council Bluffs, Iowa, on August 26, 1873, the son of Henry Swift De Forest and the former Anna Robbins. His father was a Congregational minister who became president of Talladega College in Alabama, which was created for the education of the children of former slaves. As a white boy attending the all-black elementary school at the college, De Forest did not have many friends. He therefore lost himself in the books on mechanical topics that he found at the college library. Already thinking of himself as an inventor, he avidly read the *Patent Office Official Gazette.*

Soon De Forest was designing steam hammers (large hammering machines that used steam power) and attempting to invent perpetual motion machines (machines that would run on their own power forever). When he was ten or eleven, he wanted to know how a locomotive reversed direction, so he walked to a nearby railroad yard and inspected a locomotive. By repeatedly tracing the connections from the reversing lever in the cab through the entire system, he figured out how the locomotive operated. De Forest then enlisted the help of his younger brother in building a wooden version of the locomotive, made from junk but complete with a reverse lever. The machine actually worked.

Chooses scientific education

As preparation for the ministry, De Forest was sent to a small boarding school in Mount Hermon, Massachusetts. When he was fifteen, however, he wrote a letter to his father, declaring that he intended to become a machinist and inventor. His parents granted his request to attend the Sheffield Scientific School at Yale University. Although De Forest earned a scholarship, he still had to work to meet expenses. An extremely timid and unsocial student, he tried to join in college activities by applying for the editorship of the campus magazine and entering design contests, but his efforts were in vain. After receiving his degree in 1896, De Forest stayed at Yale to earn a doctorate, studying electromagnetic waves. Upon receiving his Ph.D., he went to work in the field of telephone research for Western Electric in Chicago. He was soon fired, however, for inattention to duty.

Invents responder

When De Forest heard about the wireless telegraph (an electrical apparatus for sending coded messages), which had been invented by **Guglielmo Marconi** (see entry), he knew he had found a pursuit that would interest him. De Forest wrote

Marconi asking for a job, but he received no response. Undaunted, in 1899 he went to the international America's Cup yachting races, where Marconi had set up his wireless machine to report the event. De Forest inspected the machine carefully, noting ways it could be improved.

De Forest's first major invention was the responder, a device for detecting radio waves that contained liquid electrolyte (a nonmetallic conductor in which current is carried by the movement of ions). The electrolyte produced greater sensitivity than the coherer detector, a device that contained metal filings, which was then being used in radios. De Forest used the responder for reporting the 1901 yacht races on behalf of the Publishers' Press Association. He had invited Marconi to appear with his system, but neither man's equipment worked. Instead, the signals only jammed each other.

Starts his own business

Competing with Marconi, in 1902 De Forest and a partner organized a company called the American De Forest Wireless Telegraph Company. He found that he could raise money by demonstrating his ability to send wireless Morse code signals, which by then he could transmit a distance of six miles. He wanted to do the same with telephony—sending voices over the air, without wires. He sold equipment to the U.S. Army and Navy, and aggressively marketed his devices to the public by carrying out wireless demonstrations around the country.

In 1903 De Forest created an improved version of the responder, which was similar to a design patented by Canadian-born American physicist Reginald Fessenden. After Fessenden sued, court orders were issued in 1905 to prevent De Forest's company from marketing the responder. Disillusioned by the defeat and angered by the questionable practices of the board of directors of his own company, who were

IMPACT

Although Lee De Forest's reputation as an inventor seems to have diminished over time, the audion was more important in the development of electronics over the first half of the twentieth century than any other single invention. It eventually led to radio signals being received through airwaves, without wires.

embezzling money, De Forest took his patents and quit the company in 1907. By this time, however, he had already made a new invention of far greater importance than the responder.

Invents audion

In 1906 De Forest had developed the triode, which was based on the diode, or two-electrode tube invented by John Ambrose Fleming. Two years earlier Fleming had built a bulb with a hot filament (conductor) to boil off electrons and an electrode plate to capture them, as a way of converting alternating current into direct current. Fleming discovered that the tube was also able to detect radio signals; that is, it could convert broadcast signals from an antenna into a form suitable for moving the diaphragm of an earphone. Although it was a great advance for electronics, it had little practical value because of the weakness of the signal it received.

While experimenting with various designs of the vacuum tube, De Forest turned Fleming's diode into a triode by adding a grid between the filament and the plate. The grid was simply a bent piece of wire located between the two already-present electrodes and connected to an outer antenna. However, it possessed an amazing property: it greatly amplified (built up) the signal being received. What De Forest had found, through trial and error, was a method of amplifying the tiny amount of energy that flowed through the air and could be captured by an antenna. By connecting the antenna to the grid of his triode, he boosted the small fluctuations in electrical current to a signal strong enough to power a speaker. The triode, which De Forest called the "audion tube," was patented on January 15, 1907.

Involved in discovery of feedback

De Forest's triode was of little commercial value as long as the metals inside the tube were susceptible to rust. When a good high-vacuum pump became available two years later, it was found that a better vacuum not only prevented rust but significantly improved the performance of the tube. De Forest

Amar Bose, Founder of the Bose Corporation

Amar Bose (1929–) moved modern sound technology forward with his revolutionary design for sound systems; indeed, his name is synonymous with high-quality loudspeakers. Bose became interested in sound systems in the late 1950s while teaching at the Massachusetts Institute of Technology (MIT), where he is now a professor. He had purchased a highly rated record player, but was baffled by its poor quality when a recorded violin sounded screechy. Intent on improving loudspeakers, Bose conducted research at the MIT labs.

In 1964 Bose and five former students founded the Bose Corporation to develop and manufacture high-quality sound equipment. In 1968 the company marketed its first product, the 901 Direct/Reflecting loudspeaker system. The speaker was radically different from others on the market, in that the sound was directed only partially forward and partially reflected off the wall directly behind the cabinet, giving music a panoramic sound. Using computerized sound-measuring devices and techniques, the Bose Corporation continues to make advancements in amplified sound technology. In the mid-1990s the company introduced a compact table radio with a powerful sound system.

and other researchers soon discovered that by changing the circuitry of the tube to reconnect part of the output back into the input, it was possible to "feed back" and thus re-amplify the signal. This advance, called the feedback or regenerative circuit, proved to be an efficient method of producing strong electromagnetic waves that could be used to carry a wider range of sound. The regenerative circuit finally made it possible to transmit any type of sound over the air, including music and the human voice.

Advances commercial use of radio

The success of the audion enabled De Forest to raise capital for another company that he called the De Forest Radio Telephone Company. On January 13, 1910, using his refined audion tube, he broadcast the voices of opera stars from the

Metropolitan Opera House in New York City. The concert featured the famous Italian tenor Enrico Caruso, and was picked up by listeners over a wide area on the east coast. De Forest had won more navy contracts and at last appeared to be flourishing financially. But once again he found himself in trouble when he and a number of company officials were arrested for mail fraud. Apparently, his backers were again involved in criminal activity. Prosecutors who were determined to stop an epidemic in the radio industry charged De Forest and his associates with trying to exploit the audion, a "strange device ... that had proven to be useless."

The American Telephone and Telegraph Company (AT&T) soon bought the telephone rights to the audion for only $50,000. Shortly afterward De Forest made up for some of his losses when he sold the radio-signal rights to Western Electric for $340,000. With this money he started another company in New York, which began to manufacture tubes and equipment for the military. In 1913 De Forest was acquitted of fraud, but the president of his company was found guilty and sentenced to prison. By 1917 the refined audion tube was commercially available to consumers, who were becoming increasingly interested in radio as a hobby.

Invents "phonofilm"

By the 1920s De Forest had lost interest in the audion tube and in radio altogether. Having become intrigued by the idea of sound in motion pictures, he sold his company in 1923 and moved to Hollywood, California. He developed a sound-on-picture system that worked by printing a soundtrack on the film itself. He called his system "phonofilm" and tried to sell it to the major Hollywood studios. At the time none were interested. In 1927 the first sound movie was released, but only as a last-ditch gimmick to save the Warner Brothers film studio from bankruptcy.

The first "talkie," or motion picture with sound, did not feature De Forest's "phonofilm" system. Instead, it used a much cruder approach, synchronizing a phonograph record to the picture. Because the talking movie was an instant success, every studio seized on the potential for this new technology. Unfortunately for De Forest, Western Electric sued him over patent rights regarding certain components in the "phonofilm" system, and he was forced to stop promoting it.

After three failed marriages, De Forest found happiness at the age of fifty-seven when he wed a twenty-one-year-old Hollywood starlet, Marie Mosquini. She remained with him until his death in 1961, in Hollywood, at the age of eighty-seven. Only three years earlier De Forest had received his last patent, for an automatic telephone dialing device.

Further Reading

Heyn, Ernest, *Fire of Genius,* Anchor Press/Doubleday, 1976.

Levine, I. E., *Electronics Pioneer: Lee De Forest,* Julian Messner, 1964.

Lewis, Thomas S., *Empire of the Air: The Men Who Made Radio,* Harper Collins, 1991.

Wynne, Peter, "Wireless Wonders," *Opera News,* November 1993, pp. 30–36, 61.

Rudolf Diesel

Born March 18, 1858
Paris, France

Disappeared at sea,
September 30, 1913

German inventor Rudolf Diesel perfected a fuel-efficient internal combustion engine.

Rudolf Diesel perfected the internal-combustion engine, which is now known as the diesel engine. A keen student of thermodynamics, Diesel found a way to design an engine that converts the greatest amount of fuel energy to power. Although his engine, which was patented in 1892, never reached the efficiency he had envisioned, it was superior to gasoline-powered engines of the day. The diesel engine's efficiency has led to its widespread use in modern technology.

Excels as engineering student

Rudolf Christian Karl Diesel was born in Paris, France, on March 18, 1858, the son of Bavarian Germans from Augsburg. At the outbreak of the Franco-Prussian War in 1870, his family was expelled from France and moved to London, but Diesel's father sent his son back to Augsburg to continue the education he had begun in France. Diesel eventually found his way to the technical high school in Munich, where he excelled in engineering, passing his examinations with the highest marks on record.

Designs a more efficient engine

In 1880 Diesel went to work for the firm of his refrigeration professor, Karl Paul Gottfried von Linde. While an employee of the Linde firm, Diesel became fascinated with thermodynamics (a branch of physics that concerns the mechanical action or relations of heat), a science developed by the French physicist Nicholas Carnot. Carnot's work defined the principles of the modern internal-combustion engine, leading Diesel to design an engine that converted the greatest amount of fuel energy to usable power. Steam engines, which were in use at the time, could convert only about 7 percent of the energy contained in burnt fuel into mechanical energy.

Diesel was convinced that an engine four times as efficient as a steam engine could be built. He envisioned a process whereby fuel was injected into an engine in which the piston (a sliding piece moved by or moving against fluid pressure) compresses air in the cylinder (the chamber that holds the piston) in a ratio as great as 25 to 1. Such high compression causes the air to reach temperatures of nearly 1,000°F, which is high enough to ignite the fuel without the need for complex spark ignition systems.

Patents diesel engine

Adopting Carnot's principles, Diesel worked on various designs for his engines for over a decade. He eventually produced an engine that radically compressed the air drawn into the cylinder to a pressure of about 4,000 pounds per square

IMPACT

The efficiency of the diesel engine has led to its widespread use, and since the death of Rudolf Diesel in 1913 it has undergone several refinements. The first diesel engine was installed in a ship in 1910. Although the engine was too heavy to be used in aircraft, it was adapted for the automobile in 1922. The diesel-electric locomotive has all but replaced the steam engine on railroads, and diesel engines are put in trucks and buses as well as tractors and other agricultural machinery. Diesel power is used almost exclusively in industrial machinery throughout the world because the engine can burn relatively unrefined fuels and efficiently produce maximum fuel energy.

One of Rudolf Diesel's first engines, built in 1896.

Nikolaus August Otto, German Engineer

German engineer Nikolaus August Otto (1832–1891) was fascinated by the gas engines developed by Frenchman Jean-Joseph-Étienne Lenoir. These were two-stroke, coal gas-burning engines displayed for the first time in 1859. Five years later Otto and industrialist Eugen Langen formed the Gasmotorfabric Company to manufacture and market engines of Otto's own design. With Franz Reuleaux, Gottlieb Daimler, and Wilhelm Maybach as part of their engineering team, in 1876 they built the radically new four-stroke internal combustion engine. It was immediately called the "Otto Silent."

In the four-stroke engine the first downward motion of the piston (a sliding piece) drew the air and gas mixture into the cylinder (the chamber that holds the piston), then on the upward stroke the mixture was compressed. When the piston was near the top of this motion, the mixture was ignited, driving the piston down and providing power. The fourth stroke, moving upward again, pushed the exhaust gases out of the cylinder. The intake and exhaust actions were controlled by valves that opened at precisely the right moment by being geared directly at the crankshaft. The Otto four-cycle engine was so successful that the Otto-Langen firm sold more than fifty thousand engines in the seventeen years following its introduction.

inch. (The concept of air compression was a contribution of the German inventor Nikolaus August Otto; see box.) Diesel was granted a patent in 1892 for an engine designed to burn the cheapest fuel then available—powdered coal. By 1897 he had abandoned powdered coal, substituting kerosene as the fuel. Consistent with Diesel's calculations, the engine proved to be highly efficient.

In addition to improved efficiency, the diesel engine has other advantages over the more conventional gasoline-powered four-stroke "Otto-cycle" engine invented by Otto. Because it is self-igniting, it needs no complex ignition system. Also, its power output is regulated by the amount of fuel injected directly into the cylinder, so it requires no carburetor (a device that supplies an explosive mixture of vaporized fuel and air). Finally, diesel fuel is cheaper than gasoline and, because it is less explosive, it is a safer fuel to use.

Diesel engines also possess disadvantages. Due to the necessity of containing high compression ratios, a diesel engine must be considerably heavier than a gasoline engine that produces the same amount of usable power. Consequently, they initially cost more to build. Diesel engines run roughly at low speeds, and the exhaust systems release high levels of pollutants. The exhaust odor is considered to be more obnoxious than that emitted by conventional gasoline engines.

Finds success

Despite these disadvantages, the diesel engine's high efficiency and comparatively simple design made it commercially successful, and Diesel became a millionaire. Yet, because of the patent restrictions he placed upon manufacturers, the engines were very heavy and not suited to anything but stationary applications. For that reason early diesel engines were not adapted to power the growing automobile industry, although they became widely used in the shipping and locomotive industries.

While crossing the English Channel on the way to consult with the British Admiralty, Diesel disappeared at sea on September 30, 1913. His body was never recovered. Suicide is considered to have been a possible reason for his death, as he was known to be emotionally unstable and given to occasional breakdowns. Since his death the diesel engine has undergone several refinements and is still used in large motor vehicles and ships and for industrial power.

Further Reading

Nitske, W. Robert, and Charles Morrow Wilson, *Rudolf Diesel: Pioneer of the Age of Power,* University of Oklahoma Press, 1965.

Thomas, Donald E., Jr., *Diesel: Technology and Society in Industrial Germany,* University of Alabama Press, 1986.

Irene Diggs

Born in 1906
Monmouth, Illinois

Irene Diggs is an African American anthropologist who has studied racial and cultural differences in North, South, and Latin America. A gifted writer whose work calls attention to the issue of racial inequality, she has contributed scholarly articles to numerous publications. She also spent thirty years teaching sociology and anthropology at Morgan University in Baltimore, Maryland.

Becomes interested in race relations

Irene Diggs was born in 1906 in Monmouth, Illinois, a small college town located in the agricultural belt. Her parents were hard working and supportive, but Diggs longed to escape the poverty that surrounded her. She saw firsthand the substandard living conditions that many blacks had to endure in this region of the country and believed that education was the way out. Since Diggs had the highest average at the local school, she received a chamber of commerce scholarship to attend Mon-

"Basically, the differences between the 'problem of race' in the United States and Latin America is their different definitions of who is white."

As an African American anthropologist, Irene Diggs has made a major contribution to cross-cultural understanding through her work on Afro-Latin America, African American history, African history, and black intellectual history. *Black Chronology*, published in 1983, illustrates her view of culture and the use of historical research to document cultural change. An investigation of the African experience inside and outside Africa, it focuses on the accomplishments of black peoples through the years.

mouth College. After a year she transferred to the University of Minnesota, where she majored in sociology with a minor in psychology. Diggs graduated in 1928 with a bachelor of science degree. She then enrolled in Atlanta University (now Clark Atlanta University) for graduate work in sociology, receiving a master's degree in 1933. She earned a doctorate in anthropology from the University of Havana in Cuba in 1944.

Works with W. E. B. Du Bois

Diggs met the noted African American activist and scholar W. E. B. Du Bois during her second semester as a graduate student at Atlanta University, where he was a professor of economics, history, and sociology. Diggs registered for one of his courses and did so well that Du Bois asked her to become his summer research assistant. The "summer job" lasted eleven years. During those years Diggs helped research five of Du Bois's books, including his social commentary *Black Folk Then and Now.* Together they founded the prestigious journal *Phylon: A Review of Race and Culture.*

Spends time abroad

In the early 1940s Diggs spent time in Cuba before taking an intensive language course as a Roosevelt fellow of the Institute of International Education at the University of Havana. She studied under Fernando Ortiz, a distinguished professor of ethnography (the study of human cultures) and an expert on the African presence in Cuban culture. Diggs collected folklore, recorded music, photographed festivals, and observed rituals and dances. She spent time in cities and rural areas, writing on African culture, especially among Afro-Cuban descendants of the Yoruban and Dahomean peoples.

After World War II Diggs went to South America, where she spent almost a year in Montevideo, Uruguay, as an exchange student with the U.S. Department of State Division of International Exchange of Persons. While in Montevideo, she conducted archival research and became a participant-observer in the Afro-Uruguayan and Afro-Argentinean communities. Diggs developed an interest in fine art and wrote articles on the subject for several publications, notably "Negro Painters in Uruguay" for *Crisis* and "The Negro in the Viceroyalty of Rio de la Plata" for *Journal of Negro History.* The author soon acquired a unique place among her African American colleagues as an expert on Afro-Latin American studies.

Joins college faculty

When Diggs returned to the United States in 1947, she was invited to join the faculty of Morgan State College (now Morgan State University). During the early 1950s her work began appearing in a variety of publications. Some of her best-known articles include "Zumbi and the Republic of Os Palmares," first published in *Phylon;* "Color in Colonial Spanish America," which appeared in *Journal of Negro History;* "Cuba Before Castro," published in *The New American;* and "The Biological and Cultural Impact of Blacks on the United States," included in *Phylon.* Diggs was also coeditor of the groundbreaking 1945 work *Encyclopedia of the Negro.* Her last major project, *Black Chronology,* appeared in 1983.

Retires from academia

Diggs retired from Morgan State University in 1976, after almost thirty years of service to the department of sociology and anthropology. She served on many civic and statewide fact-finding commissions that studied the general population and issues relating to the African American community. She has participated in research on mental health, criminal corrections, and family welfare. Diggs was a founding member of the Women's Committee of the Baltimore Art Museum and served on the board of the Peabody Conservatory. She was also a member of the American Anthropological Association and the American Sociological Association. In 1978 the Association of Black Anthropologists presented her with the Distinguished Scholar Award for her outstanding achievement in scholarship and research on peoples of African descent.

Further Reading

Graces, U., and others, eds., *A Bibliographical Dictionary,* Greenwood Press, 1988.

Negro History Bulletin, Number 34, 1971, pp. 107–08.

Outreach, Number 5, 1983, pp. 1–2.

Charles Richard Drew

Born June 3, 1904
Washington, D.C.
Died April 1, 1950
North Carolina

harles Richard Drew was a renowned surgeon, teacher, and researcher who was responsible for founding two of the world's largest blood banks. Because of his research on the storage and shipment of plasma—the straw-yellow fluid left after blood cells have been removed from blood—he is credited with saving hundreds of lives during World War II. Drew was director of the first American Red Cross effort to collect and bank blood on a large scale. In 1942, a year after he was made a diplomate of surgery by the American Board of Surgery at Johns Hopkins University (meaning he passed an intensive, specialized board exam), he became the first African American surgeon to serve as an examiner on the board.

"Only extensive education can overcome this prejudice which is founded on ignorance."

Excels in school

Charles Richard Drew was born on June 3, 1904, in Washington, D.C., to Richard T. Drew, a carpet layer, and Nora (Burrell) Drew, a schoolteacher and graduate of Miner

Teachers College. Excelling in academics and sports, he graduated in 1922 from Paul Laurence Dunbar High School, which was then recognized as the best educational institution for black students. Afterward, Drew attended Amherst College in Massachusetts on an athletic scholarship.

Begins blood research

After graduating from Amherst in 1926, Drew decided to apply to medical school. He worked for two years as a biology teacher and athletics director at a Baltimore college in order to save enough money to pay for his medical training. Having been rejected from the Howard University College of Medicine because he did not have enough credits in English, he was accepted to McGill University in Montreal, Canada.

At McGill, Drew began his research in blood transfusions with Dr. John Beattie, a visiting professor from England. The four basic blood types—A, B, AB, and O—had recently been discovered. As a result, doctors knew what type of blood they were giving to patients and could avoid the harmful effects of mixing incompatible blood types. However, because whole blood was highly perishable, the problem of having fresh blood on hand for emergencies still existed. In 1930, when Drew and Beattie began their research, blood could be stored for only seven days before spoiling.

In 1933 Drew graduated from McGill with a medical degree and a master of surgery degree. After a two-year internship and residency, he returned to Washington and became an instructor at Howard University. Then, in 1938, Drew was offered a Rockefeller Foundation fellowship to continue his blood research at Columbia University in New York.

Discovers benefits of plasma

At Columbia, Drew worked with Dr. John Scudder and Dr. E. H. L. Corwin on the problem of blood storage. Drew was especially intent on exploring the use of plasma as a substitute for whole blood. Red blood cells contain the substance that determines blood type; plasma—a red blood cell-free substance—can be transferred from donor to recipient without a match, making it ideal for use in emergencies. In 1939, while supervising a blood bank at Columbia Medical Center, Drew developed a method to process and preserve blood plasma through dehydration so that it could be stored and shipped great distances. The dehydrated plasma could then be reconstituted by adding water just before transfusion.

Drew earned his doctorate from Columbia University in 1940 with a dissertation, "Banked Blood: A Study in Blood Preservation," that proved that liquid plasma lasted longer than whole blood. (Drew's conclusions were based in part on the pioneering work of nineteenth-century physiologist Henry Bowditch, who first suggested plasma as a transfusable alternative to whole blood.) Because of his discoveries, Drew was asked to become part of the World War II effort.

IMPACT

When Allied casualties began to mount during World War II, a hunt took place for someone who could find a way to preserve blood for use in battlefield transfusions. That someone turned out to be Charles Richard Drew. He made groundbreaking strides in the field of plasma research and showed that plasma was easier to preserve than whole blood. By initiating the use of "bloodmobiles"—trucks equipped with refrigerators for storing blood—he helped meet the demand for plasma caused by the war.

Contributes to war effort

German warplanes were bombing British cities regularly by 1940, creating a desperate shortage of blood to treat the wounded. Unable to tend to the growing number of casualties on its own, the British Army sought help from the U.S. Blood Transfusion Betterment Association. Drew served as medical supervisor of the association's "Blood for Britain" campaign, which was launched in cooperation with the American Red Cross.

Whole blood was deemed unsuitable for use on the battlefield because its month-long shelf life could be extended only by freezing and storing it in blood banks. Plasma, however, has a longer shelf life, is cheaper to handle, can be used

A 1951 plasma bank, in which trays of blood plasma are freeze-dried.

by patients of all blood groups, and seldom produces serious adverse reactions in recipients. With Drew's help, Britain amassed a large supply of plasma.

Encounters racial discrimination

In 1941, after the success of "Blood for Britain," Drew became director of the American Red Cross Blood Bank in New York City. He was asked to organize a massive blood drive for the U.S. Army and Navy, consisting of 100,000 donors. However, when the military issued a directive to the Red Cross that blood be typed according to the race of the donor—with the blood of African American donors actually being refused for use in transfusions—Drew was outraged. He denounced the policy as unscientific, stating there was no evidence to support the claim that blood types differed according to race. When his statements were later confirmed by other scientists, the government gradually allowed African American volunteers to donate blood. Still, the blood donation process remained segregated, since the blood from black donors could, for a time, only be given to black recipients.

Although Drew was the mastermind behind many innovations in blood plasma research, he was denied membership in the American College of Surgeons. He was also barred from membership in the American Medical Association (AMA). In 1947 Drew decided to seek AMA membership on behalf of other black physicians whose lack of membership prevented them from admitting patients to various hospitals, denied them decision-making power about nationwide medical policies, and curbed their knowledge of new research.

Tragic end

Drew did not live to see African Americans gain membership into the AMA. On April 1, 1950, he and three other doctors left Washington at about 2:15 A.M., bound for a free clinic for the poor in Tuskegee, Alabama. Drew had spent the previous day in surgery and was very tired. Shortly before 8 A.M., the car he was driving swerved out of control and crashed; Drew died in the accident. The other three doctors escaped injury.

Despite his untimely death at the age of forty-five, Drew left an impressive legacy. In 1941 he was appointed professor of surgery at Howard University and chief surgeon at Freedmen's Hospital. He later became the first black surgeon to serve as an examiner on the American Board of Surgery. Drew was an inspiration and role model to his students and received numerous honorary degrees and awards, including the prestigious Spingarn Medal from the National Association for the Advancement of Colored People (NAACP) in 1944. He wrote many articles on blood preservation and research for scientific journals and in 1946 was elected fellow to the International College of Surgeons. Drew's portrait hangs at the Clinical Center of the National Institutes of Health. His life and career were also honored with a commemorative postage stamp issued in 1980 as part of the U.S. Postal Service's "Great Americans" series.

Further Reading

Haber, Louis, *Black Pioneers of Science and Invention,* Harcourt, 1970.

Love, Spencie, *One Blood: The Death and Resurrection of Charles R. Drew,* University of North Carolina Press, 1996.

Page, Jake, *Blood: The River of Life,* U.S. News Books, 1981.

Salley, Columbus, *The Black 100,* Citadel Press, 1993.

Wolfe, Rinna, *Charles Richard Drew, M.D.,* Franklin Watts, 1991.

Wynes, Charles E., *Charles Richard Drew: The Man and the Myth,* University of Illinois Press, 1988.

Sylvia A. Earle

Born August 30, 1935
Gibbstown, New Jersey

A leading American oceanographer, Sylvia A. Earle was among the first underwater explorers to make use of modern self-contained underwater breathing apparatus (scuba) gear. She also identified many new species of marine life. With her former husband, Graham Hawkes, Earle designed and built a submersible ocean craft that could dive to unprecedented depths of 3,000 feet. She was the first woman to be named chief scientist of the National Oceanic and Atmospheric Administration (NOAA).

Interests nurtured by family

Sylvia Alice Reade Earle was born in Gibbstown, New Jersey, on August 30, 1935, the daughter of Lewis Reade Earle and Alice Freas Richie Earle. Both of her parents enjoyed the outdoors, and after the family moved to the west coast of Florida they encouraged her love and exploration of nature. "I wasn't shown frogs with the attitude 'yuk,'" Earle told an

"The idea has always been that scientists couldn't be trusted to drive a submersible [ocean craft] by themselves because they'd get so involved in their work they'd run into things."

Sylvia A. Earle was one of the first ocean biologists to take advantage of scuba gear in her studies of sea life. But the depth limitations of scuba equipment prompted Earle and her former husband, Graham Hawkes, to build *Deep Rover*, a submersible ocean craft that operates at depths of 3,000 feet. In 1993 Earle worked with a team of Japanese scientists on Ocean Everest, a manned submersible that can dive to 36,000.

interviewer for *Scientific American* magazine, "but rather my mother would show my brothers and me how beautiful they are and how fascinating it was to look at their gorgeous golden eyes."

Starts collecting algae

After Earle earned a bachelor of science degree from Florida State University in 1955, she entered the graduate program in botany at Duke University in Durham, North Carolina. The Gulf of Mexico became a natural laboratory for Earle during her work on a master's degree. Her thesis, a detailed study of algae (primitive aquatic plants) in the Gulf, became a continuing project. Earle has collected more than twenty thousand samples of Gulf algae. "When I began making collections in the Gulf, it was a very different body of water than it is now—the habitats have changed. So I have a very interesting baseline," she noted in the *Scientific American* interview.

In 1966 Earle received a Ph.D. from Duke, then became resident director of the Cape Haze Marine Laboratories in Sarasota, Florida. The following year she moved to Cambridge, Massachusetts, to take dual roles as research scholar at the Radcliffe Institute and research fellow at the Farlow Herbarium at Harvard University. Earle relocated to San Francisco in 1976 to become a research biologist and curator at the California Academy of Sciences. That same year she was named a fellow in botany at the Natural History Museum of the University of California at Berkeley.

Pioneers use of scuba gear

Although Earle's academic career could have kept her totally involved, her first love was the sea and the life within it. In 1970 Earle and four other oceanographers lived in an underwater chamber for fourteen days as part of the U.S. government-funded Tektite II Project, designed to study undersea habitats. Fortunately, technology played a major role in Earle's future. The breathing apparatus known as a scuba, which had been developed in part by **Jacques Cousteau** (see entry) in 1943, had been refined during the time Earle was involved in her scholarly research. Scuba equipment was not only an important advancement for recreational divers, it was also an indispensable tool in the study of marine biology.

One of the first researchers to don a mask and oxygen tank, Earle observed and identified many new species of plants and animals. She described her discovery of undersea dunes (sandhill habitats) off the Bahama Islands as "a simple Lewis and Clark kind of observation." Yet, as she told the *Scientific American* interviewer, "the presence of dunes was a significant insight into the formation of the area."

Designs submersible craft

Although Earle set an unprecedented record by freely diving to a depth of 1,250 feet, there were serious depth limitations to scuba diving. The study of deep-sea marine life would require the assistance of a submersible craft that could dive far deeper. In 1981 Earle and her former husband, British-born engineer Graham Hawkes, founded Deep Ocean Technology, Inc., and Deep Ocean Engineering, Inc., to design and build submersibles. Earle and Hawkes rough-sketched on a paper napkin the design for a submersible called *Deep Rover,* which could serve as a valuable tool for biologists. *Deep Rover* continues to operate as a mid-water machine in ocean depths ranging to 3,000 feet.

Urges U.S. support of ocean research

In 1990 Earle was named the first woman to serve as chief scientist at NOAA, the U.S. government agency that conducts underwater research, manages fisheries, and monitors marine spills. But she left the position after eighteen months because she felt she could accomplish more by working independently of the government.

Sylvia Earle, with the help of filmmaker Al Giddings, slips into the robot-like spacesuit she used in her September 1979 attempt to set a new world record of 1,500 feet for the deepest solo ocean dive made by a human.

Having logged more than 6,000 hours under water, Earle realizes the lack of research money being spent on deep-sea studies in the United States. Among the world's five deep-sea manned submersibles (those capable of diving to 20,000 feet or more), she points out, the States has only one, the *Sea Cliff*. "That's like having one jeep for all of North America," she said in the *Scientific American* interview. In 1993 Earle worked with a team of Japanese scientists to develop the equipment to send first a remote, then a manned submersible to 36,000 feet. "They have money from their government," she said. "They do what we do not: they really make a substantial commitment to ocean technology and science."

Continues exploration

Earle led the $10 million deep-ocean engineering project, Ocean Everest, that took her to 36,000 feet. In addition to publishing numerous scientific papers on marine life, Earle is an advocate of public education about the importance of the oceans as an environmental habitat. She is also the president and chief executive officer of Deep Ocean Technology and Deep Ocean Engineering in Oakland, California, as well as the coauthor of *Exploring the Deep Frontier.*

Further Reading

Brownlee, Shannon, "Explorers of the Dark Frontiers," *Discover,* February 1986, pp. 60–67.

Current Biography, H. W. Wilson, May 1992, pp. 21–25.

Earle, Sylvia A., "Persian Gulf Pollution," *National Geographic,* February 1992.

Earle, Sylvia A., "Wishing on a Starfish," *Sea Frontiers,* Fall 1995.

Earle, Sylvia A., with Al Giddings, *Exploring the Deep Frontier: The Adventure of Man in the Sea,* National Geographic Press, 1980.

Holloway, Marguerite, "Fire in Water," *Scientific American,* April 1992, pp. 37–40.

Orenstein, Peggy, "Champion of the Deep," *New York Times Magazine,* June 23, 1991.

Stover, Dawn, "Queen of the Deep," *Popular Science,* April 1995.

Thomas Alva Edison

Born February 11, 1847
Milan, Ohio
Died October 18, 1931
West Orange, New Jersey

American inventor Thomas Alva Edison was a pioneering figure in science whose inventions and innovations forever changed the way people lived the world over.

Thomas Alva Edison is considered one of the greatest inventors of all time. His name is virtually synonymous with the invention of the lightbulb, even though he did not invent it but only modified it. Nonetheless, over his lifetime he was awarded more than thirteen hundred patents—far more than have been credited to any other individual in American history. Among Edison's best-known inventions are the automatic telegraphy machine, the phonograph, motion picture equipment, and a modernized telephone. His major accomplishment in scientific research was the discovery of the emission of electrons from a heated cathode (or conductor), a phenomenon now known as the Edison effect. Edison is widely regarded as a virtual genius who had the ability to master an amazing array of subjects and produce a wide range of inventions.

Attends school for three months

Edison was born in Milan, Ohio, on February 11, 1847, the seventh and youngest child of Samuel and Nancy (Elliott)

Edison. When he was seven years old he moved with his family to Port Huron, Michigan, where he attended school for a total of only three months. His teacher, failing to relate to the way Edison's mind worked, dismissed him as being "addled," or retarded. Nancy Edison withdrew her son from school and from that point on educated him at home. Even though there is some evidence that Edison had dyslexia, a problem that makes reading difficult, he did learn to read, under his mother's guidance. She introduced him to natural philosophy, a mixture of physics, chemistry, and other sciences. Edison became especially interested in chemistry and built a chemical laboratory in a corner of the cellar in the family home. By the age of ten he was conducting his own experiments.

Gets first job

Edison was also fascinated by locomotives and railroads. When he was twelve years old he landed a job as a newspaper and candy salesman on the Grand Trunk Railway, which ran between Port Huron and Detroit, Michigan. During layovers in Detroit, Edison spent his time at the public library. Over time Edison expanded his activities on the train, receiving permission to use an empty part of the baggage car to set up a small chemistry laboratory and later to run a printing press on which he produced a small newspaper, the *Weekly Herald*.

Loses his hearing

One morning while Edison was running to catch the train, one of the conductors pulled him aboard by grasping his ears. Edison felt something snap inside his head. When he later became deaf he claimed this incident had caused his condition. Evidence to the contrary suggests that his deafness was probably an after-effect of scarlet fever (a severe contagious disease that occurs mainly in children and is characterized by a high fever and scarlet rash on the skin). No matter the cause, this affliction had a profound effect on his life. Edison grew increasingly solitary and studious. He also became more serious about his experiments. One of the lifelong habits he developed during this period was working long hours with only short naps to keep him going. Later in life it was not unusual for Edison to spend twenty out of every twenty-four hours at work.

Learns telegraphy

Another train incident in 1862 led to a new job for Edison. After he bravely pulled the stationmaster's son from the front of an oncoming locomotive, the boy's father offered to teach Edison telegraphy, a means of communicating over a great distance by using coded signals transmitted by wire. Edison soon mastered the art of telegraphy and for the next five years traveled throughout the country as an operator. It was during this time that he first dreamed of becoming an inventor. He spent much of each paycheck on electrical gadgets or chemicals for his laboratory.

Influenced by Michael Faraday

After returning home to Port Huron briefly in 1867, Edison moved to Boston, Massachusetts, where he found a job with the Western Union Telegraph Company. During his free time he continued studying and inventing. Two books had a particular impact on him. After reading Isaac Newton's 1687 book *Philosophiae naturalis principia mathematica* ("Mathematical Principles of Natural Philosophy"), Edison decided that he never wanted to do anything that required a knowledge of mathematics. But when he read *Experimental Researches in Electricity* by **Michael Faraday** (see entry), he noticed that Faraday seemed to conduct most of his experiments without the use of mathematics. Faraday became a model for Edison, who had decided to experiment with electrical inventions.

Receives first patent

While in Boston, Edison rented a corner of William's Electric Shop on Court Street and began to experiment. He invented a device for electronically recording the voice votes taken in a legislative assembly. In 1869 this recorder earned him his first patent (a grant made by the U.S government that assures an inventor the exclusive right to manufacture, use, and sell an invention for a stated period of time). The machine worked well, but there was just one problem—nobody was interested in buying it. Edison vowed never again to invent something no one wanted.

Goes to New York City

June 1869 marked a turning point in Edison's career as an inventor when he left Boston for New York City. He arrived in the city without a cent in his pockets and was saved by a remarkable stroke of good luck. While he was waiting to interview for a job with Law's Gold Indicator Company, the office's central transmitting machine broke down. Edison quickly found the problem and fixed the machine. The next day the owner of the company, Dr. S. S. Laws, offered Edison a job as general manager of the firm, with the then-generous salary of $300 a month.

This job allowed Edison to think more seriously about a career in invention, and he ended up forming his own electrical engineering company. Soon after, the company was bought by the Gold and Stock Telegraphic Company, which paid Edison $40,000 for a device that kept stock tickers working in unison. This was quite a fortune for a twenty-three-year-old man from Port Huron who had essentially no formal education.

Opens first "invention factory"

The profit from the Gold and Stock deal allowed Edison to act on a plan he had been thinking about for some time. First he opened a firm in Newark, New Jersey, which was, as

⩔IMPACT⩔

A Thomas Alva Edison's Menlo Park "invention factory" produced an amazing array of inventions and innovations that changed the lives of people throughout the world. Probably the best known was an inexpensive electric light. There were a variety of other inventions as well: a recording telegraph, the carbon telephone, an electric pen, the phonograph, the first electric dynamo, the phonometer (a voice transmitter), the tasimeter (to measure the Sun's heat), a dictating machine, the motion picture projector, and the cement kiln. For his amazing inventive talent and extraordinary output Edison earned the nickname "The Wizard of Menlo Park."

he called it, an "invention factory." The plant operated for six years, turning out a variety of inventions related primarily to improvements in stock tickers and telegraphy equipment. In all, Edison was granted about two hundred new patents for work completed in the Newark laboratories. Then, in 1876, when Edison had outgrown his Newark facilities, he built a new invention factory in Menlo Park, New Jersey. Over the next ten years he produced many important inventions, including three that made him famous: a more modern telephone, the phonograph, and the incandescent lightbulb. Although **Alexander Graham Bell** (see entry) was the actual inventor of the first telephone, Edison developed a transmitter that greatly improved the quality of Bell's invention.

Invents the phonograph

In 1877 Edison produced what he himself named his favorite invention: the phonograph, or record player. The idea for the phonograph came to Edison while he was studying a telephone receiver. He attached a steel stylus (a hard-pointed, pen-shaped instrument) to the diaphragm (a disk that vibrates to generate sound waves) of the receiver so he could feel the sound vibrations with his finger as they were emitted. It dawned on him that the stylus might "etch" the vibrations onto a piece of moving tinfoil. He reasoned that a similar point could then trace the grooves left on the foil and pass the vibrations onto another diaphragm to produce sound. His original phonograph used a tinfoil-covered cylinder that was hand-cranked while a needle traced a groove on it. The phonograph was very popular, and although it was improved over the years, it remained essentially the same.

Improves the lightbulb

Although Edison did not invent the incandescent lightbulb, he found a way to build it so that it would be cheap enough for everyone to buy. English chemist Sir Joseph Wilson Swan (see box) had begun working on the lightbulb back in 1848, about thirty years before Edison. The concept of the lightbulb was simple enough: when an electrical current

passes through a thin wire (a filament), it encounters resistance that causes the wire to become hot enough to glow, that is, to reach incandescence. Swan had a problem keeping the wire from oxidizing, or burning up. In theory, the solution was to encase the wire in a vacuum (a space absolutely devoid of matter). In Swan's time, however, it was impossible to make a good enough vacuum. As a result, a wire might be brought to incandescence and produce light for a short time, but it quickly burned up and the light went out.

Swan continued to work on the incandescent lightbulb for the next two decades and finally solved the problem at about the same time Edison did. An important key to Edison's success was that much better vacuums were available in 1878. In addition, Edison discovered an ideal material for use as the filament in a lightbulb, a charred length of cotton thread. On October 21, 1879, Edison first demonstrated in public an incandescent lightbulb—made with his charred cotton thread—that burned continuously for forty hours.

Achieves success

The incandescent lightbulb was, of course, a remarkable success, and Edison spent the next few years adapting it for large-scale use. He found it necessary, for example, to invent the generating, switching, and transmitting devices needed to supply electricity to a large number of lightbulbs at the same time. Within three years he had solved many of these problems and was operating the world's first power station on Pearl Street in New York City. When the plant began operation on September 4, 1882, it supplied power to four hundred incandescent lightbulbs owned by eighty-five customers.

Creates the Edison effect

While working on the incandescent lightbulb, Edison made his one and only important scientific discovery. In attempting to modify the construction of the bulb, he introduced a wire into the bulb adjacent to the filament. When the lamp was turned on, Edison observed that electrical current flowed from the filament to the wire. He saw no practical application of this discovery, so he did no further work on it. The Edison effect, as the discovery is now called, later had important applications as a way of directing electrical current.

Invents early motion picture machine

In 1887, when his laboratories outgrew the facilities at Menlo Park, Edison built an even larger invention factory in West Orange, New Jersey. By this time his labs were so productive that he was receiving an average of one new patent every five days. Probably the best-known invention to come out of this period was the kinetograph, a primitive form of the moving picture. Edison developed a method for arranging a series of photographs on a strip of celluloid film and then running the film through a projector. He used this technique in 1903 to produce *The Great Train Robbery,* one of the first moving pictures. However, he soon lost interest in the technology.

Joseph Wilson Swan, English Chemist and Physicist

Following nearly the same path as Thomas Alva Edison in America, British chemist Sir Joseph Wilson Swan (1828–1914) began experimenting with the incandescent filament lamp (the lightbulb), an electric lamp in which a filament (a conductor) gives off light when heated by an electric current. The two inventors simultaneously introduced the electric light in grand demonstrations in London and New York.

In addition to his experiments with electric lighting, Swan made several important contributions to photography that revolutionized the field. He developed the dry-plate method of developing film, a refinement of the existing method that called for chemicals in liquid form to be applied to the photographic plates. He also developed the first bromide paper (paper containing the chemical element bromine, a reddish-brown liquid), which is still widely used for printing photographs.

Almost wins Nobel Prize

In 1912 Edison was recommended as a corecipient of the Nobel Prize with **Nikola Tesla** (see entry), who had been employed in Edison's lab in the late 1880s. Soon after quitting because of a disagreement with Edison, Tesla achieved great success on his own. At the root of their hostility was their disagreement about how to supply electricity to the public. Tesla favored using a system of alternating current (AC) he had helped to develop, while Edison favored direct current (DC). Even when the superior AC system began to be accepted around the country, Edison stubbornly resisted, something the temperamental Tesla never forgot. When he refused to share the Nobel Prize with Edison, the committee awarded the prize to someone else.

Dabbled in various fields of study

Edison's active nature and inquisitive mind led him to wander from subject to subject. In some cases he stayed with a project long enough to see it to commercial production. In other instances he spent time developing the early stages of an idea and then moved on to something new. Among the inventions to which he made at least some contribution were the lead storage battery, the mimeograph machine (a copying machine), the dictaphone, and the fluoroscope (a type of X-ray machine). He also developed an interest in iron mining and processing and in cement production.

Received awards and honors

Edison was married twice, the first time on Christmas Day, 1871, to Mary Stilwell, whom he had met in Newark. They had three children: Marion Estell, Thomas Alva, and William Leslie. Mary Edison died in 1884, and two years later Edison married Mina Miller. Three children—Charles, Madeleine, and Theodore—were born during this marriage. Edison died in West Orange on October 18, 1931. In recognition of his accomplishments he was elected to the National Academy of Sciences in 1927 and the Hall of Fame for Great Americans in 1960. In addition he was awarded the Albert Medal of the British Society of Arts in 1892, the John Fritz Medal of the American Engineering Societies in 1908, and the Rumford Medal of the American Academy of Arts and Sciences.

Further Reading

Adler, David A., *Thomas Alva Edison: Great Inventor,* Holiday House, 1990.

Baldwin, Neil, *Edison, Inventing the Century,* Hyperion, 1995.

Betts, Louise, *Thomas Edison: Great American Inventor,* Barron's Educational Series, Inc., 1987.

Keller, Jack, *Tom Edison's Bright Ideas,* Raintree Publishers, 1989.

Mitchell, Barbara, *The Wizard of Sound: A Story of Thomas Edison,* Carolrhoda Books, 1991.

Parker, Steve, *Thomas Edison and Electricity,* HarperCollins, 1992.

Tames, Richard, *Thomas Edison,* Franklin Watts, 1990.

Paul R. Ehrlich and Anne H. Ehrlich

"Spaceship Earth is now filled to capacity or beyond.... People traveling first class are, without thinking, demolishing the ship's already overstrained life support systems."

Paul R. Ehrlich

Born May 29, 1932
Philadelphia, Pennsylvania

After witnessing the problems of overpopulation firsthand during a visit to India, Paul R. Ehrlich became an environmental crusader. Originally trained as an entomologist (a zoologist who studies insects), he has published many works in the fields of ecology, evolution, and behavior and gained acclaim for his plan to make the world environmentally secure. According to Ehrlich, humans must stop exploiting the earth and learn to respect it as a limited resource.

Plans career in biology

Paul R. Ehrlich was born in Philadelphia, Pennsylvania, on May 29, 1932. His father, William Ehrlich, was a salesman, and his mother, Ruth Rosenberg Ehrlich, was a Latin teacher. Ehrlich had an early interest in animals—he claims to have spent his childhood chasing butterflies and dissecting frogs. The Ehrlich family, which also included his sister Sally, moved to Maplewood, New Jersey, when Paul was still quite young. During the time he attended Columbia High School in Maplewood, Ehrlich read *Road to Survival,* a book by William Vogt that called attention the problem of supplying food for a growing population. He then became committed to a career in biology.

Trains as an entomologist

After graduating from high school Ehrlich enrolled at the University of Pennsylvania with a major in zoology. Earning a bachelor's degree in 1953, he went on to graduate study at the University of Kansas in Lawrence. The following year he married Anne Fitzhugh Howland, a biology researcher and writer with whom he would later have a daughter, Lisa Marie. In 1955 Ehrlich received a master's degree, then a doctorate two years later. While at the University of Kansas he was an associate investigator for a U.S. Air Force research project. His field work took him to the Bering Sea (part of the Pacific Ocean between Siberia and Alaska) to survey biting flies and to Africa, Alaska, Mexico, the Pacific Islands, and Asia to investigate insect genetics and behavior.

After completing his doctorate Ehrlich worked briefly as a research associate in Chicago and at the University of Kansas. In 1959 he was appointed associate professor of biology at Stanford University in Stanford, California. By 1966 he was a full professor, and ten years later he was named Bing Professor of Population Studies.

Writes on many topics

Through his writings Ehrlich has addressed a wide range of topics, including crowding in human populations, the relation of population to social and political events, and population and the environment. He has also written about butterflies, biology, immigration, extinction, and race. Ehrlich's first book, *How to Know the Butterflies,* was illustrated by his wife, who is also on the Stanford biology faculty and who has collaborated with him on a number of his works. Ehrlich's interest in butterflies resulted in a project in which he used ants to control butterfly caterpillars. In addition, he has studied migratory birds, which provide information about the environment because of their sensitivity to toxic substances and their vulnerability to destruction of their habitats.

Becomes aware of world crisis

The issue with which Ehrlich has become most closely associated is overpopulation. In 1966, while visiting Delhi, India, he had an experience that changed his understanding of the world population problem. As he and his wife were returning to their hotel by taxi one night, they passed through a section of slums. The taxi moved slowly because of the masses of people crowding the streets. The Ehrlichs saw people begging, using the streets as a bathroom, herding animals, and eating, washing, and sleeping. Shaken by the scene, Ehrlich decided to devote serious study to the overpopulation crisis. The following year he published a piece in the British journal *New Scientist.* This article resulted in a three-decade-long campaign to change the world.

Warns about environmental destruction

In his groundbreaking article and in subsequent books and shorter works Ehrlich has warned of imminent ecological disaster. The human population has been increasing faster than the food supply, threatening to destroy the environment as the planet's resources are depleted by high consumption and overcrowding. Wealthier nations, which often have lower birth rates than poorer countries, are not generally considered to be overpopulated. However, Ehrlich regards the impact of the way people live to be a more accurate measure of overpopulation than mere numbers. He maintains that populations in rich countries are harming the environment more severely than growing populations in poor countries. Therefore the United States, whose people consume a particularly high percentage of the earth's resources, is a greater threat to the environment than larger nations like China or India.

Overpopulation forces people to survive by using up and destroying natural resources—fossil fuels, the soil, fresh water, and wildlife. According to Ehrlich, measures must be taken at once to conserve resources, with particular attention to those classified as nonrenewable. Human overpopulation has already had a significant effect on the ecosystem (the community of plants and animals and the physical environment with which they interact). In addition to the depletion of minerals, soil, and other resources, a number of organisms are becoming or have become extinct. Ehrlich fears that entire species and communities will soon be lost.

Ecosystems regulate the climate, create supplies of fresh water, produce and renew soils, and facilitate crop pollination. If overpopulation destroys the biodiversity (numbers of different species of plants and animals), the ability of the planet to support life will be threatened.

Calls for zero population growth

The first and most important step toward solving the planet's problems, says Ehrlich, is to bring overpopulation to a halt and, if possible, to reverse the trend. To accomplish this goal he helped found Zero Population Growth, a political organization that supports strategies such as birth control and a two-child limit for families. Ehrlich advocates zero population growth (the number of people born equaling the number dying) as a way to begin solving serious environmental problems.

Seeks to increase awareness

Ehrlich's books and articles provide a guide to the environment along with information about crucial environmental issues and suggestions for governmental and individual action.

Lester R. Brown, American Environmentalist and Agricultural Economist

Another crusader for environmental causes is Lester R. Brown (1934–), who founded Worldwatch Institute in 1974. Based in Washington, D.C., the institute conducts studies of global environmental and economic issues such as famine, overpopulation, and scarcity of natural resources. The institute publishes *World Watch* magazine, the annual reports *State of the World* and *Vital Signs: The Trends That Are Shaping Our Future*, as well as the Environmental Alert and Worldwatch Papers series. Brown's vision is a world in which money will be redirected from military spending to programs for reforestation, environmental and agricultural research, education, and large-scale birth control and immunization programs in the developing world. Brown does not own a car; he rides his bicycle or walks to work and appointments, an example that is followed by many employees at the institute. He also uses a canvas bag to carry his groceries.

He urges better knowledge of basic science and increased global ecological education among the world's people. According to Ehrlich, the United States must do everything possible to lessen its negative impact on the environment and to encourage other nations to follow suit. Viewing population growth as a threat greater than nuclear war, Ehrlich calls upon the United States to implement a policy for immediate population reduction. In addition to curbing population growth, he advises, all government bodies should strive to preserve the integrity of ecological systems. He also identifies energy use, wastefulness, and debt in developing countries as serious global problems.

Receives international recognition

Ehrlich has won a number of awards, including the John Muir Award from the Sierra Club in 1980 and the World Wildlife Foundation Medal in 1987. In 1990 he shared the Craafoord Prize in Population Biology and Conservation of Biodiversity. He is a member of the American Academy of Arts and Sciences, the National Academy of Sciences, and the Entomological Society of America and an honorary life member of the American Museum of Natural History.

Further Reading

Ehrlich, Paul R., "Population, Plenty, and Poverty," *National Geographic,* December 1988, pp. 914–45.

Ehrlich, Paul R., with A. H. Ehrlich, *Healing the Planet,* Addison-Wesley, 1991.

Ehrlich, Paul R., with A. H. Ehrlich and others, *How to Know the Butterflies,* William C. Brown, 1961.

Ehrlich, Paul R., with A. H. Ehrlich, *The Population Explosion,* Simon & Schuster, 1990.

Ehrlich, Paul R., with Gretchen C. Daily, "Population, Sustainability, and Earth's Carrying Capacity," *BioScience,* November 1992, pp. 761–72.

Albert Einstein

Born March 14, 1879
Ulm, Germany
Died April 18, 1955
Princeton, New Jersey

"The most important human endeavor is the striving for morality in our actions."

Albert Einstein was a German-born American physicist whose name is synonymous with genius. During a single year, 1905, he produced three papers that revolutionized science. These three masterpieces dealt with Brownian motion, the photoelectric effect, and the special theory of relativity. In 1921 he was awarded the Nobel Prize in physics for his explanation of the photoelectric effect. Einstein extended his special theory of relativity into the more general theory of relativity, which he formulated into the well-known equation $E=mc^2$.

In addition to being one of the world's greatest scientists, Einstein was also a public figure. He gave generously of his time and energy to causes he supported, enduring harsh criticism and even risking death as a result of the stands he took on some of the major issues of his day. He opposed World War I, and after the nuclear attack by the United States on Japan in World War II, he became an ardent supporter of nuclear disarmament (getting rid of or reducing a nation's nuclear weapons). Despite his fame, Einstein was a solitary man who spent most of his time in isolation; although he was extremely popular, he did not seek the admiration of others.

Studies independently

Einstein was born March 14, 1879, the son of Pauline Koch Einstein and Hermann Einstein, owner of a company that made and sold electrical equipment. No one in the family was particularly gifted in science or math, and for some time it appeared that the young Einstein shared this trait—in fact, as a child he did not show much aptitude for anything. He did not talk until he was three, and for a number of years after that he still had trouble speaking fluently. In elementary school his performance was dismal at best, leading some people (including his parents) to suspect that he was retarded. From the time he was a small child, however, Einstein preferred to learn on his own, and in his early teens he taught himself advanced mathematics and science. He followed this pattern of independent study throughout his life.

Graduating from the Swiss Federal Polytechnic School in Zurich in 1900 with a degree in physics, Einstein worked at a series of temporary jobs before he secured a permanent position in 1902 as a technical expert with the Swiss Patent Office. For the next seven years he evaluated proposed inventions by day and conducted his own research in the evenings and in his spare time. Einstein applied his work toward a doctorate at the University of Zurich. He also married a former classmate at the Polytechnic, Mileva Maric, and together they had a daughter and two sons. The couple divorced in 1919; Einstein was later remarried to his cousin Elsa.

Publishes paper on Brownian motion

In 1905 Einstein published a series of papers, any one of which would have assured his fame in history. "On the Movement of Small Particles Suspended in a Stationary Liquid Demanded by the Molecular-Kinetic Theory of Heat" addressed a phenomenon first observed by the Scottish botanist Robert Brown (see box) in 1827. Brown had reported that tiny particles, such as specks of dust, move about with a rapid and random zigzag motion when suspended in a liquid.

Einstein hypothesized that the visible motion of particles was caused by the random movement of molecules (the smallest particles of an element or compound) that make up the liquid. He derived a mathematical formula that predicted the distance traveled by the particles and their relative speed. This formula was confirmed experimentally by the French physicist Jean Baptiste Perrin in 1908. Einstein's work on Brownian motion is generally regarded as the first direct experimental evidence of the existence of molecules.

Studies photoelectric effect

In his 1905 study titled "On a Heuristic Viewpoint Concerning the Production and Transformation of Light," Einstein tackled another puzzle in physics, the photoelectric effect. First observed by Heinrich Hertz in 1888, the photoelectric effect involves the release of electrons (negatively charged particles that orbit the nucleus of an atom) from a metal that occurs when light is shined on the metal. The puzzling aspect of the photoelectric effect was that the number of electrons released is not a function of the light's intensity, but of the color (that is, the wavelength) of the light.

To solve this problem, Einstein made use of the quantum hypothesis, a concept developed only a few years earlier, in 1900, by the German physicist **Max Planck** (see entry). Einstein assumed that light travels in tiny discrete bundles (quanta) of energy. The energy of any given light quantum (later renamed the photon), Einstein said, is determined by its wavelength. Thus, when light falls on a metal, electrons in the metal absorb specific quanta of energy, giving them enough energy to escape from the surface of the metal. The number of electrons released will depend not on the number of quanta (that is, the intensity of the light), but on the light's energy (or wavelength). Einstein's hypothesis was confirmed by several experiments and laid the foundation for the fields of quantitative photoelectric chemistry and quantum mechanics (the branch of physics that studies the energy levels in atoms). In recognition of this work, Einstein was awarded the 1921 Nobel Prize in physics.

Formulates special theory of relativity

A third paper Einstein wrote in 1905, for which he became best known, details his special theory of relativity. In essence, "On the Electrodynamics of Moving Bodies" discusses the relationship between measurements made by observers in two separate systems moving at constant velocity (speed) with respect to each other.

Einstein's work on relativity was by no means the first in the field. The French physicist Jules Henri Poincare, the Irish physicist George Francis Fitzgerald, and the Dutch physicist Hendrik Lorentz had already analyzed in some detail the problem attacked by Einstein in his 1905 paper. Each had developed mathematical formulas that described the effect of motion on various types of measurement. Still, there is little question that Einstein provided the most complete analysis of the subject. He began by making two assumptions. First, he said that the laws of physics are the same in all frames of reference. Second, he declared that the velocity of light is always the same, regardless of the conditions under which it is measured.

Using only these two assumptions, Einstein proceeded to uncover an unexpectedly extensive description of the properties of bodies that are in uniform motion. For example, he showed that the length and mass of an object are dependent upon their movement relative to an observer. He derived a mathematical relationship between the length of an object and its velocity that had previously been suggested by both

Robert Brown, Scottish Botanist

In 1827, while observing grains of orchid pollen suspended in fluid under a microscope, Scottish botanist Robert Brown (1773–1858) noticed particles moving within a grain. After ruling out the fluid and its gradual evaporation as possible causes for the movement, he proposed that the particle itself might be "alive." When he tested fresh pollen from other plants and expanded his experiment to powdered glass, coal, rocks, and metals, he found the same movement.

Despite his experimentation, Brown could not explain the movement, and ultimately he left it to others for interpretation. All minuscule particles that could be suspended in water exhibited what is now called Brownian motion or movement: particles are buffeted about by molecules of the fluid in which they are suspended, which are in constant, irregular motion proportional to the temperature.

Fitzgerald and Lorentz. Einstein's theory was revolutionary, for previously scientists had believed that basic measurable entities such as time, mass, and length remain the same in all frames of reference. Einstein's work established the opposite —that measurable properties will differ depending on the relative motion of the observer.

Special theory explains perception problems

Although Einstein's special theory of relativity seems abstract and complicated, it has two simple main ideas. The first is that measurements of time, space, and motion are relative. To illustrate this idea, pretend that you have just fired a gun. The bullet goes speeding off into the distance at, say, 500 miles per hour. Imagine also that an airplane has swooped down just as you fired the gun, and it, too, is going 500 miles per hour in the same direction. The pilot ends up flying along right next to the bullet. To him, the bullet looks like it is standing still. And it is—*relative to him.* Einstein believed that perceptions of time and space were also relative to the person perceiving them.

The second concept underlying special relativity is that the first idea involves a major exception—the nonrelative element in any situation is the speed of light. According to Einstein, the speed of light is constant (approximately 186,281 miles per second; a light-year measures the distance light travels in a year, roughly six trillion miles). Thus the speed of light is the same no matter who is measuring that speed. To examine a situation involving relativity and the speed of light, imagine what would happen if a train were traveling at the speed of light and the engineer turned on the headlights. According to Einstein, nothing would happen. In order for the headlights to shine—or rather, for our eyes to perceive the light shining from them—the light coming out of the lamps would have to move even faster than the train. This is impossible because the speed of light is constant. The theory of relativity, in part, was the answer to these questions.

Devises formula $E=mc^2$

In addition to his studies on the photoelectric effect, Brownian movement, and relativity, Einstein wrote two other papers in 1905. "Does the Inertia of a Body Depend on Its Energy Content?" was an extension of his earlier work on relativity. He came to the conclusion that the energy and mass of a body are closely interrelated. Two years later he stated that relationship in a formula, $E=mc^2$ (energy equals mass times the speed of light squared). Einstein submitted the final paper, "A New Determination of Molecular Dimensions," as his doctoral dissertation. He earned a Ph.D. from the University of Zurich in 1905.

Fame did not come to Einstein immediately. Indeed, when he submitted his paper on relativity to the University of Bern in support of his application to become a *privatdozent* (lecturer or teacher), the paper and the application were rejected. His work was too important to be ignored for long, however, and a second application three years later was accepted. Einstein spent only a year at Bern before taking a job as a professor of physics at the University of Zurich in 1909. He then went to the German University of Prague for a year and a half before returning to

Zurich in 1912. A year later Einstein was made director of scientific research at the Kaiser Wilhelm Institute for Physics in Berlin, a post he held until 1933.

Formulates general theory of relativity

Upon the outbreak of World War I, Einstein returned to Zurich. The war years marked the culmination of Einstein's attempt to extend his theory of relativity to a broader context. The general theory of relativity applied to motions that are not uniform and relative velocities that are not constant. Einstein was able to write mathematical expressions that describe the relationships between measurements made in *any* two systems in motion relative to each other, even if the motion is accelerated (changing) in one or both. A fundamental feature of the general theory is the concept of a space-time continuum in which space is curved. That concept means that a body affects the shape of the space that surrounds it so that a second body moving near the first body will travel in a curved path.

Proves his theory

Einstein's new theory was too radical to be immediately accepted because the mathematics behind it were extremely complex and it would replace Sir Isaac Newton's (see box) theory of gravitation that had been accepted for two centuries. Einstein therefore offered three testable proofs of general relativity. First, he predicted that relativity would cause Mercury's perihelion (a point of orbit closest to the Sun) to advance slightly more than was predicted by Newton's laws. Second, he predicted that light from a star will be bent by gravity as it passes close to a massive body, such as the Sun. Finally, Einstein suggested that relativity would also affect light by changing its wavelength, a phenomenon known as the redshift effect. Observations of the planet Mercury soon bore out Einstein's hypothesis and calculations, but astronomers and physicists had yet to test the other two proofs.

Einstein had calculated that the light passing by the Sun is bent by 1.7 seconds of an arc, a small but detectable change. In 1919, during a solar eclipse, English astronomer Arthur

Isaac Newton, English Mathematician and Physicist

Perhaps the greatest scientist who ever lived, Sir Isaac Newton (1642–1727) owed his insight into universal gravitation to an apple in an orchard. According to the famous story, Newton was sitting in an orchard in the countryside and saw an apple fall to the ground. Wondering why objects fall toward Earth, he surmised that all matter attracts other matter.

Although German astronomer Johannes Kepler (1571–1630) had earlier determined that planets move in elliptical orbits around the Sun, Newton realized that the force that draws an apple to Earth is the same as the force holding heavenly bodies in their orbits. Newton published his revolutionary findings about universal gravitation in his 1687 book *Philosophiae naturalis principia mathematica* ("Mathematical Principles of Natural Philosophy").

In *Principia* Newton also arranged the findings of Italian astronomer Galileo Galilei (1564–1642) into three basic laws of motion: a body at rest remains at rest and a body in motion remains in motion; force is equal to mass times acceleration; and for every action there is an equal and opposite reaction. These three laws allowed Newton to calculate the gravitational force between Earth and the Moon. The unity of heaven and Earth were at last grasped by reason.

Eddington measured the deflection of starlight as it passed by the Sun and found it to be 1.61 seconds of an arc, well within experimental error. The publication of this proof made Einstein an instant celebrity and made "relativity" a household word, although it was not until 1924 that Eddington proved the final hypothesis concerning redshift with the spectral analysis of the star Sirius B.

To understand the redshift of light, consider sound waves. When an automobile drives by, sounding its horn, a noticeable change in pitch is heard because the car's velocity stretches the sound waves out. Einstein predicted that gravity would stretch out light waves as they travel through space. As the waves were lengthened, a shift in color, toward the low (red) end of the spectrum, would be observed. This phenomenon, that light would be shifted to a longer wavelength in the presence of a strong gravitational field, became known as the "Einstein shift."

Opposes war

Since the outbreak of World War I, Einstein had been opposed to war, and during the 1920s and 1930s he traveled extensively, presenting lectures on his views. With the rise of National Socialism (the Nazi Party) in Germany in the early 1930s, Einstein's position became difficult. Although he was not in Germany when Nazi leader Adolf Hitler assumed power, he had renewed his German citizenship. Nevertheless, he was under suspicion as both a Jew and a pacifist. (The German Nazis systematically persecuted Jews.) Fortunately, by 1930 Einstein had become internationally famous, and a number of institutions were eager to appoint him to their faculties.

Comes to America

In early 1933 Einstein decided not to return to Germany. Instead he accepted an appointment at the Institute for Advanced Studies in Princeton, New Jersey, where he spent the rest of his life. In addition to his continued work on unified field theory (a single theory that would explain all physical phenomena, particularly gravitation electromagnetism), Einstein was in demand as a speaker and wrote extensively on many topics, especially peace. The growing fascism and anti-Semitism of Hitler's regime, however, convinced him in 1939 to sign his name to a letter written by American physicist Leo Szilard informing President Franklin D. Roosevelt of the possibility that an atomic bomb could be developed. This letter led to the formation of the Manhattan Project for the construction of the world's first nuclear weapons. Einstein's work on relativity, particularly his formulation of the equation $E=mc^2$, was essential to the development of the atomic bomb, but Einstein himself did not participate in the project. He was considered a security risk, although he had renounced his German citizenship and had become a U.S. citizen in 1940.

Receives awards and honors

After World War II, in which the United States dropped two atomic bombs on Japan, Einstein became an ardent supporter of nuclear disarmament. He also lent his support to efforts to establish a world government and to the Zionist movement to establish a Jewish state. In 1952, after the death of Israel's first president, Chaim Weizmann, Einstein was invited to succeed him as president; he declined the offer. Among the many other honors accorded Einstein were the Barnard Medal of Columbia University in 1920, the Copley Medal of the Royal Society in 1925, the Gold Medal of the Royal Astronomical Society in 1926, the Max Planck Medal of the German Physical Society in 1929, and the Franklin Medal of the Franklin Institute in 1935. Einstein died at his home in Princeton on April 18, 1955, after suffering an aortic aneurysm.

Further Reading

Einstein, Albert, *Out of My Later Years,* originally published in 1950, reprinted, Greenwood Press, 1970.

Hunter, Nigel, *Einstein,* Bookwright Press, 1987.

Ireland, Karin, *Albert Einstein,* Silver Burdett, 1989.

McPherson, Stephanie Sammarino, *Ordinary Genius: The Story of Albert Einstein,* Carolrhoda Books, 1995.

Reef, Catherine, *Albert Einstein, Scientist of the Twentieth Century,* Dillon Press, 1991.

Sayen, Jamie, *Einstein in America: The Scientist's Conscience in the Age of Hitler and Hiroshima,* Crown, 1985.

White, Michael, *Einstein: A Life in Science,* Dutton, 1992.

Sandra M. Faber

Born December 28, 1944
Boston, Massachusetts

"I really think that we will probably find that our universe is the way it is because we are in it."

Astronomer and professor Sandra M. Faber has made significant contributions to the big bang theory of the origin of the universe. Faber's work in defining and developing theories of the evolution of galaxies has resulted in a number of discoveries concerning this model of the universe, including the Faber-Jackson relation, which relates a galaxy's size to the orbital speed of its stars. In 1984, working with theoretical physicist colleagues at the Lick Observatory of the University of California at Santa Cruz, Faber further hypothesized that the universe is composed largely of cold dark matter, rather than the hot neutrino-based matter scientists had earlier supposed. (Neutrinos are uncharged subatomic particles of matter that are believed to be massless.) In 1990 Faber and six other astronomers identified the great attractor, a clumping of galaxies with a strong gravitational pull.

Sandra M. Faber was born in Boston, Massachusetts, on December 28, 1944, the only child of Donald Edwin and Elizabeth Mackenzie (Borwick) Moore. Her father, an insurance executive, pursued science in his spare time; her mother was a homemaker with an interest in medicine. During her childhood in the Midwest, Faber became involved in astronomy while stargazing with her father. Her father was forty-three when she was born, and her mother was forty-two. Faber once related that her parents' were educated at the beginning of the twentieth century—rather than in the middle of it—and as a result Faber found herself influenced by early twentieth-century scientific literature, including *The Stars in Their Courses* by James Jeans and *Frontiers of Astronomy* by English astronomer Fred Hoyle. Both books advocated the steady-state theory of the universe's existence, which proposes that the universe has neither a beginning nor an end. Although Faber no longer holds this view, the intellectual experiences of her youth did have a strong influence on her.

Determined to earn Ph.D.

Faber attended Swarthmore College in Pennsylvania, obtaining a bachelor's degree in physics in 1966. (At Swarthmore she met Andrew Leigh Faber, whom she married the following year; they have two daughters.) Faber's mentor at Swarthmore was Sarah Lee Lippincott, an astronomer who was not a member of the university faculty. Observing that Lippincott's career had been limited by her lack of a doctoral degree, Faber was determined to obtain one herself.

Faber attended Harvard University, where she completed a Ph.D. in astronomy in 1972. While she was writing her thesis, however, the idea of pursuing further graduate work was somewhat limited by her husband's acceptance of a position at the Naval Research Laboratory in Washington, D.C. For a brief period she continued her research in an office at the lab. Then she was offered a residency at the Department of Terrestrial Magnetism, where she worked with astronomers Vera Cooper Rubin and Kent Ford.

Develops Faber-Jackson relation

When Faber completed her doctoral thesis on elliptical galaxies, she accepted a position as assistant professor and astronomer at the Lick Observatory at the University of California at Santa Cruz. Her early work at Lick led her to probe the formation, structure, and evolution of galaxies. As a result of her research she hypothesized that the outer regions of certain small galaxies had been stripped away by massive companion galaxies. In 1975 she and a graduate student named Robert Jackson developed the Faber-Jackson relation. The first of many galactic "sealing laws," this theory relates the size of elliptical galaxies to the internal orbital speeds of their component stars. It was later developed into an important formula used to calculate distances between galaxies.

Formulates theory of dark matter

In 1977 Faber was promoted to associate professor of astronomy at the Lick Observatory; she became a full professor two years later. During that same year, she and a colleague, John Gallagher, wrote a review in which they concluded that galaxies are surrounded by enormous pockets of invisible matter. This idea eventually led Faber and other scientists to propose that the galaxies themselves had been formed from invisible matter. Their findings resulted in the 1984 theory of dark matter, which suggests that invisible, or dark, matter is cold and lightless, consisting of a series of weakly interacting particles that eventually cluster together to form galaxies.

Discovers great attractor

In the early 1980s Faber collaborated with six other astronomers on the Seven Samurai project that measured the distances and velocities (speeds) of elliptical galaxies. Ellipti-

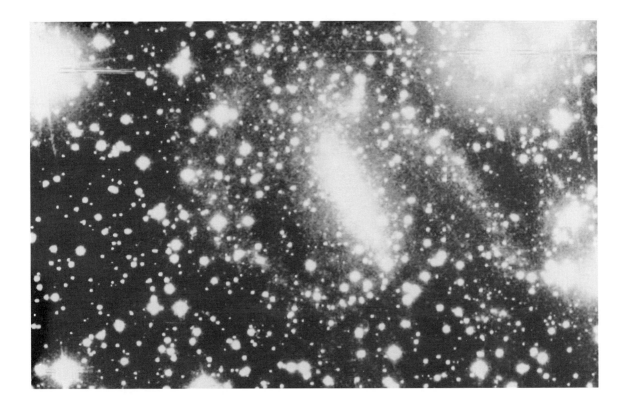

cal galaxies are collections of older stars arranged in an elliptical, or oval, pattern. Spiral galaxies contain a central nucleus
of older stars, a halo surrounding the nucleus, and smooth arms
of newer stars curving out from the center or ends. Elliptical
galaxies resemble just the nucleus and halo of their spiral
cousins. The Seven Samurai Project led to the 1990 discovery
of the great attractor. A concentrated "galaxy of clumped
galaxies" and matter that exerts a steady gravitational pull on
an area of space approximately 100,000 light-years across, the
great attractor includes our own Milky Way. (A light-year is
the distance light travels in one year, almost six trillion miles.)
The astronomers also identified over 250 galaxies—spiral and
elliptical—that are moving toward the great attractor at an
average rate of 400 miles per second.

Some scientists believe the existence of the great attractor has weakened proof of the big bang theory, which states
that the universe was created in a giant explosion of a super-
dense nucleus of matter some fifteen billion years ago. Others

*This spiral galaxy of stars
—hidden from direct view
behind the Milky Way—
was detected in 1994
through radio-wave
emissions; scientists
project that it is ten million
light-years away.*

Sandra M. Faber

contend that it contradicts Faber's own theory of dark matter. Yet Faber asserts, to the contrary, that her great attractor theory shows that dark matter consists of two new particles, one of which is massive, the other of which is light. A computer model of dark matter shows that such a mixture of particles would, in fact, produce such clumping.

Honored for achievements

In 1985 Faber was presented the Dannie Heineman Prize for astrophysics by the American Astronomical Society and the American Institute for Physics in recognition of her insights into and advancement of the theory of galaxy evolution. The following year she received an honorary doctorate of science from Swarthmore College. In addition, Faber is one of the few women to have become a member of the National Academy of Sciences. In 1990 she helped establish the Keck Observatory on the summit of Mauna Kea in Hawaii, where she is co-chairperson of the science committee. She is also a member of the wide-field camera design team for the Hubble Space Telescope, an orbiting observatory launched in 1990.

Further Reading

Bagne, Paul, "Interview With Sandra Faber," *Omni,* July 1990, pp. 62–92.

"Great Attractor Confirmed," *Sky and Telescope,* May 1990.

Hilts, Philip J., "Far Out in Space, A Giant Discovery," *New York Times,* January 12, 1990, p. 22.

Lightman, Alan, and Roberta Brawer, "Interview With Sandra Faber," *Origins,* Harvard University Press, 1990, pp. 324–40.

Pasachoff, J., "Interview With Sandra Faber," *Journey Through the Universe,* Saunders, 1992.

Travis, John, "Astronomy's Optical Illusion," *Science,* October 21, 1994.

Wilford, John Noble, "Star Clusters Astonish Astronomers," *New York Times,* January 21, 1992, p. 6.

Michael Faraday

Born September 27, 1791
Surrey, England
Died August 27, 1867
Surrey, England

Michael Faraday is often called the greatest experimental scientist of all time. In a series of brilliant experiments he confirmed that electricity and magnetism are in fact a single force and expressed his theory in Faraday's law of electromagnetic induction (1831). He also invented the electric motor, the transformer, and the generator—three devices that served as the foundation of the electrical age.

British scientist Michael Faraday is credited with discovering electromagnetism.

Divides time between school and work

Michael Faraday was born in Surrey in southeastern England on September 27, 1791, the third child of James, a blacksmith, and Margaret Hastwell Faraday. The family belonged to a small Protestant religious sect called the Sandemanians, who held beliefs similar to those of the Quakers, who are known for leading lives of simplicity, tolerance, and peace. Throughout his life Faraday was deeply religious and observed Sandemanian practices.

275

Michael Faraday's inventions initiated the electrical age. By inventing the electric motor, a revolutionary device that converted electrical energy into mechanical movement, he paved the way for the use of electrical machinery in industry. Another important innovation, the transformer, is still used to change the voltage of an electrical current, and his generator continues to be the most utilized way of creating electricity. Faraday also originated electroplating, a process that deposits a thin layer of one metal over another by means of electricity. This technique is now used to make tin cans and to coat inexpensive metal with gold or silver.

Because Faraday's father was in poor health, the family experienced periods of severe poverty. At the age of thirteen, Faraday left school to work as an apprentice to a bookseller named George Riebau. One of his tasks was to bind books between stiff leather covers. As he bound the books, he read them, keeping careful notes that he then bound for his own study purposes.

Becomes interested in science

After reading an article about electricity in the *Encyclopaedia Britannica*, Faraday became fascinated with this mysterious form of energy. By his late teens he had set up a simple lab in his room and was carrying out experiments to see if his own results would agree with what he read. He attended lectures on science and continued to take notes, which he showed to Riebau. Riebau in turn shared the notes with one of his customers, an amateur scientist named Mr. Dance, who asked to meet Faraday. Dance helped change the course of history by offering Faraday tickets to a series of lectures presented by the famous chemist **Humphry Davy** (see entry) at the Royal Institution of London, the leading scientific organization of the day. Davy is best known for discovering that electricity could break chemical compounds down into their elements.

Scientific ambitions

Faraday was captivated by Davy's four lectures. As always he took detailed notes, making drawings of the scientific instruments with which Davy carried out his demonstrations. Then he bound the notes and illustrations into a book, which he studied thoroughly. As the end of his apprenticeship with Riebau came near, Faraday needed to make a decision about his future. He wanted to be a scientist, but at that time science was viewed largely as a pastime for the upper class, not as a way to earn a living.

Takes a crucial step

Nevertheless, Faraday pursued his dream of becoming a scientist. Knowing Davy had left London after the lectures, he wrote a letter expressing his goals to Sir Joseph Banks, the president of the Royal Society, another British scientific association. When he received no answer, he called on Banks, only to be informed by a butler that Banks did not intend to reply. Determined not to be discouraged, Faraday wrote to Davy, who had by then returned to London. Davy was so impressed with Faraday's scientific zeal that he met with the aspiring scientist but told him there was no job available at the Royal Institution. Later, however, when Davy's assistant was fired, Faraday was hired on the spot.

Embarks on career and marriage

Faraday was twenty-one years old in 1813, when he began working at the Royal Institution. He remained there for the rest of his career, becoming director of the laboratory in 1825. Early on he helped Davy with various chemistry experiments while living in two rooms on the top floor of the Institution building. In 1814 and 1815 he accompanied Davy and his wife on a long trip through Europe. Although Faraday met many European scientists, much of the trip was unpleasant for him because Davy's wife insisted on treating him like a personal servant. Still, Faraday realized the value of working for Davy. By 1821 he had gained a wealth of knowledge from the elder scientist and had embarked on a new phase in his personal life as well: Faraday married Sarah Barnard, who was also a Sandemanian and the younger sister of one of his friends.

Experiments with electromagnetism

As Davy's assistant, Faraday made his share of discoveries in the fast-growing field of chemistry. A year or so before his marriage he received news from Denmark that shifted his attention back to his former interest in electricity. A Danish scientist, Hans Christian Oersted, announced his discovery that an electric current, if passed through a wire placed near a compass needle, would make the needle move. This suggested that electricity somehow creates a magnetic force, since a compass needle moves by magnetism. For the first time, a direct connection between the two forces had been confirmed experimentally.

Davy and Faraday had been hard at work on their own experiments with wires and compasses, trying to get the same results as Oersted and attempting to interpret those results. In the summer of 1821 Faraday was asked to write a summary of everything that was known about the budding field of electromagnetism. Scientists were aware that electrical and magnetic forces somehow acted over a distance, sending out some kind of invisible push or pull on each other. Since ancient times it was understood that magnets mysteriously attracted certain metals. Similarly, the resinous (semisolid) substance called amber (*elektron* in Greek), when rubbed with fur, was known to attract things like feathers. But the question remained as to how the seemingly magical force of electromagnetism actually worked.

Invents the electric motor

Faraday's first major breakthrough came in an experiment he conducted later in 1821. He filled a bowl with mercury, a liquid metal, and put a magnet upright in the middle, with the top just above the surface. Over the bowl he hung a wire whose lower end, tipped with cork, floated in the mercury just beside the top end of the magnet. The upper end was connected to the positive terminal of a battery. Taking another piece of wire, he attached one end to the negative terminal and put the other over the side of the bowl into the mercury. When the wire touched the mercury, the electrical circuit was completed, and the corked end of the first wire began moving in a circle around the magnet. Faraday had converted electrical energy into mechanical movement. He had invented the electric motor.

Produces other revolutionary inventions

As Faraday continued his experiments over the next decade, his understanding of electromagnetism grew. Soon after his invention of the electric motor, he devised the transformer, which is still used to change the voltage of an electrical current. Then, after improving his electric motor, he began experiments on reversing the process that made it work. If an electric current plus a magnet could produce mechanical movement, he reasoned, then mechanical movement plus a magnet should be able to produce a current. Faraday thus originated the scientific principle of induction, which explained how such a transfer of energy occurs. In 1831 came his third invention: the dynamo, or generator, which produced electricity by moving a magnet through a coil of wire. Faraday's generator remains the leading way to create electricity.

Retires because of ill health

In the 1830s Faraday developed techniques for electroplating, or depositing a thin layer of one metal over another by means of electricity. This technique is still used to make tin cans and to coat a cheaper metal with a more expensive one like gold or silver. By the 1840s, however, Faraday's health began to fail. He was soon forced to stop his experiments, and in 1861 he retired from teaching. Nevertheless, between 1839 and 1855 he wrote a three-volume work titled *Experimental Researches on Electricity,* which explained his work and ideas. Faraday died on August 27, 1867.

Further Reading

Brophy, Michael, *Michael Faraday,* Bookwright Press, 1991.

Gutnick, Martin J., *Michael Faraday: Creative Scientist,* Childrens Press, 1986.

Kendall, James, *Michael Faraday: Man of Simplicity,* Faber, 1955.

Anthony S. Fauci

Born December 24, 1940
Brooklyn, New York

"We've learned that AIDS is a ... disease of overlapping phases, progressing from infection to viral replication to chronic smoldering disease to profound depression of the immune system."

Since the beginning of his career Anthony S. Fauci has conducted research in immunology, the branch of medicine that studies how the human body protects itself from infections and diseases. In 1981 he began to focus on the human immunodeficiency virus (HIV), which causes acquired immunodeficiency syndrome (AIDS). His work has led to breakthroughs in understanding the progress of the virus, especially during the latency (inactive) period between infection and full-blown AIDS. Now the director of the National Institute of Allergy and Infectious Diseases (NIAID) and the Office of AIDS Research at the National Institutes of Health (NIH), Fauci has a significant involvement in AIDS research performed in the United States. Among his responsibilities is supervising the investigation of how the disease works and the development of vaccines and drug therapy to treat and cure it.

Anthony Stephen Fauci was born on December 24, 1940, in Brooklyn, New York, to Stephen A. Fauci, a pharmacist, and Eugenia A. Fauci, a homemaker. He attended a Jesuit (a

Roman Catholic religious order) high school in Manhattan, where he was an outstanding student and athlete. After high school Fauci entered Holy Cross College in Worcester, Massachusetts, as a premedical student, earning a bachelor's degree in 1962. He then attended Cornell University Medical School, from which he received a medical degree in 1966. He also completed both his internship and residency at Cornell.

In 1969 Fauci became a clinical associate in the Laboratory of Clinical Investigation of NIAID. Except for a year he spent as chief resident at the New York Hospital Cornell Medical Center, he has remained at NIH throughout his career. Fauci focused his earliest studies on the functioning of the human immune system and the impact of infectious diseases on the system. While he served as a senior staff fellow at NIAID, Fauci worked with two other researchers to identify the mechanisms (basic physical and chemical processes) of Wegener's granulomatosis, a relatively rare and fatal disease of the immune system involving the inflammation of blood vessels and organs. By 1971 Fauci had developed a blood regimen (systematic plan) for treating the disease that is 95 percent effective. He also found cures for lymphomatoid granulomatosis and polyarteritis nodosa, two other diseases of the immune system.

IMPACT

Searching for an effective drug therapy for AIDS, Anthony S. Fauci and his laboratory staff at the National Institutes of Health have run hundreds of clinical tests on medications such as azidothymidine (AZT). Fauci has promoted early use of drugs like AZT by terminally ill AIDS patients. Although no truly effective antiviral drug yet exists, researchers have developed drug therapies that can prolong the lives of AIDS victims. Potential AIDS vaccines are still being investigated, a process complicated by the difficulty in finding willing research volunteers. Since animals do not develop AIDS in the same way as humans, available research subjects are further limited. No viable vaccine is therefore expected before the year 2000.

Conducts innovative AIDS research

In 1972 Fauci became a senior investigator at NIAID, then two years later he was named head of the Clinical Physiology Section. By 1977 he had become deputy clinical director of NIAID, which has eleven divisions. Within a few years he

An azidothymidine (AZT) crystal magnified twenty-five times; AZT is the first therapeutic agent that seems to hold promise for some AIDS patients.

had shifted the focus of the Laboratory of Clinical Infection toward the investigation of the nature of AIDS. AIDS is a very difficult disease to study, treat, and cure because it destroys the body's immune system. Fauci's lab was responsible for an important step forward in AIDS research when it demonstrated how the HIV virus affects T4 helper cells (white blood cells that are an important part of the body's immune system) and thus causes AIDS to be fatal. Fauci also worked to use early therapeutic techniques, including bone-marrow transplants, to save the lives of AIDS patients.

Fauci was appointed director of NIAID in 1984, and the following year became coordinator of all AIDS research at NIH. During his tenure he has worked not only against AIDS but also against governmental indifference to the disease by winning increasingly larger budgets for research. In 1988, when the Office of AIDS Research was founded, Fauci became director of the new division while also retaining his position as head of NIH. Since then he and his laboratory

Flossie Wong-Staal, Chinese-born American virologist

One of the world's leading authorities on the study of viruses, Flossie Wong-Staal (1947–) is credited as a discoverer of HIV, the virus that causes AIDS. Along with her colleagues at the National Cancer Institute, Wong-Staal was the first researcher to clone, or make a copy of, the human immunodeficiency virus (HIV)—the virus that causes the acquired immunodeficiency virus (AIDS)—which allowed them to decipher its structure. In 1990 Wong-Staal left the National Cancer Institute to become the Florence Riford Chair in AIDS Research at the University of California at San Diego. In that position, Wong-Staal is focusing on developing a vaccine to combat the AIDS virus and on therapies to treat those already suffering from the disease.

teams have established a threefold approach to combating AIDS: researching the mechanism of HIV, developing and testing drug therapies, and creating an AIDS vaccine.

Makes important discovery

In 1993 Fauci and his team disproved the theory that HIV remains dormant (not actively growing) for approximately ten years. They showed that, to the contrary, the virus attacks the lymph nodes (places in the body where white blood cells are made) and reproduces itself in white blood cells known as CD4 cells. This discovery could lead to new and different approaches in the early treatment of HIV-positive patients. Other discoveries coming from Fauci's lab include the finding, in 1987, that a protein substance known as cytokine may be responsible for triggering full-blown AIDS. Fauci and his researchers also recognized the macrophage (a type of immune system cell that destroys germs in the body) as the means for transmission of AIDS.

Honored for contributions

Fauci married Christine Grady, a clinical nurse and medical ethicist (a specialist in medical ethics), in 1985. They have three daughters: Jennifer, Megan, and Allison. Widely recognized for his research, Fauci is the recipient of numerous prizes and awards. Among them are the Arthur Flemming Award (1979), the U.S. Public Health Service Distinguished Service Medal (1984), the National Medical Research Award from the National Research Council (1989), and the Dr. Nathan Davis Award from the American Medical Association (1992). Fauci is also a fellow of the American Academy of Arts and Sciences and holds several honorary degrees. He is the author or coauthor of more than eight hundred scientific articles and has edited a number of medical textbooks.

Further Reading

Breo, Dennis L., "The U.S. Race to 'Cure' AIDS," *Journal of the American Medical Association,* June 9, 1993, pp. 2898–2900.

Current Biography Yearbook: 1988, H. W. Wilson, 1989, pp. 153–56.

Fauci, Anthony, "Multifactorial Nature of Human Immunodeficiency Virus Disease," *Science,* November 12, 1993.

Hilts, Philip J., "AIDS Advocates Are Angry at U.S. But Its Research Chief Wins Respect," *New York Times,* September 4, 1990, p. A14.

Russell, Christine, "Anthony Fauci: A Hard-Driving Leader of the Lab War on AIDS," *Washington Post,* November 3, 1986, pp. A12–13.

Enrico Fermi

Born September 29, 1901
Rome, Italy
Died November 28, 1954
Chicago, Illinois

Italian scientist Enrico Fermi was an experimenter, a theorist, and an educator who helped shape the field of modern physics, the study of matter and forces. He exhibited intellectual talents early on, and by the age of twenty-five he had developed a statistical method, later known as Fermi-Dirac statistical mechanics, for describing the behavior of a cloud of electrons. While teaching in Italy he devised an explanation for beta decay (a process of radioactive decomposition within an atomic nucleus) and identified the neutrino (a fundamental particle of matter). For his experiments with neutrons he was awarded the 1938 Nobel Prize for physics. Fermi also created the first self-sustaining nuclear chain reaction. This research led to his participation in the U.S. government's top-secret Manhattan Project, which yielded the first atomic bomb.

Enrico Fermi made astounding advancements in the field of nuclear physics. He was awarded the Nobel Prize for physics for his work in nuclear bombardment.

Masters physics on his own

Fermi was born in Rome, Italy, on September 29, 1901, to Alberto Fermi, a railway employee, and Ida de Gattis Fermi, a

Enrico Fermi changed the face of modern physics with his ground-breaking studies of atomic nuclei. His experiments with nuclear bombardment earned him the 1938 Nobel Prize for physics and helped lead to the development of the first nuclear reactor—and, ultimately, the first atomic bomb.

teacher. While Fermi was still a teenager he became interested in physics and taught himself the basics of the subject. A friend of his father, Adolfo Amidei, assumed some responsibility for Fermi's intellectual development, supplying him with books on mathematics and physics. By the time Fermi graduated from high school he knew as much classical physics as the typical university graduate student.

Invents mathematical system

When Fermi applied for a scholarship at the Reale Scuola Normale in Pisa in 1918, he wrote his entrance essay on the mathematics and physics of vibrating reeds. The essay convinced the examiners he was a candidate of unusual promise. Four years later, at the age of twenty-one, Fermi earned a Ph.D. in physics with highest honors. Since Germany offered better opportunities for advanced students of science, he continued his graduate studies at the German universities of Göttingen and Leiden. In 1924 he returned to Italy and took a teaching position at the University of Florence. During his first year at Florence, Fermi wrote a paper that established his growing reputation among physicists.

Fermi's paper outlined a new application of a revolutionary theory on the behavior of particles of matter—a theory that had been formulated by Austrian-born American physicist Wolfgang Pauli earlier that same year. The theory, called Pauli's Exclusion Principle, restricts the possible location of electrons in atoms, allowing no two electrons to exist in the same quantum state (restricted orbits). Fermi postulated that the same rules developed by Pauli might also explain the behavior of "clouds" of electrons in a gas. The mathematical system he invented, later developed independently by English mathematician and physicist Paul Dirac, came to be known as Fermi-Dirac statistical mechanics, and it describes the actions of subatomic particles.

Helps revitalize Italian physics

Fermi's accomplishment came at an opportune time. In Rome, physicist Orso Mario Corbino had just begun a campaign to revitalize Italian science, a field that had experienced a long period of decline. As both chairman of the physics department at the University of Rome and a powerful figure in the Italian government, Corbino obtained authorization to create a new chair of theoretical physics at the university. In 1926 Fermi left Florence to assume this new position. Over the next six years a number of first-class physicists and students were attracted to Rome. During this period of scientific renaissance, Fermi and his colleagues focused their energies on the latest developments in atomic theory. By 1930 Fermi had embarked on a study of the atomic nucleus.

Discovers neutrino and weak force

One of the first problems Fermi tackled was beta decay. Beta decay is the process by which a neutron in an atomic nucleus breaks apart into a proton and an electron. The electron is then emitted from the nucleus as a beta particle. The mechanics of beta decay appeared to violate known physical principles (conservation laws) and were therefore the subject of intense research in the early 1930s. Pauli had suggested that the apparent violation of conservation laws observed during beta decay could be explained by assuming the existence of a tiny particle that was also released during the event. Fermi later named that particle the neutrino ("little neutron").

In 1933 Fermi proposed his own theory for beta decay. He said the event occurs because a neutron moves from a state of higher energy to one of lower energy as it undergoes conversion to a proton and electron. To explain the process by which this occurs, Fermi postulated the existence of a new kind of force, now known as weak force.

Conducts neutron bombardment

Fermi's interest in atomic nuclei prompted him to return to the laboratory and design a number of experiments. An important factor motivating his research was the then-recent discovery of artificial radioactivity by Irène Joliot-Curie and her husband, Frédéric Joliot-Curie. The Joliot-Curies had found that bombarding stable isotopes (atoms in chemical elements) with alpha (positively charged) particles would convert the original isotopes into unstable, radioactive forms. Fermi reasoned that this type of experiment might be even more effective if neutrons, rather than alpha particles, were used as the "bullets." Neutrons have no electrical charge and are, therefore, not repelled by either the negatively charged electrons or the positively charged protons in an atom.

Beginning in 1934 Fermi and his colleagues systematically subjected one element after another to bombardment by neutrons. Over a period of months he was able to show that thirty-seven of the sixty-three elements he studied could be converted to radioactive forms by neutron bombardment. The element among all others that especially intrigued Fermi was uranium.

But the physicist did not recognize the revolutionary nature of his experimental results. Bombardment of uranium with neutrons resulted not in a simple nuclear transformation but in nuclear fission, a process during which the uranium atom is split, unleashing tremendous amounts of energy. The significance of this reaction was later explained by **Lise Meitner** (see entry) and Otto Robert Frisch.

Wins Nobel Prize, defects to U.S.

In 1938 Fermi was informed that he had won the Nobel Prize for physics in recognition of his research on neutron bombardment. After accepting the prize in Stockholm, Sweden, he and his family headed directly for the United States. Fascist dictator Benito Mussolini had come to power in Italy and the first signs of World War II, including widespread anti-Semitism (prejudice against Jewish people), were becoming evident throughout Europe. Because his wife was Jewish, Fermi no longer felt comfortable working in Italy. He accepted a new post as professor of physics at Columbia University in New York City.

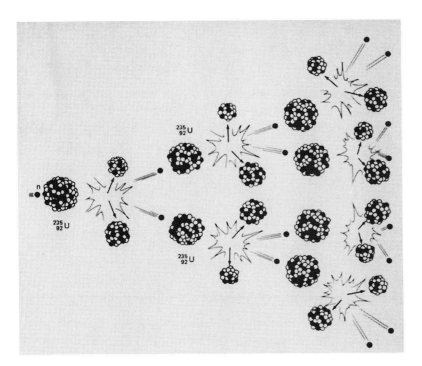

A nuclear chain reaction: the successive fissioning of ever-increasing numbers of uranium-235 atoms.

Joins Manhattan Project

The timing of Fermi's arrival in the United States was indeed fortuitous. At almost the same time, **Niels Bohr** (see entry) was informing American physicists of the discovery of nuclear fission by Otto Hahn and Fritz Strassmann in Germany. A movement was soon under way to alert the U.S. government to the political and military implications of the Hahn-Strassmann discovery. That movement culminated in the famous August 2, 1939, letter to President Franklin D. Roosevelt written by Hungarian-American physicist Leo Szilard and signed by the great German-born American physicist **Albert Einstein** (see entry). The scientists feared the prospect of nuclear weapons being developed and used by the enemy forces during World War II.

Fermi's immediate future was now laid out for him. He became involved in the Manhattan Project, a secret research effort sponsored by the U.S. government that involved the nation's top scientists. Their task was to determine whether a controlled nuclear chain reaction was possible, and, if so, how

Lloyd Albert Quarterman, American Chemist

As a member of the Manhattan Project team, Lloyd Albert Quarterman (1918–1982) helped split the first atom and create the first atomic reactor. He was one of only six African Americans assigned to the project. Although his specific duties were kept secret, it is known that Quarterman worked with two of the laboratories in the overall network, at Columbia University in New York City and at the hidden University of Chicago facility in Illinois. The Columbia team was involved in splitting an atom, which would provide the energy necessary to fuel the atom bomb. Quarterman played a key role in developing a uranium isotope, a fundamental step in this process. Working under Enrico Fermi as part of the Chicago team, Quarterman participated in developing and building the first nuclear reactor or pile.

After the Manhattan Project officially closed in 1946, the government converted the Chicago lab into the Argonne National Laboratories and brought it above ground to a Chicago suburb. Quarterman remained with the Argonne project, and contributed to the construction of the first nuclear power plant.

it could be used in the construction of a nuclear weapon. Although Fermi's initial work was carried out at Columbia, he eventually moved to the University of Chicago.

Creates nuclear chain reaction

The effort to produce a sustained nuclear chain reaction came to a successful conclusion in Fermi's lab under the squash courts at the university on December 2, 1942. At 3:21 P.M., instruments indicated that a self-sustaining chain reaction was taking place in the world's first atomic "pile," a primitive nuclear reactor. For the next two years Fermi continued his research on nuclear fission at the Argonne National Laboratory outside of Chicago. In 1944 he and his wife became naturalized citizens of the United States. That same year the Fermis moved to Los Alamos, New Mexico, where final assembly of the first nuclear weapons was to occur.

At Los Alamos, Fermi was put in charge of his own division (the F division) with the job of solving special problems as they arose during construction of the first atomic bombs. After the testing and eventual dropping of the bombs on Japan in 1945, Fermi concluded his work with the Manhattan Project. He returned to the University of Chicago, where he became Charles H. Swift Distinguished Service Professor of Physics and a member of the newly created Institute for Nuclear Studies.

Fermi remained at Chicago for the rest of his life. He received numerous honorary degrees and other awards, among them the Civilian Medal of Merit in 1946 for his work on the Manhattan Project, the Franklin Medal from the Franklin Institute, and the Transenter Medal from the University of Liége in Belgium. Fermium, atomic element 100 (Fm), and the fermimeter, the unit for nuclear dimensions, were named for Fermi.

After Fermi's health began to fail in 1954, exploratory surgery revealed that he had stomach cancer. He refused to quit working, however, and continued his research up to the very end of his life. He died in his sleep on November 28, 1954. The U.S. Atomic Energy Commission later named him the recipient of the first Enrico Fermi Award.

Further Reading

Epstein, Sam, *Enrico Fermi, Father of Atomic Power,* Garrard, 1970.

Fermi, Laura, *Atoms in the Family: My Life with Enrico Fermi,* University of Chicago Press, 1954.

Garraty, John, ed., *Dictionary of American Biography,* Supplement 5, Scribner, 1955, pp. 219–21.

Gillispie, Charles Coulson, ed., *Dictionary of Scientific Biography,* Volume 4, Scribner, 1975, pp. 576–83.

Lichello, Robert, *Enrico Fermi, Father of the Atomic Bomb,* SamHar Press, 1971.

McGraw-Hill Modern Men of Science, Volume 1, McGraw-Hill, 1984, pp. 168–69.

Alexander Fleming

Born August 6, 1881
Lochfield, Scotland
Died March 11, 1955
London, England

"I had no suspicion that I had got a clue to the most powerful therapeutic substance yet used to defeat bacterial infections in the human body."

As the result of a routine laboratory accident Alexander Fleming discovered penicillin, which was eventually called a "wonder drug" because of its ability to cure a wide range of often-fatal bacterial illnesses. Nevertheless, more than ten years passed between the time Fleming first identified penicillin and another team of researchers successfully produced it in mass quantities. The discovery of penicillin ushered in an age of life-saving antibiotics, such as streptomycin, aureomycin, terramycin, and bacitracin.

Studies medicine

Alexander Fleming grew up on a sheep farm near Dorval, Scotland, one of eight children of Hugh Fleming and Mary Morton Fleming. Faced with limited career opportunities in his native country, he left home at the age of thirteen. Fleming then lived with an older brother in London, where he attended classes for two years at Regent Street Polytechnic, an applied sciences school. He worked as a clerk in a shipping company until an inheritance enabled him to enroll at St. Mary's Hospital Medical School in 1901. Fleming performed brilliantly, winning numerous class prizes for high test scores, including a scholarship that paid his tuition for the first year.

Upon being licensed as a doctor by the Royal College of Physicians in 1906, Fleming accepted a research position at St. Mary's in bacteriology, the scientific study of bacteria. He worked in the inoculation department (later renamed the Wright-Fleming Institute of Microbiology) as an assistant to Sir Almroth Wright, a distinguished British physician who pioneered the use of vaccine therapy to fight bacterial infections such as typhoid. He also became one of the first to use Salvarsan, an arsenic compound developed by German bacteriologist Paul Ehrlich (see box), to treat syphilis in Great Britain. Two years later Fleming passed his final medical examinations and was awarded the gold medal of the university for academic excellence.

Pursues research

Fleming divided his time between a research post at St. Mary's and a professorship in bacteriology at the University of London. He preferred working in the laboratory and even managed to continue his research during World War I as a member of the Royal Army Medical Corps. Disturbed by the high rate of death from infected wounds, Fleming began to question the effectiveness of treating dead or damaged tissue with certain antiseptics. In a series of ingenious experiments, he proved that the antiseptics then in use actually did more harm than good by killing the white cells of the immune system and thus making it easier for infection to develop.

Fails to convince scientists

After the war Fleming returned to St. Mary's and resumed his study of bacteriology, focusing primarily on identifying some naturally occurring substance that could fight bacteria without harming healthy tissue or weakening the body's self-defense mechanisms. In 1921 he took a major step in that direction when he discovered that human tears and nasal mucus as well as egg whites all contain a similar chemical that dissolves some bacteria. He called the new antibiotic lysozyme and published several articles on its capabilities, but most scientists dismissed his findings.

Notices something unusual

Despite the lack of enthusiasm among his colleagues, Fleming continued his research on bacteria-fighting agents. One day in 1928 he was in his basement laboratory checking some staphylococci bacteria cultures. A particular culture caught his eye. Accidently left uncovered for several days, it had been contaminated by a mold spore that had blown in through a window. Fleming was about to rinse off the dish when he noticed something highly unusual: in the area surrounding the greenish-blue spot of mold, the staphylococci had completely disappeared; elsewhere on the plate, however, it was still thriving.

Discovers penicillin

Intrigued, Fleming immediately began to grow more of the mold so that he could study its amazing properties. Over the next eight months he discovered that it secreted a powerful substance, which he named penicillin after the *Penicillium Chrysogenum notatum* mold (often found in rotting fruit or bread) from which it originated. That substance destroyed not only staphylococci but a number of other deadly bacteria, including streptococci and pneumococci. Testing small doses first on laboratory animals and later on himself, he also learned it was not toxic.

The *Penicillium* mold proved to be extremely difficult to grow in the laboratory, however, and the meager amount of penicillin that could be extracted from a culture was unstable and tainted with foreign proteins. Fleming turned to a biologist friend for help, but neither scientist was able to find a way to produce enough pure penicillin to treat ill patients. Therefore, they failed to demonstrate the unusual mold's potential as an antibiotic.

Hoping to interest others in tackling the problem, Fleming presented a report on his experiments at a meeting of bacteriologists in May 1929. Unfortunately, the presentation coincided with a surge of interest in new sulfa drugs, which were then being heralded as the cure-all for infectious diseases. Fleming moved on to other research, but he did not give up on penicillin; he always kept a strain of the original mold growing in a corner of his laboratory.

Fleming's discovery revived

By the late 1930s it was clear that the sulfa drugs had been greatly overrated, for they exhibited a variety of toxic side effects—such as kidney damage—in some patients. With the prospect of another world war breaking out, there was an urgent need for a new substance to combat wound infections. At Oxford University, Australian-born pathologist Howard W. Florey searched through old professional journals for clues to a possible breakthrough. (A pathologist is a doctor who is an expert in the causes, symptoms, and results of diseases.) In 1938, after coming across Fleming's report on penicillin, Florey paid him a visit. Fleming gave Florey a sample of the *Penicillium* mold he had been keeping alive in his laboratory.

Working with the chemist Ernst Chain, Florey verified all of Fleming's observations, including the difficulty of producing sufficient amounts of penicillin for use on patients. Although the experiments they ran on lab animals proved that penicillin worked, early tests on humans were less conclusive.

Paul Ehrlich, German bacteriologist

Through his comprehensive study of the effects of chemicals in the human body, Paul Ehrlich (1854–1915) fathered the fields of chemotherapy (the treatment of disease with chemical agents) and hematology (the study of blood). He also made important contributions to the understanding of immunity (the body's ability to fight disease) and discovered the first effective treatment of the sexually transmitted disease syphilis. Caused by a microorganism called spirochete (pronounced SPY-ruh-keet), syphilis meant a slow and painful death for thousands of people. In 1910 Ehrlich announced that chemical 606, which he called Salvarsan, could cure syphilis.

For several years Ehrlich suffered personal and professional attacks because of his work with syphilis. Some felt the disease was just punishment for sinful sexual behavior and attacked Ehrlich for searching for a cure. The administration of the drug was also complicated, even risky at first, and when a few patients died because doctors administering the drug failed to follow Ehrlich's instructions, Ehrlich was accused of fraud. The attacks finally ceased in 1914 when the German parliament finally endorsed his claim as authentic. Unfortunately, the strain surrounding his controversial efforts to cure syphilis took its toll on his health, and Ehrlich suffered a series of strokes during his last year that led to his death in Bad Homburg, Germany, in 1915.

Mass produces penicillin

Florey and Chain then concentrated on producing enough purified penicillin to demonstrate its power on humans; by 1941 they documented nearly two hundred cases in which penicillin therapy had destroyed potentially fatal infections. The next step was to find financial and technical assistance in mass producing the antibiotic. By mid-1943 factories in England and the United States had geared up to produce 400 million units of penicillin in a five-month period, a number that increased to over nine billion units per month by the end of the year. The therapeutic power of penicillin, the "miracle drug," had been clearly established. Although initial production was designated for military use only, penicillin became available to the civilian population in 1944.

Achieves recognition and fame

As codiscoverers of this wonder drug, Fleming and Florey were showered with honors. Both were knighted in 1944, and in 1945 Fleming, Florey, and Chain shared the Nobel Prize in medicine. None of them profited financially from the sale of penicillin, however. Fleming routinely gave any money he received to St. Mary's for research. Because of the rather dramatic circumstances surrounding his discovery, Fleming, more so than Florey or Chain, became an international celebrity. But he was always quick to credit the others with developing penicillin into a readily available substance that doctors could use to treat their patients.

Fleming continued to spend as much time as possible in his laboratory, his efforts focused on examining the bacteria-fighting capabilities of other molds. In 1946 he was named director of the Wright-Fleming Institute, a position he held until November 1954, when he retired to pursue his own research. On March 11, 1955, he died of a heart attack in London.

Further Reading

Kaye, Judith, *The Life of Alexander Fleming,* Holt, 1993.

MacFarlane, Gwyn, *Alexander Fleming: The Man and the Myth,* Harvard University Press, 1984.

Smithsonian, November 1990, pp. 173–87.

Tames, Richard, *Alexander Fleming,* F. Watts, 1990.

Sally Fox

Born in 1956
Menlo Park, California

"It's a real Jack and the Beanstalk story."

S ally Fox has built an innovative and successful business on an ancient agricultural product: she developed a natural color cotton fiber called FoxFibre that is free of chemical coloring agents and pesticides. FoxFibre is marketed worldwide through her company, Natural Cotton Colours.

Colored cotton fiber is not new; it has been grown for thousands of years. However, as Fox noted in an interview for *Discover* magazine, "All of the brown cottons were pretty much native to the Americas, but their fibers were too short to be machine spun for commercial use." Commercial white cotton is brown cotton that has been bleached; colored cotton is made from brown cotton that has been bleached and then dyed. These processes are hazardous to the environment because bleaching and dyeing produce toxic chemicals, whereas natural colored (undyed brown) cotton is environmentally safe.

Sally Fox was born in Menlo Park, California, in 1956. As a child she avidly pursued the hobby of hand-spinning her own yarn and weaving it into cloth items. Before starting her business in 1986, she worked at various jobs and served a tour of duty as a Peace Corps volunteer. After earning a degree in biology in 1982, she began work as an entomologist (a scientist who studies insects), specializing in pest resistance in cotton seeds. Her adventure as an entrepreneur (a person who risks his or her own money to organize a business venture) began that year, when the father of one of her friends handed her a bag of brown cotton seeds and lint. Although he had asked Fox to test the pest resistance of the seeds, she was more interested in the color because she knew hand-spinners and weavers preferred undyed, natural brown cotton to chemically treated fibers. Curious to know whether she could in fact grow brown cotton, she began her experiment by planting some of the brown-bagged seeds in plastic pots in the backyard of her mother's home in Menlo Park.

Develops raw brown cotton

Fox did not have success overnight; it took a few years for her to see results in her experiments. While working at agricultural jobs in California, she planted seeds wherever she could find space. Each year she planted seeds from the previous season's best plants to produce the strongest colors and extend the length of the cotton fibers. For instance, her colored cotton fibers in the 1982 crop were three-fourths of an inch long, too short to be spun into yarn. (They had to be at least one inch.)

In 1983 Fox grew her crop in thirty pots on the back porch of her apartment, then in 1984 and 1985 she planted half an acre at a friend's farm. By 1986 she had expanded her test plot to two acres on a farmer's property. She began to see results: the brown seeds produced both brown and green cotton, and the fibers were one inch in length. Although she still faced the problem of developing seeds that would yield a consistent color, she opened a mail-order business offering raw brown cotton to hand-spinning hobbyists.

Meets opposition

Again Fox did not experience instant success. During the first year of her business, orders for cotton totaled less than $1,000. She continued improving her crops, and by 1988 the fibers were long enough to be spun by machine. After a Japanese mill bought half of her 12-acre crop of brown and green cotton for making naturally colored towels, she recognized she could sell the cotton to a commercial market. She obtained a trademark for her process, naming it "FoxFibre," and then quit her job studying insect-killing bacteria.

With a loan from relatives Fox bought a farm in the San Joaquin Valley, a prime cotton-growing area, and began promoting her company, Natural Cotton Colours. In 1990, however, she encountered a major obstacle. She had received an order for 800,000 pounds of cotton, totaling $4 million, a crop that would require 2,000 acres of land. Before commissioning farmers to grow so much cotton, however, she had to obtain permission from the San Joaquin Valley cotton board. Her request was turned down because other farmers feared that her colored cotton would contaminate their white cotton by cross-pollination.

Having no time to waste because the planting season was about to begin, Fox traveled to Texas and Arizona in search of farmers who could grow the cotton. Although she finally found growers, they were able to plant only 400 acres, substantially reducing her potential income. Yet luck was on her side. Executives at Levi Strauss, the denim manufacturer based in San Francisco, had seen newspaper accounts of Fox's problem with the cotton board and bought some of her cotton for research. By the end of the year, Levi Strauss had contracted to buy cotton from her 1991 and 1992 crops.

Expands business

After making a modest profit and paying off her debts, Fox was able to expand her business. She contacted other manufacturers and distributors who bought FoxFibre for making clothing and bed sheets. Consumer response was enthusiastic, primarily because people liked buying products made from materials free of chemical dyes and pesticides. They also liked the colors produced by the cotton—Coyote, a reddish brown; Buffalo, a bronze brown; and Palo Verde, an olive green—which manufacturers frequently combine with white cotton fibers to produce other shades and hues. In addition Fox created stripes, checks, and plaids in combinations of the basic browns and greens.

Continues experiments

In 1993 Fox suffered yet another setback when the San Joaquin cotton board reduced the amount of land she was allotted for testing and research, or breeding, from 40 acres to 10. Since most of her growers were already in Arizona, Fox decided to move Natural Cotton Colours headquarters to Wickenburg, Arizona, where the business is now thriving.

When Fox discovered that FoxFibre is fire resistant, she began work on a nonflammable cotton for children's sleepwear. She is also experimenting with other colors. While she may never produce blue or pink fibers, Fox told her *Discover* interviewer that she predicts a wider variety of natural hues someday: "Cotton, like wood, is mainly cellulose, and has the same molecules that give wood its colors. You'll see the same color range in cotton that you see in wood—everything from the greens of the young wood to yellow, to red, to ebony."

Further Reading

Discover, October 1994, p. 72.

Forbes, August 15, 1994.

House Beautiful, November 1993, pp. 72–73.

Rosalind Franklin

Born July 25, 1920
London, England
Died April 16, 1958
London, England

Rosalind Franklin was a geneticist who was instrumental in the discovery of DNA.

Rosalind Franklin was a geneticist whose work on X-ray diffraction helped lead to the discovery of the molecular structure of deoxyribonucleic acid (DNA), which directs cell growth. Her research provided the scientific evidence upon which American biologist **James D. Watson** and British physicist **Francis Crick** (see entries) based their double-helix molecular model of DNA. Watson, Crick, and biophysicist Maurice Wilkins won the Nobel Prize in 1962 for this discovery. Franklin's failure to receive recognition in her lifetime sparked controversy in the scientific world, considering her significant role in untangling the complex structure and function of DNA.

Excels in science

Rosalind Elsie Franklin was born in London, England, on July 25, 1920. Both of her parents were socialists, advocates of a political and economic system based on government control of the production and distribution of goods—a system intended to lead to the attainment of a classless society. Ellis Franklin devoted his life to teaching at the Working Men's College, while his wife, Muriel Waley Franklin, cared for their five children. From an early age Franklin excelled at science. She attended St. Paul's Girls' School, one of the few educational institutions in Britain that offered physics and chemistry to female students. As a foundation scholar at the school, Franklin decided at the age of fifteen to pursue a career in science, despite her father's advice to consider social work. In 1938 she enrolled at Newnham College in Cambridge.

Learns X-ray diffraction

After graduating in 1941 Franklin accepted a research scholarship at Newnham to study gas-phase chromatography —chemical separation and analysis—with future Nobel Prize winner Ronald G. W. Norrish. Finding Norrish difficult to work with, she quit graduate school the following year. Franklin then took a job as assistant research officer with the British Coal Utilization Research Association, where she studied the micro-structures of coals. In 1947 she moved to Paris to work with the Laboratoire Central des Services Chimiques de l'Etat (Central Laboratory of State Chemical Services). There she became fluent in French and learned X-ray diffraction (the method of determining the structure of crystals through the way in which they scatter X rays). Using this technique, Franklin was able to describe in exacting detail the structure of carbon and the changes that occur when carbon is heated to form graphite.

Joins DNA research team

In 1951 Franklin left Paris for London, where she had received a fellowship to join a research team headed by Sir John T. Randall at King's College at the University of London. She was given the task of setting up an X-ray diffraction unit in the laboratory to take pictures of DNA, a long, chainlike molecule in the nucleus of most living cells that carries the

The story of a great scientific discovery usually involves a combination of inspiration, hard work, and good fortune. In the case of the discovery of DNA, controversy also played a role. Despite the fact that Rosalind Franklin may have been the first scientist to determine the structure of DNA, she never received official recognition for her important scientific contribution. Franklin died in 1958, so Francis Crick, James D. Watson, and Maurice Wilkins received the 1962 Nobel Prize for this discovery. (The Nobel committee honors only living recipients.) Many critics believe Franklin's work was underestimated because of her insistence on working independently, her untimely death, and the prejudices against women in the English scientific community during the 1950s.

genetic (hereditary) material in all organisms. Franklin thus had the opportunity to work on one of the most challenging research problems of the time—figuring out the structure and function of DNA.

When Franklin arrived at Randall's laboratory she began working with Raymond Gosling, a student who had been attempting to capture pictures of the elusive DNA. Another scientist on the team, Maurice Wilkins, was already involved in the project assigned to Franklin. Wilkins and Franklin immediately had a personality conflict. Franklin's biographers have not been able to determine exactly why they could not find common ground, although some have suggested that Wilkins felt threatened because Franklin was a woman who considered herself his equal. But the animosity apparently did not distract Franklin from her work; shortly after arriving at King's College she began X-raying DNA fibers Wilkins had obtained from a Swiss investigator.

Encounters Watson

In November 1952, a few months after joining Randall's team, Franklin gave a talk describing preliminary pictures she had obtained of the DNA molecule as it transformed from a crystalline form, or A pattern, to a wet form, or B pattern, through an increase in relative humidity. She suggested the pictures showed that phosphate groups (phosphoric acids, later shown to be among the building blocks of DNA) might lie outside the molecule. In the audience was James Watson, an American biologist. He and British physicist Francis Crick were working at Cambridge on unraveling the molecular structure of DNA. Franklin reportedly refused to set aside the data she had obtained from X-ray diffraction pictures of the crystalline form of DNA, making Watson and Crick's goal of building a model of the DNA molecule that much more difficult. Perhaps for that reason Franklin publicly criticized the notion, which was then gaining acceptance, that DNA had a helical (spiral) structure. Nevertheless, in her unpublished reports she suggested the probability that the B (wet) form of DNA showed a helical structure as did, perhaps, the A (crystalline) form.

Provides evidence of double-helix structure

In 1952 Franklin and Gosling continued to investigate DNA's A pattern. By January 1953 Franklin had started model-building, but she could think of no structure that would accommodate all of the evidence she had gathered from her X-ray diffraction pictures. She ruled out both single and multiple-stranded helices in favor of a figure-eight shape. In the meantime Watson and Crick had begun their own model building at Cambridge because they suspected that American chemist **Linus Pauling** (see entry) was about to make a DNA discovery of his own. Watson had also grown quite close to Wilkins. As Watson recalls in his book *The Double Helix,* Wilkins showed him (without Franklin's permission) DNA diffraction pictures that Franklin had taken.

Upon seeing the evidence he needed to prove the helical structure of DNA, Watson and Crick began writing what would become one of the best-known scientific papers of the century, "A Structure for Deoxyribose Nucleic Acid," in which they described a double-helix DNA molecular model. Franklin and Gosling quickly revised a report of their own so it could appear along with Watson and Crick's paper. It is unclear how close Franklin had come to making a similar discovery; however, unpublished drafts of her paper reveal she had determined the sugar-phosphate backbone of the helix before Watson and Crick's model was made public.

Watson and Crick claim discovery

On April 25, 1953, Watson and Crick published their article in the British science journal *Nature*. Accompanying it was the article by Franklin and Gosling, which provided essential evidence for the double-helix theory. Watson and Crick's model showed that the building blocks of DNA—sugars, phosphates, and pairs of substances known as bases—form bonds in a regular sequence, much like the structure of a spiraling ladder. Knowledge of the distances between the atoms in the molecule was necessary to the researchers in establishing the structure of DNA. For this reason Franklin's X-ray diffraction pictures, which Wilkins had shown Watson, furnished the crucial evidence that solved the puzzle.

Studies TMV

Although Franklin and Gosling published another paper on DNA in *Nature* in July 1953, Franklin had by this time lost interest in DNA research. She had instead become involved in the study of the tobacco mosaic virus (TMV), a group of virus diseases of plants of the nightshade family, especially tobacco. She had also decided to move on to a position at Birkbeck College. By 1956 Franklin had obtained some of the best pictures of the crystallographic structure of TMV and, along with her colleagues, disproved the then-standard notion that TMV was a solid cylinder with RNA in the middle and protein subunits on the outside. (RNA, or ribonucleic acid, is a close relative of DNA and is also involved in protein production.) While Franklin confirmed that the protein units did lie on the outside, she also showed that the cylinder was hollow, and that the RNA lay embedded among the protein units. Later she initiated work that would support her hypothesis that the RNA in TMV is single stranded.

Praised by Watson and Crick

Franklin had two cancer operations in 1956. Despite her weakened physical condition and lowered resistance, she began researching the dangerous and highly contagious polio virus. She died within two years, at the age of thirty-seven, on April 16, 1958. Four years later Watson, Crick, and Wilkins won the Nobel Prize in medicine or physiology for the discovery of the structure of DNA. Watson later published *The Double Helix,* his account of this important scientific achievement. Although he remained critical of Franklin, he toned down his earlier opinion of her as a brash feminist scientist. He wrote that he and Crick "both came to appreciate greatly her personal honesty and generosity, realizing years too late the struggles that the intelligent woman faces to be accepted by a scientific world which often regards women as mere diversions from serious thinking."

Further Reading

Judson, Horace Freeland, *The Eighth Day of Creation: Makers of the Revolution in Biology,* Simon & Schuster, 1980.

Sayre, Anne, *Rosalind Franklin and DNA,* Norton, 1975.

Watson, James D., *The Double Helix: A Personal Account of the Discovery of the Structure of DNA,* Norton, 1968.

Sigmund Freud

Born May 6, 1856
Freiberg, Austria
(now Pribor, Czech Republic)
Died September 23, 1939
London, England

Sigmund Freud is known as the father of psychoanalysis.

Sigmund Freud began his career as a neurologist, a doctor who studies the nervous system. His years of practice led him to believe that some illnesses originate in the mind, not the body. Freud conducted extensive research on his patients, publishing a substantial body of work and formulating numerous theories on human personality and behavior. While collaborating with physician Josef Breuer on research into hysteria, Freud came up with an idea that would form the core of psychoanalysis: he concluded that neurotic behavior is motivated by unconscious desires that can be revealed through a method known as "the talking cure."

Considered the family favorite

Sigismund Solomon Freud was born on May 6, 1856, in the small Central European village-state of Freiberg, then part of the Austrian empire (now Pribor, in the Czech Republic).

His father, Jacob Freud, was descended from German Jews who had migrated to escape anti-Jewish persecution. His mother, Amalie Nathanson, was Jacob's third wife. Freud, who began calling himself Sigmund when he was a teenager, was born the year after his parents were married. He had two older half-brothers from his father's first marriage; seven more siblings would be born later.

The Freuds were poor, occupying a single room in a house in Freiberg. When young Freud was four they moved to Vienna, where the family fortunes improved slightly. Both of Freud's parents recognized their son's unusual intelligence. From an early age, he was openly treated as the family favorite. When his sister's piano practice disturbed his studying, for example, their parents reportedly got rid of the piano without a second thought. The fact that Sigmund came first was soon taken for granted by the rest of the family. This left him with a lifelong sense of confidence in his abilities and in his destiny as a man of great accomplishment.

Decides to study medicine

A hard-working honors student, Freud ranked first in his class in six of his eight years of schooling. In 1873, at the age of seventeen, he entered the University of Vienna as a medical student. Because his interests were so diverse, he took eight years to finish his studies instead of the customary five. For a while he studied zoology, performing detailed research on river eels. Then, in 1876, he began to concentrate on physiology, the study of the functions of living things. He worked in the field of physiology for six years, making it the cornerstone of his medical training.

After graduating from the university in 1881 Freud planned to continue his research in physiology. The following year, however, he met and fell in love with Martha Bernays. She agreed to marry him, but Freud knew there was little money in research, probably not enough to support a family. It was time, he decided, to shift from medical research to the actual practice of medicine.

Begins studying psychology

Soon after becoming engaged Freud accepted a position at Vienna Central Hospital. From 1882 through 1885 he worked in one department after another: surgery, skin diseases, internal medicine, nervous diseases, psychiatry. Highly ambitious, he looked for a way to combine his interests with a position that would provide a decent income and the promise of advancement. Slowly, he began to focus on the human mind, studying the rapidly growing fields of psychology and psychiatry.

At the same time Freud's friend, Josef Breuer, who was also a doctor, began telling Freud about a young patient named Bertha Pappenheim, whom he had been treating. In 1880, while caring for her terminally ill father, Pappenheim had begun suffering from a number of physical complaints: headaches, loss of appetite, weakness, and coughing among them. These symptoms worsened, until she was regularly reporting periods of memory loss, extreme mood swings, and hallucinations involving black snakes, skulls, and skeletons. Sometimes she seemed to have two separate personalities; while normally she could speak French, English, and Italian, at times she could speak only one of these languages. Her problems became even more severe after the death of her father in 1881.

Develops "talking cure"

Pappenheim—who by now was known as "Anna O." to protect her identity—was unusually intelligent and strong willed. Gradually, during daily visits to Freud and Breuer, the doctors discovered that some of her symptoms were alleviated merely by discussing her memories and the feelings they created in her. Breuer realized that the symptoms had first begun to appear when she held back—or "repressed"—her reaction to an uncomfortable situation. When Freud encouraged Anna O. to recall a given situation and express the reaction she had earlier repressed, her symptoms vanished. During these discussions the doctors often used hypnosis:

sometimes Anna O. would hypnotize her-self; other times Breuer would hypnotize her. She called it her "talking cure."

Freud and Breuer did not publish arti-cles about Anna O. until the early 1890s. In the meantime Freud had spent two months in 1884 doing research on cocaine and its effects on the mind and body. Later he stud-ied briefly in Paris with Jean-Martin Char-cot, a noted authority on the human brain. Charcot impressed Freud with the power of hypnosis. Freud, however, did not impress Charcot with his "talking cure."

Treats new patients

Freud had finally married Bernays in 1886 after a long engagement. Within a year their first child was born; as five other chil-dren followed, family life became increas-ingly important to Freud. He soon moved his medical practice to the family home. Between patients he spent time with his wife and children.

Freud's patients often complained of problems similar to Anna O.'s. If he could find no physical reason for the symptoms—such as swelling or tumors in the brain, for example—he would focus on the possibility of a psychological disease. Freud soon identified a mysterious factor—the "libido," or sexual drive—that he felt was central to understanding problems of the mind.

Defines cause of hysteria

Nineteenth-century Western culture denied human sexu-ality. Strict rules governed people's behavior, especially inter-actions between men and women, and sexual matters were literally unmentionable. By the 1890s Freud was beginning to see sex—or rather, society's attitudes toward sex—as more and more responsible for certain psychological problems.

The symptoms Freud and Breuer had observed in Anna O.'s behavior were not uncommon. They occurred especially in women, but also from time to time in men. Doctors lumped all such symptoms together under the general name "hysteria." In 1895 Freud and Breuer published observations from years of research in a book called *Studies in Hysteria*. Freud asserted that the stress of always holding back or "repressing" sexual memories, thoughts, or impulses could actually create hysterical symptoms. This radical conclusion about the workings of the unconscious mind clashed with Breuer's more traditional methods of psychological diagnosis and treatment, and after 1895 he lost interest in further research. Freud, however, was just beginning to refine his theories.

Uses "self-analysis" for new discovery

As Freud began to develop his ideas about hysteria and sexual repression, he examined his own memories, thoughts, and impulses, effectively becoming his own patient. His "self-analysis," which began in the 1890s, would continue for the rest of his life. Among his findings were many childhood memories that seemed sexual, violent, or aggressive in nature. For example, Freud remembered being attracted to his mother and viewing his father as a rival. He also recalled feeling extreme jealousy toward his younger brother, which resulted in intense feelings of guilt when the brother fell ill and died. Such feelings, he believed, were not unique to him; on the contrary, he was convinced that every child had similar experiences.

The feelings Freud recalled having toward his mother, father, and brother became the basis of psychoanalysis. They reveal what he saw as the two strongest factors shaping human behavior: sexuality and aggression. Freud coined the terms "Oedipus complex" (in boys) and "Electra complex" (in girls) to describe a child's attraction to the parent of the opposite sex and jealousy toward the parent of the same sex. (Oedipus, the

title character in a Greek tragedy, unknowingly kills his father and marries his mother.) In addition, Freud called feelings of jealousy directed at a brother or sister "sibling rivalry." Like so much of Freud's psychoanalytical lingo, these terms are now commonly used.

Sigmund Freud in his home office.

Begins dream analysis

In 1899 Freud published *The Interpretation of Dreams,* in which he first laid out the basic principles of his psychoanalytic theory. As the title suggests, the book also introduces another idea fundamental to his theory—the importance of dreams. If aggression and sexuality are the two strongest motivations behind our behavior, Freud argued, then dreams are the best clue we have to understanding how these forces are at work in our minds. He theorized that dreams are messages from our unconscious that offer stunning insights into the deepest recesses of the human mind.

Organizes Vienna Psycho-Analytical Association

At first *The Interpretation of Dreams* attracted little attention, even though Freud continued with a steady stream of writings in which he developed his ideas. Slowly, as these works were read and understood, they won an increasingly large following of physicians. In 1902 a group began meeting at Freud's house every Wednesday evening to discuss his discoveries. The "Psychological Wednesday Circle" became the Vienna Psycho-Analytical Society in 1908, then the International Psycho-Analytical Association in 1910. By this time Freud had achieved fame throughout the world.

Lasting impressions despite controversy

Many of Freud's early followers were brilliant thinkers in their own right, however, and disagreements soon arose. The International Psycho-Analytical Association broke up in 1911 as men like Alfred Adler and **C. G. Jung** (see entry) devoted more time to their own ideas. Nonetheless, psychoanalysis had become firmly established as a method of treatment. Though deeply disappointed by the bitterness that often accompanied these philosophical disagreements, Freud kept up his remarkable pace of writing, lecturing, and treating patients.

One of Freud's best-known and most influential books of the 1920s, published in English as *The Ego and the Id,* introduces a framework for the structure of the human mind. Freud divided the mind into three components: the *id,* the *superego,* and the *ego.* He proposed that internal clashes between the instinct-driven *id,* the conscience-driven *superego,* and the reality-based mediator known as the *ego* can lead to mental disturbances if they go unresolved.

In 1923 Freud had the first of many operations for cancer of the jaw, caused by his heavy cigar smoking. As his health failed with advancing age, his daughter Anna, who was a psychologist, became his primary assistant and source of support. In 1938, after the Germans took control of Austria, she helped him move to London. Freud died there on September 23, 1939.

Further Reading

Bloom, Harold, ed., *Sigmund Freud,* Chelsea House, 1985.

Freud, Ernst, and others, *Sigmund Freud: His Life in Pictures and Words,* Harcourt, 1978.

Gay, Peter, *Freud: A Life for Our Time,* Anchor Books, 1989.

Gay, Peter, ed., *The Freud Reader,* Norton, 1989.

Mann, Barry, *Sigmund Freud,* Rourke, 1993.

Charlotte Friend

Born March 11, 1921
New York, New York
Died January 13, 1987

Charlotte Friend was the first scientist to discover a direct link between viruses and cancer.

Charlotte Friend was a microbiologist who made important breakthroughs in the treatment of leukemia, a potentially fatal disease of the white blood cells and a leading killer of children. She was successful in immunizing mice against leukemia and in pointing a way toward new treatment methods for patients stricken with the disease. Because of her work, medical researchers have developed a greater understanding of leukemia and other cancers and how they can be fought.

Influenced by parents

Friend was born on March 11, 1921, in New York City to Russian immigrants. Her father died of endocarditis (inflammation of the heart) when she was three years old, a factor that may have influenced her early decision to become a microbiologist. Her mother's job as a pharmacist also exposed her to the medical field. After graduating from Hunter College in

1944, Friend immediately enlisted in the U.S. Navy to serve in World War II. She rose to the rank of lieutenant junior grade.

Discovers cause of leukemia

After the war Friend entered graduate school at Yale University in New Haven, Connecticut, where she obtained her Ph.D. in bacteriology in 1950. Soon afterward she was hired by the Sloan-Kettering Institute for Cancer Research in New York City. In 1952 Friend became an associate professor of microbiology at Cornell University, which had just established a joint program with the institute. Around that time she developed an interest in the study of cancer, particularly leukemia. Her research on the disease led her to believe—contrary to the prevailing medical opinion of the time—that leukemia was caused by a virus.

To confirm her theory, Friend took samples of leukemia tissue from mice; then, after putting the tissue through a filter to remove cells, she injected the strained disease sample into healthy lab mice. These animals developed leukemia, indicating that the cause of the disease was a substance smaller than a cell. Using an electron microscope, which uses a beam of electrons to produce a picture many times more detailed than an optical microscope, Friend was able to discover and photograph the virus she believed was responsible for leukemia.

Findings greeted with skepticism

Friend presented her findings at the April 1956 annual meeting of the American Association for Cancer Research. Other researchers refused to believe that a virus was responsible for leukemia. However, over the next year, support for her theory mounted. Dr. Jacob Furth declared that his experiments had confirmed the existence of such a virus in mice with leukemia. Furthermore, Friend provided her own support. She tried vaccinating mice against leukemia by injecting a weakened form of the virus (now called the Friend virus) into healthy mice. These mice developed antibodies to fight off the regular strain of the virus. Her presentation of a report on this vaccine at the 1957 meeting of the association dispelled all doubts about the validity of her claims.

Continues research

In 1962 Friend was honored for her work with the Alfred P. Sloan Award for Cancer Research and an award from the American Cancer Society. The following year she became a member of the New York Academy of Sciences. In 1966 Friend left Sloan-Kettering to assume the dual posts of professor and director at the Center for Experimental Cell Biology at Mount Sinai Hospital in New York. During this time she continued her research on leukemia. In 1972 she announced her discovery of a method of altering a leukemia mouse cell in a test tube so that it would no longer multiply. Through chemical treatment, the malignant (or diseased) red blood cell could once again be made to produce hemoglobin, the iron-containing pigment present in normal red blood cells.

Honored for her work

In 1976 Friend was elected president of the American Association for Cancer Research. This was the same organization whose members had so strongly criticized her twenty years earlier. She was also chosen as the first woman president of the New York Academy of Sciences. Friend was active in supporting other women scientists and in speaking out on women's issues. During her later years she expressed concern over a lack of adequate progress in basic cancer research in the United States. She felt that without sufficient funding for research, new breakthroughs in patient care would be impossible. Friend died on January 13, 1987, of lymphoma, a tumor in the tissue surrounding the lymph nodes.

Further Reading

Annals of the New York Academy of Sciences, Volume 567, August 4, 1989.

Beattie, Edward, *Towards the Conquest of Cancer,* Crown Publishing, 1988.

Marget, Madeline, *Life's Blood,* Simon & Schuster, 1992.

New York Times, January 16, 1987.

Noble, Iris, *Contemporary Women Scientists,* Julian Messner, 1979.

Karl von Frisch

Born in 1886
Vienna, Austria
Died in 1982
Munich, Germany

"Every single-species of the animal kingdom challenges us with all, or nearly all, the mysteries of life."

Karl von Frisch won the Nobel Prize in 1973 for his pioneering work in the field of animal physiology and behavior. A leading researcher in the study of insect behavior, he conducted studies that proved that fish have highly sensitive hearing and that bees communicate effectively through a ritual dance. Frisch's discoveries and subsequent Nobel Prize were also significant because this was the first major acknowledgment of advances made in ethology, the study of animal behavior.

Shows early interest in animals

Karl von Frisch was born in Vienna, Austria, in 1886, into a family dedicated to science. His father, Anton Ritter von Frisch, was a physician, and his mother, Marie Exner, came from a long line of distinguished scientists and scholars. From his earliest years Frisch was exposed to the natural world. When his family vacationed at a home in the country every summer, he spent his time collecting various species of animals. "Even before I went to school," he wrote in his autobiography *A Biologist Remembers,* "I had a little zoo in my room." But Frisch was not simply a collector; he was also a keen observer. A few of his early observations—most notably that the sea animals he collected in an aquarium in his room waved their tentacles when he turned on the lights—prompted a curiosity about the sensory systems of animals that would last throughout his life.

By the time Frisch reached college age, his interests were clearly focused on zoology (the study of animals). Nevertheless his father thought medicine was a more practical field, so Frisch enrolled as a student of medicine at the University of Vienna in 1905. He studied with his uncle, Sigmund Exner, a renowned physiologist (one who studies the physical and chemical processes of the body) and lecturer. Although Exner taught physiology, he encouraged Frisch to pursue his interest in animals. Exner assisted him in a research project on the position of pigments in the compound eyes of certain beetles, butterflies, and crustaceans. Exner's openness toward the study of animals was unheard of at the time. Comparing the physiology of animals and humans would only later be seen as so invaluable that it was defined as a separate field of study.

Changes career goal

During his third year as a medical student, Frisch found himself increasingly frustrated by the "medical character" of the curriculum. Dropping out of medical school, he decided to pursue ethology. He transferred to the Zoological Institute at the University of Munich in Germany. He continued to cultivate the interests he had developed under his uncle's leadership, researching light perception and color changes in minnows. At this time he discovered that minnows have an area in the forehead filled with sensory cells—a "third, very primitive eye," as he called it. This explained why blind minnows reacted to light by changing color in the same way as minnows with sight. Frisch wrote his doctoral thesis on this subject; he received his degree in 1910.

Challenges scientific assumptions

Frisch began to question the common assumption of the time that fish and all invertebrates (animals lacking a spinal column) were color blind. He successfully trained minnows to respond to colored objects, proving that they could perceive color. These findings were not welcomed by the scientific community, however. His most notable opponent was Karl von Hess, director of the Munich Eye Clinic. The debate arose partly because of the connections between Frisch's findings and the views of the famous naturalist **Charles Darwin** (see entry). Frisch accepted Darwin's theory that the survival of certain species of animals depended on the development of their senses. He hypothesized that animal behavior, rather than simply being a fixed mechanism, had an "adaptive biological significance." Such assumptions were still a source of disagreement among scientists at the time. Despite the opposition to his research, Frisch was offered a faculty position at the University of Munich in 1921.

Conducts innovative studies of bees

While teaching at Munich, Frisch continued to study color perception in animals during vacations at his family's summer home. Having proved that fish are not color-blind he turned to the task of proving the same fact about bees. That bees could be color-blind was unacceptable to Frisch. He suggested that the purpose of the bright coloration of flowers was to guide bees to the nectar in the flowers. The bees, in turn, aided the reproduction of flowers through pollination.

To test his hypothesis, Frisch used research methods similar to those he had developed with fish. He conditioned the bees' behavior by placing drops of sugar water on squares of blue-colored cardboard. He then placed the squares among plain gray cardboard squares. Eventually he placed blue squares without sugar among the gray squares. He found that the bees continued to go to the blue squares for their food, even when the squares did not contain sugar—thus proving they could differentiate color.

Works with Red Cross

In 1914 Frisch's research was interrupted by the outbreak of World War I. Although he could not serve in the military because of poor eyesight, he answered a plea from his brother, a physician, to volunteer at a Red Cross hospital that was in dire need of help. Because of his medical background Frisch was able to establish a bacteriologic laboratory that aided in the rapid diagnosis of diseases such as cholera, dysentery, and typhoid. While at the hospital Frisch met Margarethe Mohr, whom he married in 1917. They would later have three daughters and a son.

Frisch continued his research on bees. During the war he took a few weeks' leave every summer, returning to the country house to study bees. As the war came to an end his work at the hospital lessened and his students returned to the Zoological Institute. After four years with the Red Cross, in 1919 he returned to teaching as an assistant professor.

Discovers the "dance of the bees"

In the course of his research Frisch became interested in scout bees (bees that have left the hive to explore for food). He set out dishes of sugar water, then observed the bees' behavior. When a dish was empty a scout bee only occasionally came to the dish, but when a dish was full the scout would return in a matter of minutes with a whole company of bees. "It became clear to me that the bee community possessed an excellent intelligence function," Frisch wrote in his autobiography, "but how it functioned I did not know."

In 1919 Frisch constructed a glass cage in which he placed a single honeycomb that could be observed from all sides. Through continuous observation and experimentation,

IMPACT

In the course of his research on animal behavior, Karl von Frisch reached conclusions that surprised —even troubled—the scientific community. He proved that honeybees can see colors, bees can distinguish the scents of flowers, and fish can even hear. One of his most interesting experiments involved honeybees, which he discovered to have a simple language in the form of ritual dances. Frisch's work was important because it revealed the similarities between animal communication and human language.

he reached an intriguing conclusion: when the scout bees found food on the honeycomb, they conveyed this information to the other bees by performing a kind of dance. The dance excited the other bees, who then flew directly to the food. By 1923 Frisch had determined that the bees performed two different dances: "round" dances and "waggle" dances. Round dances mean that food is nearby, and waggle dances signal that food is at a distance. When the scout bee is moving in a straight line during the waggle dance it points the way to the food; the length of the dance indicates the distance of the food. In retrospect, Frisch called his first discovery of the bees' dance "the most far-reaching observation of my life."

Finds that fish can hear

In 1921 Frisch was appointed professor of zoology and director of the Zoological Institute at Rostock University. While he was at Rostock he expanded his research to an investigation of whether fish could hear. The physiology of fish suggested they could not hear: they do not have any of the characteristics thought to be necessary for the sense of hearing, such as ear lobes, auditory canals, or middle ears. In addition, fish do not have a cochlea in the inner ear, which was considered the center of hearing in humans. Using his proven methods of behavior conditioning, Frisch tested the hearing of fish. He whistled to blind catfish before feeding them. When he whistled but did not feed the fish, they continued to respond. The answer seemed simple—or, as one skeptical scientist put it, "There is no doubt. The fish comes when you whistle." With the help of his students, over time Frisch eventually refined his research, discovering other facts that supported his initial findings.

Wins Nobel Prize

In 1925 Frisch moved to the Zoological Institute of the University of Munich, where he worked until the institute was destroyed during World War II. After spending a few years at his country home and at the University of Graz, he returned to

Munich in 1950 to rebuild the institute as its director. During this time he wrote several books for the general public as well as the scientific community. He retired in 1958. Fifteen years later he was awarded the Nobel Prize, which he shared with the Austrian-born German ethologist **Konrad Lorenz** (see entry) and Dutch ethologist Nikolaas Tinbergen. Honoring animal behaviorists was a departure for the Nobel Committee, for to that point there had never been such public recognition of the interactive study of animals and humans. Frisch died in 1982, at the age of ninety-six.

Further Reading

Current Biography, H. W. Wilson, 1974.

Frisch, Karl von, *Bees: Their Vision, Chemical Senses, and Language,* Cornell University Press, 1950.

Frisch, Karl von, *A Biologist Remembers* (autobiography), translated by Lisbeth Gombrich, Pergamon, 1960.

Frisch, Karl von, *The Dancing Bees: An Account of the Life and Senses of the Honey Bee,* Methuen, 1954.

Frisch, Karl von, *Ten Little Housemates,* translated by Margaret D. Senft, Pergamon, 1960.

Tetsuya Theodore Fujita

Born October 23, 1920
Kitakyushu, Japan

"After I pointed out the existence of downbursts, the number of tornadoes listed in the United States decreased for a number of years."

Tetsuya Theodore Fujita, a Japanese-born American meteorologist, became the first scientist to identify the microburst, a particularly strong and isolated form of wind shear later blamed for several devastating plane crashes in the 1980s. The development of Doppler radar allowed Fujita to track and explain the microburst phenomenon, which in the 1990s is far better understood and avoided by aviators. Fujita also developed the "F Scale," used to measure the strength of tornadoes by analyzing the damage they cause on the ground.

Observes ruins of Hiroshima and Nagasaki

Fujita was born in Kitakyushu, Japan, on October 23, 1920, to Tomojiro, a schoolteacher, and Yoshie (Kanesue) Fujita. He became interested in science early in his life. When he was twenty-three, Fujita obtained the equivalent of a bachelor's degree in mechanical engineering from the Meji College of Technology in 1943. While he was working as an assistant professor of physics at Meji, U.S. forces dropped the atom bomb on the Japanese cities of Hiroshima and Nagasaki to end World War II. Fujita visited the ruins three weeks after the bombings. By measuring the scorch marks on bamboo vases in a cemetery in Nagasaki, Fujita was able to show that only one bomb had been dropped. Surveying the damage in Hiroshima, Fujita calculated how high above the ground the bombs had exploded in order to create their unique starburst patterns on the ground. These observations became important to his later work.

Comes to America

Leaving Meji College in 1949, Fujita became an assistant professor at Kyushu Institute of Technology while pursuing his Ph.D. in atmospheric science at Tokyo University. Like others involved in atmospheric science, he had read the published articles of Horace R. Byers of the University of Chicago, who had conducted groundbreaking research on thunderstorms in 1946 and 1947. Fujita translated two of his own articles on the same subject into English and sent them to Byers. Byers was impressed with Fujita's work, and the two men began a correspondence. In 1953, the year Fujita received his doctorate, Byers extended an invitation to the Japanese scientist to work at the University of Chicago as a visiting research associate.

Fujita remained at the University of Chicago as a senior meteorologist until 1962, when he became an associate professor. For two years beginning in 1961, he was the director of the Mesometeorological Research Project, then in 1964 he became the director of the Satellite and Mesometeorology Research Project. Fujita was made a full professor in 1965 and has held the Charles E. Merriam Distinguished Service Professorship since 1989. He became a naturalized U.S. citizen in 1968 and adopted the first name Theodore for use in the United States. He married Sumiko Yamamo in June 1969, and has a son, Kazuya, from his first marriage.

As a result of Tetsuya Theodore Fujita's study of wind phenomena such as tornadoes, microbursts, and wind shears, scientists can now do more to prevent airline accidents. His work has led to the use of Doppler radar, which helps aviators and airports detect air systems that cause tornadoes and other wind disturbances that endanger aircraft.

Develops the "F Scale"

Fujita and his graduate students performed extensive aerial surveys of tornadoes (a violent, destructive, whirling wind accompanied by a funnel-shaped cloud that progresses in a narrow path over the land). Having logged over 40,000 miles flying in small planes under the worst of weather conditions, Fujita developed his tornado "F Scale" in the 1960s. Traditionally, meteorologists (scientists who study the atmosphere and its phenomena and weather with weather forecasting) had listed only the total number of tornadoes that occurred, having no objective way to measure storm strength. Fujita constructed a system of measurement that correlates ground damage to wind speed. His six-point system operates on an F-0 (very weak) to F-6 (inconceivable) scale, which is similar to the Richter scale invented by **Charles F. Richter** (see entry) used to measure the strength of earthquakes.

Fujita did not actually witness a tornado until June 12, 1982, so the mainstay of his work was research on the aftermath of tornadoes. While at the National Center for Atmospheric Research in Denver, Colorado, Fujita spotted a tornado in the region early and collected some of the best data on the phenomenon ever accumulated.

Analyzes microbursts

In 1974 Fujita began analyzing the phenomenon of microbursts, violent, short-lived localized downdrafts (downward currents of air) that create extreme wind shear (a radical shift in wind speed and direction between slightly different altitudes) at low altitudes and are usually associated with thunderstorms. Flying over the devastation wrought by a tornado, he noticed patterns of damage similar to those he had witnessed in Hiroshima and Nagasaki. "If something comes down from the sky and hits the ground it will spread out; it will pro-

duce the same kind of outburst effect that was in the back of my mind, from 1945 to 1974," Fujita explained in *The Weather Book: An Easy to Understand Guide to the U.S.A.'s Weather.*

Meteorologists knew by the mid-1970s that severe storms produce downdrafts. However, because they assumed those downdrafts lost most of their force before they hit the ground and therefore did not cause much damage, the phenomenon was

Vilhelm Bjerknes, Norwegian Physicist and Geophysicist

Tetsuya Theodore Fujita and other meteorologists are indebted to the pioneering work of Vilhelm Bjerknes (1862–1951), who established modern meteorology as an exact science. In the late 1890s Bjerknes formulated the theory of "physical hydrodynamics," based on the principle that the Sun's heat is converted into motion in the atmosphere, and that the friction of atmospheric motion itself generates heat, which is again converted into motion. Since atmospheric motion creates weather patterns, Bjerknes's work held great promise for meteorological forecasting.

In 1917 Bjerknes founded the Western Bergen Weather Service at the University of Bergen in Norway to issue detailed reports for the government and military. Eventually the weather service furnished sophisticated local forecasts to fishers, farmers, and the commercial aviation industry. Continued research by the Bergen team—which became known as the Bergen School of Meteorology—resulted in theories relating to weather fronts and cyclone system motion.

largely ignored. Encouraged by Byers, Fujita coined the term "downburst" for the powerful downdrafts that strike the ground and deflect in all directions, causing danger for low-flying aircraft. He began research to prove his thesis that downdraft is a significant weather phenomenon. Aided by the National Center for Atmospheric Research, he set up a project near Chicago that detected fifty-two downbursts in forty-two days.

Discovers wind shear

Fujita was eventually able to show that downdrafts cause wind shear, which poses a particular hazard in aviation. Wind speeds up to F-3 are common for downbursts (higher F Scale readings usually indicate tornadoes). Fujita's research finally gained national attention in the 1980s. A shear caused by a downdraft was cited as a contributing factor in the July 1982 crash of a Pan Am 727 airliner in New Orleans, Louisiana, which killed 154 people. During that event, the plane was observed sinking back to the ground shortly after takeoff as the apparent result of a wind shear. Another accident occurred in August 1985, when Delta Flight 191 crashed at the Dallas-Ft. Worth Airport, killing 133 people. Again a wind shear was suspected to be the cause of the catastrophe.

Leads to the development of Doppler radar

Air safety has improved dramatically because of Fujita's research, which led to the development of Doppler radar. (The Doppler effect is a change in frequency with which sound or light waves reach an observer when both the source and the observer are in motion. The Doppler effect explains, for example, why the sound of a train grows louder as it approaches and then softens once it has gone by. Doppler radar systems use the Doppler effect to measure wind velocity). Doppler radar is so sensitive it actually picks up particles of debris in the air that are as fine as dust. Movements of these particles are tracked to measure shifts in wind velocity. By the mid-1990s the National Weather Service and the U.S. Air Force together will have installed 137 Doppler systems, essentially blanketing the continental United States. Because of these radar systems, which give aviators twenty to twenty-five minutes' warning of approaching tornadoes, there has already been a decrease in airline accidents.

Receives awards and honors

Since 1988, Fujita has directed the Wind Research Lab at the University of Chicago. Among his many awards have been the 1989 Medaille de Vermeil from the French National Academy of Air and Science for his work identifying microbursts; the 1990 Fujiwara Award Medal from the Meteorological Society of Japan for his research on mesometeorology; the 1991 Order of the Sacred Treasure, Gold and Silver Star from the Government of Japan for his tornado and microburst work; and the 1992 Transportation Cultural Award from the Japanese government for his contributions to air safety.

Further Reading

Frank, James, "Mr. Tornado," *Chicago Tribune,* May 10, 1990.

McClellan, J. Mac, "Technicalities: Tracking the Elusive Wind Shear," *Flying,* October 1992, pp. 22–23.

McKean, Kevin, "Solving the Mystery of Wind Shear," *Discover,* September 1982, pp. 78–81.

Taubes, Gary, "Ted Fujita: On the Tornado's Tail," *Discover,* May 1983, pp. 48–53.

Williams, Jack, *The Weather Book: An Easy to Understand Guide to the U.S.A.'s Weather,* Vintage Books, 1992, pp. 122–23.

R. Buckminster Fuller

Born July 12, 1895
Milton, Massachusetts
Died in 1983

O ne of the most creative thinkers of the twentieth century, R. Buckminster Fuller devoted his life to inventing techno-logical designs that would improve modern living. He is best known for creating the geodesic dome, a complex of triangle-like shapes balanced together to form an extremely sturdy structure that resembles a large soccer ball. Among his other revolutionary developments are the streamlined Dymax-ion automobile and the Dymaxion house. An early advocate of solar power, resource recycling, and gaining the maximum strength from minimal use of materials, Fuller coined the term "Spaceship Earth" to describe the need for technology to be self-contained and to avoid waste.

Mission inspired by tragedy

Richard Buckminster (Bucky) Fuller was born on July 12, 1895, in Milton, Massachusetts, an isolated island fishing village where he spent his childhood learning seamanship and

American architect and engineer R. Buckminster Fuller produced revolutionary technological designs—including the geodesic dome—for the improvement of modern living.

333

Despite his many innovations in housing design and construction, R. Buckminster Fuller is best remembered for his geodesic dome. Two years after Fuller patented the design for the geodesic dome in 1951, the Ford Motor Company gave him his first major contract—to build a dome over the courtyard of the company headquarters in Detroit. A conventional dome would have weighed about 160 tons and was technically unfeasible; the materials on the Fuller project weighed only 8.5 tons. The U.S. Defense Department eventually became Fuller's largest customer, using the domes as temporary housing units and—since they can withstand 200-mile-an-hour winds—as shelter for sensitive radar equipment in harsh environments, such as the Arctic. Today dome homes can be found in all fifty of the United States and in Europe, Africa, and Asia.

all its related skills. From an early age he was fascinated with how humans solve problems in attempts to adapt to—or at least deal more effectively with—the constraints of their environments. Fuller attended the Milton Academy, then entered Harvard University in 1913. After being expelled two years later for irresponsible conduct, he found work as a machinist at a textile mill in Sherbrooke, Quebec. During World War I he served briefly in the U.S. Navy. These experiences prompted Fuller to focus his problem-solving interests on engineering.

In 1917 Fuller married Anne Hewlett, the daughter of well-known architect and artist James Monroe Hewlett. Fuller and his father-in-law formed a construction company, but after supervising the construction of several hundred houses, Fuller concluded that custom homes were inefficiently built. In 1922 one of the Fullers' two daughters, Alexandra, died in an epidemic. Blaming her death partly on a poor physical environment, Fuller became obsessed with the potential of modern technology to address and resolve the problems of poor housing and living conditions worldwide.

Develops first inventions

The following year Fuller invented the stockade brick-laying method, which consists of reinforcing bricks by pouring concrete and cement into vertical holes in the bricks. He then went to Chicago, where his mother was from, to start his own construction company, the Stockade Building System. Fuller found he had to battle strong construction workers' unions, which opposed the reinforced brick and other, more efficient building methods he

R. Buckminster Fuller in 1980 at the dedication of Monterey One, a 3,500-square-foot, solar-powered geodesic dome house in Riverside, California, that he designed.

introduced as a threat to their jobs. By 1927 he was forced to sell the business.

Fuller then turned to designing Dymaxion objects. "Dymaxion" was a term Fuller used to refer to anything that derived maximum output from minimum material and effort. His Dymaxion house was a factory-assembled "house on a pole" that was suspended from a central mast. It was self-contained and dust-free and included a complete recycling system.

In 1928 Fuller designed the Dymaxion automobile, a vehicle that could drive in several directions and gave minimum resistance to the wind. His two-year-old daughter, Allegra, called the teardrop-shaped car the "zoommobile." While the vehicle could seat twelve passengers, make 180-degree turns, and average 28 miles (45 kilometers) per gallon, the venture was unprofitable because Fuller was unable to sell his idea to an automobile manufacturer. He finally

Buckminsterfullerene

In 1965 chemist Richard Smalley identified a large molecule that had the shape of a soccer ball and contained sixty carbon atoms. This molecule was named buckminsterfullerene because of the structure's resemblance to the geodesic domes designed by R. Buckminster Fuller. Since that time, other stable, large, even-numbered carbon clusters have been produced. This new class of molecules has been called "fullerenes" since they all seem to have the structure of a geodesic dome.

managed to pay off his debts, but the project bankrupted him and his family.

Achieves success with DDU

Although Fuller's motives were mainly unselfish, he became financially successful in 1940 when he designed the Dymaxion Deployment Unit (DDU), a circular, self-cooled living unit made of corrugated steel and containing pie-shaped rooms. The British purchased DDUs for use during World War II, and before long Fuller was shipping orders all over the world. Following the war Fuller went on the lecture circuit and became somewhat of a celebrity. In 1948 he was appointed dean at Black Mountain College in North Carolina, where he developed the Tensegrity Dome, which used tetrahedrons for balance. (A tetrahedron is a solid structure with four flat, triangular-shaped sides.)

Designs innovative geodesic dome

Fuller left Black Mountain in 1949 and commenced work on the design for a geodesic dome. He based his concept on the geodesic line, which is the shortest distance between two points across a surface. If that surface is curved, a geodesic line across it will usually be curved as well. A geodesic line on the surface of a sphere will be part of a great circle. Fuller realized the surface of a sphere could be divided into triangles by a network of geodesic lines, and that structures could be designed so that their main elements either followed those lines or were joined along them.

Fuller's geodesic dome was generally spherical in shape and constructed of many light, straight elements arranged in a framework of triangles (tetrahedrons). Made of enormously strong aluminum and glass or plastic, the geodesic dome is lightweight, resistant to wind, and capable of covering acres of ground with no internal support. It can also be erected in a very short period of time. Fuller constructed a model on the lawn of the Pentagon, then applied for a patent in 1951.

Dome earns Fuller fame

Fuller was appointed research professor at Southern Illinois University in Carbondale, Illinois, in 1959. His stipend of $12,000 was insignificant, but he was given use of an entire building and staff. He went on to propose domes for whole cities such as East St. Louis, Missouri, to protect them from industrial smog. Constructed in 1959 and 1960 was the American Society of Metals dome, located east of Cleveland, Ohio, and made of open lattice-work. Among the largest geodesic domes is the gigantic Houston Astrodome, which was completed in 1965. Fuller also designed the twenty-story geodesic dome that housed the United States' Exhibition at the 1967 World's Fair. By the time of his death in 1983, Fuller's name had become synonymous with the geodesic dome throughout the world.

Further Reading

Aaseng, Nathan, *More With Less: The Future World of Buckminster Fuller,* Lerner, 1986.

Baldwin, James T., *Buckyworks: Buckminster Fuller's Ideas Today,* Wiley, 1996.

Edmondson, Amy C., *Fuller Explanation,* Van Nostrand Reinhold, 1992.

Pawley, Martin, *Buckminster Fuller,* Taplinger, 1991.

Potter, Robert R., *Buckminster Fuller,* Silver Burdett Press, 1990.

Picture Credits

Jane Goodall

The photographs appearing in *Scientists: The Lives and Works of 150 Scientists* were received from the following sources:

On the cover (clockwise from top right): Luis Alvarez, Robert H. Goddard (**AP/Wide World Photos. Reproduced by permission.**); Margaret Mead (**The Bettmann Archive. Reproduced by permission.**). On the back cover (top to bottom): Edwin H. Land (**AP/Wide World Photos. Reproduced by permission.**); George Washington Carver (**The Bettmann Archive. Reproduced by permission.**).

Courtesy of the Library of Congress: pp. v, 11, 30, 66, 82, 96, 98, 102, 135, 137, 185, 188, 197, 200, 203, 206 (top and bottom), 208, 211, 224, 244, 260, 267, 275, 296, 308, 316, 339, 371, 374, 395, 399, 405, 441, 444, 487, 490, 506, 524, 527, 529, 568, 573, 599, 616, 620 (top and bottom), 648, 654, 680, 686, 693, 723, 726, 746, 759, 772, 787, 794, 803, 822, 855, 858, 905, 908, 945, 959, 990, 996, 1004, 1023; **AP/Wide World Photos. Reproduced by permission.:** pp. xv, xliii, 7, 19, 34, 72, 92, 105, 121, 124, 128, 141, 142, 233, 236, 239, 242, 254, 258, 273, 280, 282, 283, 320, 326, 333, 335, 367, 376, 384, 389, 397, 408, 415, 418, 422, 425, 432, 438, 466, 468, 474, 478, 483, 498, 502, 512, 523, 556, 575, 581, 585, 588, 642, 652, 660, 665, 674, 733, 735, 737, 738, 743,

769, 783, 797, 801, 814, 838, 845, 862, 882, 901, 917, 921, 957, 962, 969, 980, 992, 999, 1012; **The Bettmann Archive. Reproduced by permission.**: pp. xxix, 65, 144, 174, 181, 226, 458, 609, 631, 670, 728, 750, 810, 889, 923, 926, 995; **UPI/Corbis-Bettmann. Reproduced by permission.**: pp. xxxi, 112, 115, 117, 178, 251, 378, 448, 454, 515, 593; **Courtesy of Keiiti Aki:** p. 1; **Photograph by Robert T. Eplett. California Governor's Office of Emergency Services.**: p. 3; **The Granger Collection, New York. Reproduced by permission.**: pp. 27, 37, 41, 85, 168, 184, 217, 249, 392, 543, 607, 628, 651, 658, 753, 805, 825, 876, 893, 948, 987, 1017; **UPI/Bettmann. Reproduced by permission.**: pp. 48, 51, 56, 75, 95, 127, 131, 150, 155, 292, 341, 412, 463, 493, 495, 578, 603, 604, 622, 635, 639, 695, 755, 757, 836, 867, 933, 936, 951, 1010, 1025; **AT&T Bell Laboratories. Reproduced by permission.**: p. 62; **UPI/Bettmann Newsphotos. Reproduced by permission.**: pp. 80, 134, 149, 161, 780, 819, 832, 870; **Washington University Photographic Services. Reproduced by permission.**: p. 165; **From *Undersea World of Jacques Cousteau*. American Broadcasting Company. Reproduced by permission.**: p. 171; **Courtesy of Francisco Dallmeier:** p. 192; © **Zefa Germany, Stock Market. Reproduced by permission.**: p. 195; **Los Alamos National Laboratory:** p. 285; **Illustration by Robert L. Wolke. Reproduced by permission.**: p. 289; **Archive Photos, Inc. Reproduced by permission.**: p. 313; **Photri/Bikderberg. Stock Market. Reproduced by permission.**: p. 329; **Reuters/Bettmann. Reproduced by permission.**: pp. 363, 508, 565; **U.S. National Aeronautics and Space Administration (NASA):** p. 437; **J. W. Cappelens Forlag. Reproduced by permission.**: p. 451; **Courtesy of Louis Keith:** p. 549; **Photograph by Yousuf Karsh. Reproduced by permission of Woodman Camp:** p. 536; © **1990 Peter Menzel. Reproduced by permission.**: p. 562; **Mary Evans Picture Library. Reproduced by permission.**: p. 591; **Anthony Howarth/Science Photo Library. Reproduced by permission.**: p. 596; **Courtesy of Raymond Kurzweil:** p. 668; © **Scott Camazine, The National Audubon Society Collection/Photo Researchers, Inc. Reproduced by permission.**: p. 689; **Conservation International. Reproduced by permission.**: p. 767; **Royal Institute of Technology. Reproduced by permission.**: p. 791; **Photograph by Allen Furbeck. Reproduced by permission.**: p. 827; **Courtesy of Dr. Susan Leeman.**: p. 851; © **The Alan Mason Chesney Medical Archives of The Johns Hopkins Medical Institutions. Reproduced by permission.**: p. 897; **Courtesy of New York Public Library Picture Collection:** p. 911; **Courtesy of Dr. Levi Watkins:** p. 929; **Photograph by Brent Clingman. *Time* Magazine. Reproduced by permission.**: p. 973.

Index

Italic type indicates volume numbers;
boldface *type indicates entries and their page numbers;*
(ill.) indicates illustrations.

James D. Watson

Drew, Charles Richard
1: **233–38,** 233 (ill.)
Drosophila 2: 623–24
Du Bois, W. E. B. *1:* 230
Dymaxion automobile
1: 333, 335
Dymaxion Deployment Unit
1: 336
Dymaxion house *1:* 333, 335
Dynamite *2:* 670, 672

E

Earle, Sylvia A. *1:* **239–43,**
239 (ill.), 242 (ill.)
Earthquakes *1:* 1–4, 3 (ill.), 328;
3: 780–85
Easter Island *2:* 451
Eastman Kodak *2:* 558
Eckert, J. Presper *2:* 367,
367 (ill.)
E. coli (*Escherichia coli*)
1: 77, 79; *2:* 386
Ecology *1:* 192, 194; *3:* 977
Ecosystems *1:* 193; *2:* 598
Ectotoxicology *3:* 735
Eddington, Arthur Stanley *1:*
150, 152–53, 266–268
The Edge of the Sea 1: 140
Edgerton, Harold *1:* 172
Edison, Thomas Alva *1:* 66,
244–53, 244 (ill.), 249 (ill.);
2: 557, 614; *3:* 891–92,
894–95, 983, 985
Edwards, Robert G. *3:* 883–87
E=mc² *1:* 260, 265, 269
Ego *1:* 314
The Ego and the Id 1: 314
Ehrlich, Anne H.
1: 254 (ill.), 255
Ehrlich, Paul *1:* 296, 296 (ill.)
Ehrlich, Paul R. *1:* **254–59,**
254 (ill.)
Eight Minutes to Midnight 1: 129
Einstein, Albert *1:* **260–69,**
260 (ill.), 289; *2:* 434; *3:*
764–65, 813
Eisenhower, Dwight D. *2:* 690
Eldredge, Niles *2:* 417

Electra complex *1:* 312
Electricity, alternating-current
1: 251; *3:* 889, 891–93
Electricity, direct-current *1:* 251;
3: 890–92
Electrochemistry *1:* 211–13;
3: 775
Electrogasdynamics (EGD)
2: 422, 424
Electrolytes *1:* 30–34
Electromagnetic radiation *1:* 263;
2: 610
Electromagnetic spectrum
2: 619
Electromagnetic theory *2:* 618;
3: 789
Electromagnetism *1:* 275–76,
278; *2:* 374; *2:* 610, 619;
3: 806
Electroweak force *3:* 832,
834–35
Elementary Seismology 3: 785
Elementary Theory of Nuclear
Shell Structure 2: 403
Elementary Treatise on
Chemistry 2: 572
The Elements 2: 374
Elion, Gertrude Belle
2: **468–73,** 468 (ill.)
ELIZA *2:* 566
The Emperor's New Mind:
Concerning Computers,
Minds, and the Laws of
Physics 2: 436
Encephalitis lethargica
(sleeping sickness) *3:* 829
Enders, John F. *3:* 818, 840, 843
Endocrine system
3: 847–48, 1009
ENIAC (electronic numerical
integrator and computer)
2: 367, 676
Environmental Protection Agency
1: 138
Eötvös force *3:* 955–56
Epps, Maeve *2:* 584
Estés, Clarissa Pinkola *2:* 540
Ethology *1:* 320–21; *2:* 405–06,
588, 590
Euclid *2:* 373–74, 374 (ill.), 456

Galileo Galilei *1:* 267;
2: 444–46, 490; *3:* 789
Gallagher, John *1:* 272
Galle, Johann Gottfried *2:* 373
Game theory *3:* 962
Gates, Bill *2:* **363–70,** 363 (ill.)
Gauss, Carl Friedrich *2:*
371–75, 371 (ill.)
Gayle, Helene D. *2:* **376–79,**
376 (ill.)
Gay-Lussac, Joseph *1:* 215
Geiger counter *3:* 808; *3:* 920
Geiger, Hans *3:* 808–11,
810 (ill.)
Geissler, Heinrich *3:* 1020
Gelfond, A. O. *2:* 458
Geller, Margaret *2:* **380–83,**
380 (ill.)
*Genes and Genomes: A Changing
Perspective 3:* 874
Genes, Mind and Culture 3: 977
Genetic code *1:* 78, 179, 209
Genetic engineering *1:* 76–78,
80; *3:* 870, 873–74
Genetic transposition *2:* 622,
624–25, 627
Geodesic dome *1:* 333–34,
336–37
George III (of England)
2: 443–47
Germ theory *3:* 726
Gilbert, Walter *1:* 81;
2: **384–91,** 384 (ill.)
Glaser, Donald *1:* 11
Glashow, Sheldon L.
3: 832, 835, 836 (ill.)
Glass, nonreflecting *1:* 92, 94
Glaucoma *2:* 531
Gliders *3:* 989–93
Global warming *2:* 597
Goddard, Robert H. *2:* **392–98,**
392 (ill.), 397 (ill.)
Gödel, Kurt *2:* 372, 461
Goeppert-Mayer, Maria
2: **399–404,** 399 (ill.)
Gold, Lois Swirsky *1:* 21–22
Gold, Thomas *1:* 71
Golka, Robert *3:* 891
Gombe Stream Reserve, Tanzania
2: 405, 407, 409

Gondwanaland *3:* 956
Goodall, Jane *2:* **405–14,** 405
(ill.), 412 (ill.)
Gorillas in the Mist 2: 408
Gosling, Raymond *1:* 304–06
Gough, John *1:* 198
Gould, Gordon *2:* 601, 604,
604 (ill.)
Gould, Stephen Jay *2:* **415–21,**
415 (ill.); *3:* 976
Gourdine, Meredith *2:* **422–26,**
422 (ill.), 425 (ill.)
Grand unification theory *2:* 435
Graphophone *1:* 62, 67
Gray, Elisha *1:* 64, 66, 66 (ill.)
*The Great Train Robbery
1:* 250
Greenhouse effect *1:* 30, 33–35
*The Greenhouse Effect, Climate
Change, and Ecosystems 1:* 34
Green Revolution *1:* 105,
107–09
Greylag geese *2:* 589
*Growing Up in New Guinea
2:* 636
Guillemin, Roger *3:* 1009,
1010 (ill.)
Gutenberg, Beno *3:* 781, 784
Guyots *3:* 954
Gypsum *2:* 569

H

Hadar, Ethiopia *2:* 519–20, 523
Hadrons *2:* 500
Hahn, Otto *1:* 289; *2:* 401,
641–42, 644–45, 647
Hale, George E. *2:* 489
Half-life, radioactive *3:* 807, 809
Hall, Lloyd A. *2:* **427–31**
Hardy, G. H. *3:* 960
Hardy-Weinberg law *2:* 552
Hargreaves, James *1:* 24–25
Harrar, George *1:* 107
Harris, Geoffrey W. *3:* 1009
Hawkes, Graham *1:* 239–41
Hawking, Stephen *2:* **432–40,**
432 (ill.)

M

MacArthur, Robert H. *3:* 971
Macrophage *1:* 284
Magic numbers *2:* 403
Magnetic core memory *3:* 923, 925
Magnetohydrodynamics *2:* 424
Maiman, Theodore *2:* **601–06**
Mall, Franklin P. *3:* 823
Manhattan Project *1:* 7, 10, 103, 268–69, 285, 289–91; *2:* 399, 402; *2:* 680, 683–85; *3:* 779, 1002
Manus (people) *2:* 635, 635 (ill.)
The Man Who Mistook His Wife for a Hat *3:* 827, 830
Marconi, Guglielmo *1:* 218–19; *2:* **607–15,** 607 (ill.), 609 (ill.); *3:* 806, 896
Mark I *3:* 924, 926
Marriage and Morals *3:* 802
Marsden, Ernest *3:* 809, 811
Martin, Pierre-Emile *1:* 86
Marx, Karl *3:* 797
Maser *2:* 602
A Matter of Consequences *3:* 880
Mauchly, John William *2:* 367, 367 (ill.)
Maury, Antonia *1:* 133
Maxam, Allan *2:* 387
Max Planck Society *3:* 765
Maxwell, James Clerk *2:* 610, **616–21,** 616 (ill.); *3:* 789, 906, 908
Maybach, Wilhelm *1:* 227
Mayer, Joseph E. *2:* 400–01
Mayer, Julius *2:* 527
McCarthy, Senator Joseph *2:* 690
McClintock, Barbara *2:* **622–27,** 622 (ill.)
McCoy, Elijah *2:* **628–32,** 628 (ill.)
Mead, Margaret *2:* **633–38,** 633 (ill.), 635 (ill.)
Meaning of Evolution *2:* 416
The Mechanism of Mendelian Heredity *2:* 626
Meiosis *2:* 624–25

Meitner, Lise *1:* 288; *2:* 401, **639–47,** 639 (ill.)
Meltdown, nuclear *1:* 127
Mendel, Gregor *1:* 209; *2:* 626, **648–53,** 648 (ill.)
Mendel, Lafayette B. *3:* 857
Mendeleev, Dmitry *2:* **654–59,** 654 (ill.)
Menlo Park, New Jersey *1:* 248
Menninger, Charles *2:* 660
Menninger Clinic *2:* 660–61
Menninger, Karl *2:* **660–64,** 660 (ill.)
Menninger, William *2:* 661
Mental illness *2:* 660–62; *3:* 827, 830
Mercalli scale *1:* 3; *3:* 781–82
Mesometeorology *1:* 331
Mesoscaphe *3:* 758
Metric system *2:* 569
Michelson, Albert *2:* 620–21, 620 (ill.)
Microbursts *1:* 326, 328, 331
Microchips *2:* 674, 676–77
Microsoft *2:* 363–64, 368
Microwaves *2:* 603, 614; *3:* 943
Mid-oceanic ridges *3:* 954
Migraine *3:* 829
Milky Way *2:* 445, 447
Minkowski, Hermann *2:* 455
Minsky, Marvin *2:* **665–69,** 665 (ill.)
Mirowski, Michel *3:* 931
The Mismeasure of Man *2:* 419
Miss Goodall and the Wild Chimpanzees *2:* 410
Missile Envy: The Arms Race and Nuclear War *1:* 129
Moi, Daniel Arap *2:* 585
The Molecular Biology of the Gene *3:* 937
Monod, Jacques Lucien *2:* 386
Monterey One *1:* 335 (ill.)
Morgan, Lewis Henry *3:* 719
Morgan, Thomas Hunt *2:* 626
Morgenstern, Oskar *3:* 962
Morley, Edward *2:* 620–21, 620 (ill.)
Morse code *2:* 611; *3:* 983–84

Morse, Samuel F. B. *2:* 375; *3:* 984
Moseley, Henry *2:* 656–58
Mount Palomar Observatory *2:* 495 (ill.), 496
Mount Wilson Observatory *2:* 487, 489
mRNA (messenger ribonucleic acid) *2:* 384–85
MS-DOS (Microsoft Disk Operating System) *2:* 368
Muller, Hermann *3:* 934
Multiple births *2:* 549–54
Myers-Briggs personality assessment *2:* 538
Mysterium Coniunctionis 2: 541

N

Nagasaki, Japan *2:* 688
National Aeronautics and Space Administration (NASA) *1:* 59; *2:* 598
National Earthquake Information Center *1:* 4
National Foundation for Infantile Paralysis *3:* 841
National Oceanic and Atmospheric Administration *1:* 239
Natural History 2: 417
Natural History of Invertebrates 1: 208
Natural philosophy *1:* 245
Natural selection, theory of *1:* 203–04, 207; *2:* 589–90, 653; *3:* 747
The Nature of the Chemical Bond and the Structure of Molecules and Crystals 3: 740
Navajo (people) *1:* 58, 60
Nazism (National Socialism) *1:* 268; *2:* 461, 593
Nebulae *2:* 441–42, 444, 446
Neddermeyer, Seth *2:* 685, 687
Neptune *2:* 373
Nereis 2: 545
Nervous system *3:* 847–48

Neuroendocrinology *3:* 847–48, 851–52, 1009
Neuroendocrinology 3: 852
Neurohormones *3:* 849
Neurons *3:* 848, 852
Neurosecretion *3:* 847–50, 853
Neutrino *1:* 285, 287
Neutron stars *1:* 71, 153
New Guinea *2:* 635
The New Science 3: 764
A New System of Chemical Philosophy 1: 202
New York State Archeological Association *3:* 721
Newcomen, Thomas *3:* 947
Newlands, J. A. R. *2:* 656
Newton, Isaac *1:* 38, 41, 246, 266, 267, 267 (ill.); *2:* 435; *3:* 764
NeXT Company *2:* 513–14
Nez Percé (people) *3:* 721
Night vision *3:* 1022
Nipkow, Paul *3:* 1018
Nitroglycerin *2:* 671
Nitrous oxide *1:* 211, 213; *3:* 773
Nobel, Alfred *2:* 670–73, 670 (ill.)
Nobel Foundation *2:* 672–73
Nobel Peace Prize *1:* 105, 109, 129; *2:* 684, 686; *3:* 738, 740, 744
Nobel Prize for chemistry *1:* 30, 33, 75, 81, 91, 96, 189, 251; *2:* 389, 474, 477, 639, 647, 654; *3:* 738, 740, 805–06, 809, 895–96
Nobel Prize for literature *3:* 802
Nobel Prize for physics *1:* 7, 13, 98, 101, 150, 153, 156, 181, 187–88, 260, 263, 285, 288; *2:* 399, 403, 607, 613; *3:* 759, 764, 787, 792, 832, 834–35, 862, 865–66, 868, 1003, 1012, 1016
Nobel Prize for physiology or medicine *1:* 161, 166, 178, 297, 302, 304, 306, 320, 325; *2:* 468, 472, 483, 486, 588, 594, 622, 627; *3:* 746, 749,

Pugwash Conferences on Science and World Affairs *2:* 684
Pulsars *1:* 69, 71, 73
Punctuated equilibrium *2:* 417
Putnam, Frederick Ward *3:* 719
Pyramids *1:* 13
Pyroelectricity *1:* 183
Pythagoras *2:* 458, 458 (ill.), 460
Pythagorean theorem *2:* 460

Q

Quantum mechanics *1:* 101, 262; *2:* 680–82; *3:* 739–40
Quantum theory *1:* 99–100; *3:* 759–60, 763–64
Quarks *3:* 835
Quarterman, Lloyd Albert *1:* 290
Quasars *1:* 70, 117, 119–22, 121 (ill.)
Quasi-Stellar Objects 1: 120
Quimby, Edith H. *3:* 776–79

R

Ra 2: 452
Ra II 2: 452
Rabies *3:* 731
Radar *1:* 7, 9; *3:* 939–41, 943
Radiation *1:* 125–26; *3:* 776–79, 790, 807–09
Radiation sickness *1:* 187; *2:* 688
Radio *1:* 217, 222; *2:* 614
Radioactive fallout *2:* 688
Radioactive isotopes *3:* 776
Radioactivity *1:* 181, 186–88; *3:* 789, 805, 807–09
Radioimmunoassay (RIA) *3:* 1004, 1006–09, 1011
Radiological Research Laboratory *3:* 778
Radio waves *2:* 607–08, 610–12; *3:* 893–94
Radium *1:* 181, 186, 189
Rain forests *1:* 257; *3:* 766, 768–70

Raman, Chandrasekhar V. *1:* 151
Ramart-Lucas, Pauline *2:* 643
Randall, John T. *1:* 303
Rayleigh, John *3:* 763
The Realm of the Nebulae 2: 496
Redshifting *1:* 120–21, 266, 268; *2:* 381, 492
Reflections on the Decline of Science in England and on Some of Its Causes 1: 43
Reflex, conditioned *3:* 746, 749–50, 752
Reflex, unconditioned *3:* 749
Reifenstein, Edward *1:* 73
Relativity, theory of *1:* 260, 263–67, 269; *3:* 764
Repression *1:* 310, 312
Reuleaux, Franz *1:* 227
Revelle, Roger *1:* 17
Revolution of the Heavenly Spheres 2: 444
Rheumatoid arthritis *2:* 530
Ribet, Kenneth *2:* 460
Rice *1:* 108–10
Richter, Charles F. *1:* 1, 4, 328; *3:* 780–86, 780 (ill.), 783 (ill.)
Richter scale *1:* 1, 4, 328; *3:* 780, 782
RNA (ribonucleic acid) *1:* 76, 90–91, 304, 306
The Road Ahead 2: 370
Roads to Freedom: Socialism, Anarchism and Syndicalism 3: 802
Road to Survival 1: 255
Robbins, Frederick *3:* 818, 841, 843
Roberts, Ed *2:* 365–66
Rockets *2:* 393–94, 396
Rockoon *3:* 920
Röntgen, Wilhelm *1:* 132; *3:* 787–93, 787 (ill.)
Roosevelt, Franklin D. *1:* 268
Rosenwald, Julius *2:* 546
Rosing, Boris *3:* 1018
Rotblat, Joseph *2:* 684
Royal Society *1:* 39–40
Russell, Bertrand *3:* 794–804, 794 (ill.), 801 (ill.), 960
Russell, Frederick Stratten *1:* 17

Rutherford, Ernest *1:* 99, 102; *2:* 400, 641; *3:* **805–13,** 805 (ill.), 810 (ill.)

S

W

Walden Two *3:* 878–79

Wang, An *3:* **923–28,** 923 (ill.)

Wang Laboratories *3:* 923–25, 927

War Crimes Tribunal *3:* 804

War of the Worlds *2:* 393

Washkansky, Louis *2:* 506

Wassermann, August von *2:* 465

Water frame *1:* 25, 27 (ill.)

Water pollution *3:* 734–36

Watkins, Levi, Jr. *3:* **929–32,** 929 (ill.)

Watson, James D. *1:* 174, 176, 178, 180, 302, 304–06; *2:* 384–85, 469; *3:* **933–38,** 933 (ill.), 936 (ill.)

Watson, Thomas A. *1:* 63–65

Watson-Watt, Robert *3:* **939–44**

Watt, James *3:* **945–50,** 945 (ill.)

Weak force *1:* 287; *3:* 833

Weber, Wilhelm *2:* 373

Webster, Arthur Gordon *2:* 393

Wegener, Alfred *3:* **951–58,** 951 (ill.)

Wegener's granulomatosis *1:* 281

Weinberg, Steven *3:* 832, 834–35, 836 (ill.)

Weinberg, Wilhelm *2:* 552

Weizenbaum, Joseph *2:* 566

Weller, Thomas *3:* 818, 841, 843

Wells, H. Gideon *3:* 857

Westinghouse, George *3:* 892; *3:* 1020

What Mad Pursuit: A Personal View of Scientific Discovery *1:* 179–80

Wheat *1:* 107–09

Wheatstone, Charles *2:* 375

Wheelwright, George *2:* 558

Whitehead, Alfred North *3:* 796–97, 797 (ill.), 799

Whitehouse, E. O. W. *3:* 909

Whiting, Sarah Frances *1:* 132

Why Men Fight: A Method of Abolishing the International Duel *3:* 800

Wien, Wilhelm *3:* 762–63

Wiener, Norbert *3:* **959–63,** 959 (ill.)

Wigner, Eugene Paul *2:* 403

Wiles, Andrew J. *2:* 460

Wilkins, A. F. *3:* 941

Wilkins, Maurice *1:* 176–77, 302, 304, 306; *3:* 933–36

Williams, Robin *3:* 828

Williamson, James S. *3:* **964–68**

Wilson, Edward O. *3:* **969–79,** 969 (ill.)

Wilson, Woodrow *3:* 801

Wind shear *1:* 326, 330–31

Wireless receiver *2:* 609, 609 (ill.)

Women Who Run with the Wolves *2:* 540

Wonderful Life: The Burgess Shale and the Nature of History *2:* 420

Wong-Staal, Flossie *1:* 283, 283 (ill.)

Woods, Granville T. *3:* **980–86,** 980 (ill.)

Woods Hole Oceanographic Institute *1:* 49; *2:* 544, 547

Woodwell, George M. *1:* 142, 142 (ill.)

Worlds in the Making *1:* 35

Worldwatch Institute *1:* 258

Wozniak, Stephen *2:* 508–11, 513

Wright, Almroth *1:* 293

Wright Flyer I *3:* 993

Wright Flyer III *3:* 994

Wright, Orville *3:* **987–98,** 987 (ill.), 992 (ill.)

Wright, Wilbur *3:* **987–98,** 987 (ill.), 995 (ill.)

Wu, Chien-Shiung *3:* **999–1003,** 999 (ill.), 1012, 1015

X

X-ray crystallography *1:* 177;
    2: 474–76, 478
X-ray diffraction *1:* 175–76,
    303–04, 306
X-ray imaging *1:* 44–45, 47
X-ray photograph *3:* 791 (ill.)
X rays *2:* 483; *3:* 776–77, 779,
    787, 789–93, 807
X-ray spectroscopy *2:* 657
X-ray telescope *1:* 45

Y

Yalow, Rosalyn Sussman *3:*
    1004–11, 1010 (ill.), 1004 (ill.)
Yang, Chen Ning *3:* 999, 1002,
    1012–16, 1012 (ill.)
The Year of the Greylag Goose
    2: 592

Yerkes Observatory (University
    of Chicago) *2:* 489
Young, Thomas *2:* 617
Yukuna (people) *3:* 768

Z

Zero Population Growth *1:* 257
Zinjanthropus *2:* 579–80
Zion, Élie de *3:* 747
Zionist movement *1:* 269
Zoological Institute, University
    of Munich *1:* 321, 324
Zoological Philosophy *1:* 208
Zooplankton *1:* 15, 17–18
Zwicky, Fritz *1:* 156
Zworykin, Vladimir
    3: **1017–22,** 1017 (ill.)